Hegel, Kant and the Structure of the Object

Hegel, Kant and the Structure of the Object

Robert Stern

London and New York

First published 1990
by Routledge
11 New Fetter Lane, London EC4P 4EE

Simultaneously published in the USA and Canada
by Routledge
a division of Routledge, Chapman and Hall, Inc.
29 West 35th Street, New York, NY 10001

Reprinted 1991

Typeset in 10/12 Times by Megaron, Cardiff, Wales
Printed in Great Britain by Antony Rowe Ltd.,
Chippenham, Wiltshire

British Library Cataloguing in Publication Data
Stern, Robert
Hegel, Kant and the structure of the object.
  1. German philosophy. Hegel, Georg Wilhelm Friedrich,
  1770–1831
  I. Title
  193

  ISBN 0-415-02593-1

Library of Congress Cataloging in Publication Data
also available

Contents

Preface

The primary aim of this book is to provide an interpretation of the metaphysics of G. W. F. Hegel. According to this interpretation, a central theme of Hegel's metaphysics is to show how the structure of things is fundamentally holistic: that is, to show how the world contains concrete objects which cannot be treated as compounds of more fundamental atomistic entities, and that these objects have a unity which is not properly analysable into a plurality of self-subsistent and externally related parts.

This interpretation has been arrived at principally by looking in detail at the last section of Hegel's *Logic*, which contains his account of the categories of universal, particular, and individual. There, I will argue, we find that Hegel puts forward an account of the individual as the exemplification of a substance-universal, which cannot be reduced to a plurality of attributes, sensible properties, or simple ideas; thus, it is argued, *qua* man, rose, or whatever, the individual exists as a given totality, and the unity of the individual is explained by virtue of its being an exemplification of such and such a kind.

In order to bring out the implications of this metaphysical model of the object, I have tried to highlight the significance of Hegel's position by contrasting it with that of his great predecessor, Immanuel Kant. One of the central features of the latter's idealism is that he follows the empiricist tradition of treating objects as reducible to a plurality of sensible attributes or intuitions, while the unity of this plurality is derived from the synthesizing activity of the supervening subject. By contrast, Hegel's account of the object as the embodiment of a substance-universal enables him to argue that the object has a unity *in itself*, without having to be 'taken up' and synthesized by the experiencing consciousness. In freeing the object from the subject in this way, Hegel's holistic treatment of the object has profound philosophical implications, and marks the break between subjective and absolute idealism.

Throughout this book I have sought to emphasize Hegel's holistic model of the object as a major theme in his philosophical system, and have tried to get across the depth and importance of this conception of things. As a consequence, I have avoided making too much of Hegel's minor errors, and overlooked the implausibility of some of his arguments, aiming instead at highlighting the whole picture, the grand sweep of Hegel's metaphysical vision. What follows is therefore in no way an attempt to disprove or 'go beyond' Hegel, or to fully condone him either; it is merely an attempt to understand him, and to do justice to his philosophy.

I would like to thank the following most warmly for their criticisms, suggestions, and comments on previous versions of this book, including the PhD dissertation on which it is based: Ares Axiotis, Jens Brockmeier, Gerd Buchdahl, Michael Hampe, Bill Hart, Stephen Houlgate, Michael Inwood, Fraser MacBride, Sue Morgan, Michael Petry, and Nick Walker. Special gratitude and mention must go to Edward Craig and to Michael Rosen, both of whom have been most generous in offering their help, ideas, and encouragement over many years. I should also like to thank the Master and Fellows of Churchill College, Cambridge, and the Master and Fellows of St John's College, Cambridge: without the support of these two institutions, I would not have been able to complete this work.

Thanks of a different sort must go to my parents and to my wife, Crosby, and I should like to dedicate this book to them, for having faith and confidence that it could be written at all.

Note on editions and conventions

The following abbreviations are used for translations of works by Kant that are cited in this volume:

CJ   *Critique of Judgement*, translated by James Creed Meredith (Oxford University Press, Oxford, 1952)

CPR   *Critique of Pure Reason*, translated by Norman Kemp Smith, 2nd edn with corrections (Macmillan, London, 1933)

Prol.   *Prolegomena to any Future Metaphysics that Will be Able to Present Itself as a Science*, translated by P. Gray Lucas (Manchester University Press, Manchester, 1953)

In the case of CPR, references are given in the standard pagination for the first and second editions; as this is the same in both German and English versions of the text, only one reference is given. In the case of the other works mentioned, the following German edition of Kant's writings is also cited:

KW   *Kants gesammelte Schriften, Akademie Textausgabe* (Georg Reimer (subsequently W. de Gruyter), Berlin, 1902–)

The following abbreviations are used for translations of works by Hegel:

DFS   *The Difference between Fichte's and Schelling's System of Philosophy*, translated by W. Cerf and H. S. Harris (State University of New York, Albany, 1977)

EL   *Hegel's Logic*, translated by William Wallace, 3rd edn (Oxford University Press, Oxford, 1975)

EM   *Hegel's Philosophy of Mind*, translated by William Wallace and A. V. Miller (Oxford University Press, Oxford, 1971)

EN   *Hegel's Philosophy of Nature*, translated by M. J. Petry (3 vols, George Allen & Unwin, London, 1970)

FK   *Faith and Knowledge*, translated by W. Cerf and H. S. Harris (State University of New York, Albany, 1977)

HPW   *Hegel's Political Writings*, translated by T. M. Knox (Oxford University Press, Oxford, 1964)

ILHP   *Introduction to the Lectures on the History of Philosophy*, translated by T. M. Knox and A. V. Miller (Oxford University Press, Oxford, 1985)

LA   *Aesthetics: Lectures on Fine Art*, translated by T. M. Knox (2 vols, Oxford University Press, Oxford, 1975)

LHP   *Lectures on the History of Philosophy*, translated by E. S. Haldene and F. H. Simson (3 vols, Humanities Press, London, 1892–6)

LPH   *Lectures on the Philosophy of History*, translated by J. Sibree (George Bell & Sons, London, 1881)

LPR   *Lectures on the Philosophy of Religion*, translated by E. B. Spiers and J. B. Sanderson, new edn (3 vols, Humanities Press, London, 1962)

LPWH   *Lectures on the Philosophy of World History; Introduction: Reason in History*, translated by H. B. Nisbet (Cambridge University Press, Cambridge, 1975)

NL   *Natural Law*, translated by T. M. Knox (University of Pennsylvania Press, Pennsylvania, 1975)

PP   *The Philosophical Propaedeutic*, translated by A. V. Miller, edited by Michael George and Andrew Vincent (Basil Blackwell, Oxford, 1986)

PR   *Hegel's Philosophy of Right*, translated by T. M. Knox (Oxford University Press, Oxford, 1952)

PS   *Hegel's Phenomenology of Spirit*, translated by A. V. Miller (Oxford University Press, Oxford, 1977)

SL   *Hegel's Science of Logic*, translated by A. V. Miller (George Allen & Unwin, London, 1969)

When Hegel's works are cited, the first reference is to one of the translations given above; I have indicated if the translation has been modified in any way. In the case of those works in which Hegel's text is divided into numbered paragraphs or sections, no further reference is given to a German text, as this system of paragraphing makes it easy to locate the reference in the original, should this be required. If the text quoted or referred to is from one of the student notes attached to a paragraph, this is indicated by adding a 'Z' to the paragraph number (e. g. §32Z). In the case of those works where no paragraphing is used, the second reference is to the following edition of Hegel's works, giving volume and page number:

HW   *Theorie Werkausgabe*, edited by Eva Moldenhauer and Klaus Markus Michel (20 vols and Index, Suhrkamp, Frankfurt am Main, 1969–71)

In those instances where it has been necessary to refer to another edition of Hegel's works, references are given in full in the relevant note.

Das Vereinigen ist eine größere Kunst, ein größeres Verdienst. Ein Einungskünstler wäre in jedem Fache der ganzen Welt willkommen.

J. W. von Goethe, *Die Wahlverwandtschaften*

I would make a pilgrimage to the Deserts of Arabia to find the man who could make me understand how the *one can be many*! Eternal universal mystery! It seems as if it were impossible; yet it *is* – & it is every where.

Samuel Taylor Coleridge, Notebooks, October 1803

Mais les parties du monde ont toutes un tel rapport et un tel enchaînment l'une avec l'autre que je crois impossible de connaître l'une sans l'autre et sans le tout.

Blaise Pascal, *Pensées*

Introduction

The question of unity is one of the great questions of metaphysics. What is the structure of an apparently unified totality (such as an ordinary individual object, an organism, a self, a thought, or a state), and what does its unity consist in? Are these totalities constructed in some way out of simpler atomistic elements, to which they can be reduced? Or are the parts that make up the totality unintelligible outside the whole, and is it impossible to explain the totality by combining together such pre-existing simpler elements? Those who argue that a given whole *can* be treated as the unification of more basic entities I will call pluralists,[1] while those who argue that it *cannot* I will call holists.

According to upholders of the pluralistic account, a given unity is in fact a compound of more fundamental and independently existing separable elements: that is, it is reducible to a plurality of intrinsically unrelated individual components out of which the pluralist claims the whole is constructed, through some process of unification. (The process of unification will of course depend on the nature of the components in question.) Thus, on this view, there are certain stable and independent entities[2] which form the basic 'building blocks' for the totality, out of which it is said to be constituted, much as a wall is constituted out of bricks or a wood out of trees. It is because the pluralist takes these entities to be ontologically prior to and independent of their instantiation in the whole that he or she explains the existence of the whole through the combination of such separable elements, and argues that these are the parts into which it should be analysed.

Against this, the holist wants to claim that it is a mistake to think that totalities can be understood in this way, as a construction out of a complex of independently existing atomistic entities. On the contrary, he or she insists, it is the totality *as a unity* which is the ontologically primary individual substance, because the parts into which it is *properly* analysable cannot exist outside the whole. The holist therefore claims that the totality in question should not be treated as a compound of self-subsistent elements, for there are no such elements into which this whole as such can be reduced. The holist argues that the pluralist makes a fundamental error, which leads the latter to suggest that the totality is constructed from a plurality of ontologically self-subsistent elements: the error is to treat the parts into which the totality *can* be properly analysed[3] as if they were intelligible *in abstraction from* and *prior to* their existence in the whole; the holist, however, denies that the parts which make up the whole *have* any such ontological independence, and so claims the pluralist is mistaken in thinking that it is from the combination of such elements that the existence of the whole can be explained.

An illustration of the difference in outlook between the pluralist and holist might help here. Consider the structure of languages. According to the pluralist, languages are constructed out of certain basic elements or units of meaning (e.g. sentences or words), which are combined using various rules and operators into the language as a whole. Words or sentences are therefore treated by the pluralist as the fundamental and intrinsically distinct units out of which the language is formed. Against this, however, the holist might claim that it is the language *as a whole* that should be treated as primary, and although the language is analysable into words, sentences, etc., these are not to be understood as the self-subsistent units which the pluralist takes them to be: rather, the holist might argue, words and sentences are only intelligible in the context of the language as a whole, and the latter is not reducible to the sort of independently existing separable units from which the pluralist claims the language is constructed.

Now, the dispute between pluralists and holists has often centred on the proper account to be given of the nature of material objects. On the one hand, pluralists have argued that a given individual entity (such as a table, a plant, a man, and so on) should be treated as constituted through the compounding together of simpler independent elements; on the other hand, holists have argued that these entities cannot be reduced to a plurality of such pre-existing elements, as the parts into which it *can* be analysed could not exist as such outside or prior to their instantiation in the whole. At the metaphysical level, this debate about the structure and realization of the object has revolved around the relationship between the object and its properties: pluralists have argued that the object is constituted out of an atomistic plurality of attributes, simple ideas, sense-data, or intuitions; while holists have claimed that, although the object is analysable into different aspects, it is not compounded out of a plurality of more basic atomistic entities of this sort. In these terms, three models of the nature of objects (in this general, metaphysical sense) have been put forward: substratum models, bundle models, and what I will call (following M. J. Loux[4]) substance-kind models.

According to upholders of the substratum model, the object is not just a plurality of properties, but is fundamentally an indivisible 'bare particular', which grounds these properties and constitutes their unity. According to upholders of the bundle model, by contrast, the object is no more than a collection of properties and has no underlying substratum in which these properties inhere: it is a mere bundle or cluster of attributes, simple ideas, or sense-data, and nothing more besides.

As is well known, each of these models faces its own difficulties. The proponent of the substratum model must make sense of the idea that an 'unknown *something*'[5] underlies the plurality of properties, which is itself *lacking* in any qualities; and the defender of the bundle model faces the difficulty of explaining how it is that the plurality of properties into which the object is analysed in fact form a unity, and what the relation between these properties consists in.

In what follows I will argue that Kant's doctrine of synthesis was intended to shore up this bundle model of the object, by deriving the unity of the object from the unity of the *subject*. I shall also argue that, although Kant uses the subject as a 'ground' for the unity of the object in this way, he is not in fact putting forward a substratum model, since the underlying unity of the subject is merely *formal*, and the subject *itself* is only constituted by its synthesizing activity. In short, I will suggest, Kant developed a very sophisticated version of the bundle model of unity, in which the object is nothing more than a compound of atomistic intuitions which are formed into a relational unity by the transcendental subject. The Kantian model of the object therefore remains essentially pluralistic in character, as the unity of the object is reducible to a complex of more basic and intrinsically unrelated entities (the manifold of intuitions) out of which the object is constructed.

Now, the third model of the object that I have mentioned can be seen as a way of avoiding the problems of both the substratum and bundle models; for it does not treat the object *either* as a bare particular or indeterminate 'one' underlying a manifold of qualities (as does the substratum model), *or* as reducible to a plurality of attributes, simple ideas, or sensible properties (as does the bundle model). Instead, the substance-kind model treats the object as an irreducible whole, in so far as it exemplifies a universal from the category of substance (like 'man', 'dog', or 'rose'), which constitutes the essential nature of the individual as a totality. The defender of the substance-kind model is thereby able to argue (against the substratum model) that *qua* man, dog, or whatever, the individual is not bare, but can be determined using a substance-universal; and, as a result of not treating the individual in this indeterminate manner, he or she can allow that it can be further particularized, for it is *as* a man or a dog that the individual can have many other less overarching qualities. At the same time, however, where he or she objects to the bundle model is in the way that the latter moves from this particularization of the individual to a *reduction* of the object into *isolated* and *self-subsistent* properties, by mistakenly treating the individual as if it were constituted by bringing together just these qualities alone. Against this, the substance-kind model suggests that while the individual may have many properties (brown, hairy, four-legged, and so on) as a result of being a dog, this does not mean that *qua* dog it is a construction out of these properties. Thus, it is claimed on this account that the individual as a whole, *qua* dog, man or whatever, is ontologically primary, in so far as its essential nature is not reducible to those atomistic properties, simple ideas, or sense-data out of which the pluralist claims it is constructed.

It should be clear, I hope, that this ontological model of the object, as the exemplification of a determinate but irreducible substance-universal, is closely allied to the holistic account of unity that I mentioned earlier. The aim of the model, as I have explained, is to show that the object is neither a combination of atomistic, self-subsistent properties, simple ideas, or whatever (and thus reducible to a plurality), *nor* a bare particular (and thus an unanalysable 'this'). Against both these views, the substance-kind model is meant to suggest that, as the exemplification of a universal, with a definite nature, the object is not simply bare, or an indeterminate 'one'; on the other hand, it is also meant to suggest that this universal essence of the object as a whole is not a construction out of atomistic elements, and to imply that the individual should be treated as an irreducible unity.

In Chapter 3, which forms the core of the book, I will suggest that in his *Logic* Hegel attempts to construct a metaphysics designed to challenge the pluralistic assumption behind the bundle theory, that an object is nothing more than a combination of attributes. Hegel argues, along Aristotelian lines,[6] that, properly conceived, the individual is an irreducible substance, and this irreducibility is explained by virtue of its being of such and such a kind; for as such the individual object is not a mere combination of properties, or a bare particular in which these properties inhere, but the manifestation of a universal substance-form which confers unity upon it.

I will argue that Hegel's defence of this holistic model should be understood in conjunction with his more general dissatisfaction with the atomistic outlook of the physical sciences, a dissatisfaction which he shared with many of his contemporaries. In my account of his *Philosophy of Nature* in Chapter 4 I will set out to show how Hegel uses his ontological model of the object to challenge the reductionist and atomistic claims of physics and chemistry, and how this account of nature must be read against the background of his metaphysics.

Now, because Hegel holds that any unified object must be the exemplification of a substance-universal, he is inevitably led towards a *realist* account of concepts, as constituting the essential nature of the individual as a whole. At the same time, I will argue, he frees the unity of the object from the synthesizing activity of Kant's transcendental subject; for, on Hegel's account (to put it simply), the object does not need to be organized or unified by *us*, because, as the exemplification of a substance-universal, it is no longer treated as reducible to the kind of atomistic manifold that *requires* this synthesis. In this way, the split between the Hegelian and Kantian varieties of idealism can be traced back to their differing conceptions of the metaphysical structure of material objects.

In what follows, therefore, my aim will be to show how Hegel took Kant's 'constructivism' to rest on his assumption that the apparent unity of objects as we experience them can be reduced to a plurality of self-subsistent and independently existent elements, that then only constitute a unity as a result of the activity of the synthesizing consciousness. In contrast, I will argue, Hegel held that in so far as the individual object manifests a substantial form, its reduction to a plurality of supposedly more fundamental yet intrinsically unconnected elements is not possible. He therefore rejected any account (such as Kant's) which *begins* with such elements, and then attempts to connect them externally, as reversing the true order of ontological priority. For Hegel, such elements are ontologically *subsequent* to the whole: thus (put crudely) whereas Kant began with the former and saw the latter as a product of synthesis, Hegel argues that he should have begun with the latter and seen the former as products of a false analysis.[7] In this way, Hegel took Kant's constructivism to be founded on the wrong ontological premisses, and on the wrong model of the object.

Though my treatment of this contrast between the Kantian and Hegelian accounts of the nature of individual objects will mainly confine itself to an interpretation of these two thinkers, I believe that the issue which lay between them is of more than merely historical interest. For the debate between the pluralistic and holistic standpoints remains one of the great 'central disputes' of philosophy; that is why philosophers still contend over the proper account to be given of the structure of the object, as well as of the structure of consciousness and the self, thought and language, states and communities, and physical reality in general.[8] Now, I would argue that those modern philosophers who treat these totalities as compounds of intrinsically separate elements are adopting the sort of empiricist, reductionist standpoint that we find in Kant; on the other hand, those who argue that each of these elements is no more than 'an artefact of analysis'[9] abstracted from a given whole are, like Hegel, following more Aristotelian, non-reductionist lines, in treating the given entity as an indivisible totality. The aim of the following study is to make explicit how far this long-running debate between pluralism and holism was a pivotal issue between Kant and Hegel.

Chapter one

Kant and the doctrine of synthesis

Kant's way of accounting for the existence of ordinary concrete objects is, in essence, to show how the content of our experience must exhibit a definite connectedness and relational structure, and to argue that objects are nothing more than 'centres' of such connectedness. None the less, he holds that these relations and forms of connection are not inherent in reality *per se*:[1] he argues that they rest on the synthesizing activity of the transcendental subject, which organizes our experience using certain *a priori* categories. If Kant's position is to be made comprehensible, something must be said about the background to his doctrine of synthesis and an outline must be given of his general philosophical project; I will then discuss his account of the categories as the source of relational unity in our experience, and show how he uses the unity of the subject to ground this relational unity of the object.

THINGS, QUALITIES, AND RELATIONS

In order to understand the evolution of Kant's doctrine of synthesis, it is first necessary to see how he inherited a pluralistic conception of the object from Locke and Hume, and an idealistic account of relations from Leibniz. Instead of treating ordinary individual objects as the primary, ontologically basic entities, in the Aristotelian manner,[2] Locke and Hume began the empiricist tradition of viewing the object as a bundle of qualities, by reducing it to a plurality of simple ideas that are treated as self-subsistent and independent of one another and of the whole. At the same time, Leibniz had raised doubts over the reality of relations, and gave them 'only a mental truth'.[3] I will argue that in developing his doctrine of synthesis, and deriving the relational unity of the object from the synthesizing activity of the transcendental subject, Kant took advantage of both these conceptions, and that they lie behind his own philosophical position. In this section I will first analyse the pluralistic model of the object developed by Locke and Hume, and then discuss Leibniz's theory of relations, as a background to my account of Kant in the remainder of the chapter.

Locke's account of the constitution of things is embedded within his representational theory of knowledge; he does not talk about objects as such, but about our *ideas* of objects. None the less, his account of how we come to represent objects in our experience implies a certain doctrine about the structure of objects, and of how objects must be if we are to perceive and know them.

The idea of an object for Locke is a complex idea, made up of an aggregate of simple ideas to which it is reducible. These simple ideas are treated as basic elements out of which the representation of the object is constituted. The question arises, however, as to how these simple ideas come to form a unity. As we shall see in what follows, Locke was never really able to answer this question satisfactorily, because while on the one hand he dismissed any notion of substance as a substratum underlying and unifying the object, on the other hand he never really developed a theory of relations capable of explaining the unity of simple ideas.

Locke's attack on substance as an underlying basis for the unity of simple ideas is well known. He argues that our conception of this unifying substratum only arises because we treat the collection of simple ideas which represent an object as if they formed one single totality, with the result that we are led to *project* a substratum as a *ground* for this unity:

> The Mind being, as I have declared, furnished with a great number of the simple *Ideas*, conveyed in by the *Senses*, as they are found in exteriour things, or by *Reflection* on its own Operations, takes notice also, that a certain number of these simple *Ideas* go constantly together; which being presumed to belong to one thing, and Words being suited to common apprehensions, and made use of for quick dispatch, are called so united in one subject, by one name; which by inadvertency we are apt afterward to talk of and consider as one simple *Idea*, which indeed is a complication of many *Ideas* together; Because, as I have said, not imagining how these simple *Ideas* can subsist by themselves, we accustom our selves, to suppose some *Substratum*, wherein they do subsist, and from which they do result, which therefore we call *Substance*.[4]

Locke bases his rejection of substance on its apparent unknowability, as a *hidden* support for unrelated sensible attributes. He therefore dismisses substance as 'a supposed, I know not what',[5] and suggests that it can be excluded from our ontology as an unverifiable postulate of our over-active imaginations.

However, having dismissed the concept of substance in this way, as the ground of unity for the various attributes united in an object, Locke then needed to give some other account of how this unity comes about, if he was to treat it as anything more than an arbitrary aggregation. The account Locke gives, however, is notoriously ambiguous, as it contains both subjective and objective elements.

The source of this ambiguity lies in a distinction Locke draws between *modes* and *substances*. Modes are defined as being either homogeneous or heterogeneous complex ideas (i.e. complex ideas made up out of the same sort of simple ideas, which he calls simple modes, or complex ideas made up of different sorts of simple ideas, which he calls mixed modes). Modes are also defined as being predicable or dependent on substances. Substances are defined as complex ideas that are independently existent.[6] Now, whereas Locke is happy to talk of mixed modes as complex ideas that are related together or compounded together by the mind, he is less happy to talk of the unity of the complex ideas of *substances* in this way. Thus, while the unity of a mode is *subjective* in origin and relational in structure, the unity of a substance is not, but seems to be *given* to us in experience.[7] Locke's account of the activity of mind in relating together simple ideas therefore only answers *half* of the question of unity: it answers the question with respect to modes, but not with respect to substances, which appear to have a unity *independent* of our subjective activity of 'compounding'.

What, then, is the source of the unity of substance, if it is *neither* the underlying but mysterious 'substratum' postulated by traditional metaphysics, *nor* the result of the compounding activity of mind? The answer Locke gives to this question arises out of his doctrine of sortal concepts or natural kinds, and is an answer closer to the substratum model, in its objectivity, than his own subjective account of the unity of modes. This comes about as follows.

According to Locke, the names of natural kinds (such as 'gold', to use his favourite example) stand for complex ideas, made up of a conjunction of simple ideas (yellowness, malleability, being of a certain weight, and so on). These complex ideas constitute the *nominal essence* of the natural kind.[8] Now, the co-existing simple ideas that make up our complex idea of gold 'carry with them, in their own Nature, no visible necessary connexion, or inconsistency with any other simple *Ideas*, whose *co-existence* with them we would inform our selves about'.[9] That is, the simple ideas in themselves have no necessary relation to one another: 'there is no discoverable connexion between *Fixedness*, and the

Colour, Weight, and other simple *Ideas* of that nominal Essence of *Gold*.'[10] The simple ideas that make up the nominal essence of gold are in themselves self-subsistent, and ontologically independent of one another.

However, this account of the nominal essence leaves unexplained the regular unity of properties that we find in objects which are members of a natural kind. It is in order to explain *this* unity that Locke puts forward his doctrine of *real* essence:

> By this *real Essence*, I mean, that real constitution of any Thing, which is the foundation of all those Properties, that are combined in, and are constantly found to co-exist with the *nominal Essence*; that particular constitution, which every Thing has within it self, without any relation to any thing without it.[11]

Now, this postulation of a real essence (based on a distinction between observable qualities and microscopic structures) is used by Locke to replace what M. R. Ayers has called the 'dummy concept' of substance with something apparently more intelligible as an explanation for the unity of attributes that we find in the object: that is, insensible particles on which the observable qualities of objects are based.[12]

The doctrine of real essence therefore makes the unity of properties in the object independent of the 'compounding' activity of the subject: but does it make it intelligible? The difficulty Locke's theory faces is that although he insists on the emptiness of substance as an explanation for the unity of the object as a bundle of simple ideas, he seems merely to have replaced the unknowable substratum of metaphysics with the unknowable substratum of contemporary physics. Moreover, the success of Locke's theory as an account of the unity of the object depends on accepting that the structure of insensible particles on which it is based is *itself* unified and cohesive: but given Locke's insistence that this cohesion of particles is itself unknown, this objective account of the unity of the object remains unstable.

With Hume's more consistent acceptance of the consequences of an atomistic theory of representation, this instability is revealed even more clearly. We have seen that the unity of the object had threatened to fall apart as a consequence of Locke's attack on substance, and that this unity was only restored via the ambiguous re-introduction of the quasi-substratum of real essence as the new basis for the unity of the object. Locke had taken the object to the brink of a crisis, only to return to something like the status quo. It took Hume's more thoroughgoing radicalism to repeat the crisis, and this time not to draw back from its consequences; for, unlike Locke, Hume never accepted the postulation of *any* ground of unity underlying the object (be it an indeterminate substratum or Locke's real essence). Instead, Hume insisted that the object is nothing more than a bundle of simple qualities, which only seem to be grounded in some unity as a consequence of being associated together by the imagination. Let us examine Hume's position in more detail.

Hume was as convinced as Locke that substance as a substratum is unknowable, and for that reason of dubious ontological status:

> I wou'd fain ask those philosophers, who found so much of their reasonings on the distinction of substance and attribute, and imagine we have clear ideas of each, whether the idea of *substance* be deriv'd from the impressions of sensation or reflexion? If it be convey'd to us by our senses, I ask, which of them; and after what manner? If it be perceiv'd by the eyes, it must be a colour; if by the ears, a sound; if by the palate, a taste; and so of the other senses. But I believe none will assert, that substance is either a colour, or a sound, or a taste. The idea of substance must therefore be deriv'd from an impression of reflexion, if it really exists. But the impressions of reflexion resolve themselves into our passions and emotions; none of which can possibly represent a substance. We have therefore no idea of substance, distinct from that of a collection of particular qualities, nor have we any other meaning when we talk or reason concerning it.[13]

Hume's point is that as we have no experience of substance, this idea cannot explain why it is that we think a particular collection of qualities forms a unity in an object. Instead, Hume believes that he can explain our feeling that these qualities constitute *one* object in some other way.

The way he chooses is to argue that we take various qualities to form a unified object if, when we think of the object, our minds move from one of its qualities to another without any sense of 'transition'. It is the fact that we feel no 'transition' in thinking of these qualities which he uses to explain why we take them to be attributes of a single, unified object:

> The imagination conceives the simple object at once, with facility, by a single effort of thought, without change or variation. The connexion of parts in the compound object has almost the same effect, and so unites the object within itself, that the fancy feels not the transition in passing from one part to another. Hence the colour, taste, figure, solidity, and other qualities, combin'd in a peach or melon, are conceiv'd to form *one thing*; and that on account of their close relation, which makes them affect the thought in the same manner, as if perfectly uncompounded.[14]

According to Hume, therefore, because the connection between various qualities in the mind (or imagination) is very strong, we are not aware of any transition between them, and take them to constitute one object.

Now, Hume explains this close connection between qualities in our minds using his theory of association. According to this theory, the relations that we feel to hold between simple ideas or impressions are based on what Hume calls the three 'uniting principles' or 'principles of association', viz. resemblance, contiguity in time and place, and cause and effect. Hume's theory is that these 'associating qualities' make up a 'gentle force' that operates on the mind, and leads it to connect together various perceptions into a unity, of the sort that we feel when we look at a unified object, such as (to use the above example) a peach or a melon.[15] Hume therefore argues that in the case of a thing that we take to be a substance (as opposed to a mode), there is no 'unknown *something*' in which the collection of simple ideas inhere, but rather a collection of 'particular qualities' which are 'closely and inseparably connected by the relations of contiguity and causation'.[16] Hume therefore hopes to have explained why we feel that an object is *one* unified object, on the grounds that the qualities that make up the object are very strongly related together in our minds, without any 'transition'; and he hopes to have explained this relation by appealing to the mind's association of ideas on the basis of its three 'uniting principles'. In this way, Hume tries to do without the need to postulate any substratum in which the qualities of the objects inhere.

The difficulty with Hume's account, however, is that while it seems to explain why it is we might take various qualities to constitute one object, it does not show how these qualities are related together *in the object*, but only how perceptions are connected together in our minds; furthermore, it fails to explain why certain qualities are *invariably* found to be united together in our experience of the object. Now Hume was of course notoriously sceptical in his approach to these kinds of questions: he held that no real relation can be discovered between matters of fact, and that the relation is only *felt* by us to be objective and necessary as a result of our habitual association of certain ideas, based on the regular but contingent and external association of the corresponding impressions in our experience. As a consequence of this atomistic account of impressions, therefore, Hume holds that no real connecting link or objective relation can be discovered *in the world* which holds together various qualities into an object: the object is merely a collection of qualities that are regularly found together and consequently strongly associated with each other in our minds, but this connection is only one *felt* by us, as we cannot come to know whether qualities in themselves have any real relational unity.

The upshot, then, is that while we may *feel* that a particular collection of qualities constitutes a unified object with real relations between its various attributes, in fact the object is nothing more than a bundle, with no internal connection or necessary relatedness between its properties. It turns out, therefore, that Hume's 'principles of association' are too weak and too subjective, and as such cannot give an account of the object which is capable of explaining its unity.

With this outline of the Humean theory of association, one thing should now be clear: any account that rejects the notion of a simple substance and reduces the object to a plurality of atomistic properties must give an account of the relations that link up these simple properties, if it is to explain how the plurality of properties that make up the object come to form a unity. However, philosophers in the pluralist tradition have raised doubts about the intelligibility of relations holding between such atomistic entities. It is necessary to examine the nature of these doubts in order to understand the development of Kant's position.

That many metaphysical systems have not been hospitable to relations has been noted recently by Reinhardt Grossmann, in his attempt to reconstruct Aristotle's list of categories. Grossmann gives as the primary reason for this, that relations do not fit easily into Aristotle's ontology of substance and accident; for the conception of substances with accidents produces serious difficulties when the existence of relations comes to be defined.[17] On this conception, an accident always inheres in a substance which grounds its existence, and this account works well enough with monadic, non-relational properties. The problem with relations, however, is that they appear to belong to two different substances at the same time, and this is incompatible with the strict concept of an accident. Thus, to take a simple example, while there is no difficulty on the substance/attribute model with saying that Tim has the attribute of being 5 feet 6 inches tall, and Tom the attribute of being 6 feet tall, the relation 'taller than' appears not to belong exclusively to *either* of them, but only to hold when both substances are taken *together*. The problem is that relations have no distinct and independent reality such as belongs to substances, but neither are they exclusively grounded in a single substance in the manner of accidents.

This ancient and Scholastic problem had been taken up prior to Kant by Leibniz.[18] As Bertrand Russell has argued, Leibniz too was led to question the reality of relations as a result of his bias towards subject–predicate logic, and thus towards an ontology of substances or monads.[19] Following the Aristotelian conception of substances, Leibniz also maintained that every property or modification belongs exclusively to an individual monad in which the modification is grounded.

However, once again, relations do not fit easily into this ontology, as they appear to belong to two monads at the same time: thus, as Leibniz puts it in his correspondence with Clarke, a relation seems to be an accident with one foot in one substance and one foot in another, which, given Leibniz's doctrine of monads, is impossible.[20]

Given these difficulties, both Leibniz and the Scholastics deny the reality of relations, giving them the status of transcendentals. As Gottfried Martin has pointed out, however, though this means denying that relations have the reality of substances, they do have reality in a certain sense; for they have an *ideal* existence in the mind of God, who compares and contrasts the non-relational properties of the individual substances. Thus, although relations are only representations, they have the advantage of being represented by the divine understanding: while being phenomena, they are phenomena to be found in the mind of God, not merely illusions belonging to the realm of sheer appearances.[21]

None the less, despite rescuing relations in some degree from the status of mere illusions, the fact remains that the assumptions implicit in the Aristotelian ontology of individual substances made the status of relations problematic, as did the doctrine that all real properties must belong exclusively to a single substance. Thus, as we also saw with Hume, the pluralist tradition prior to Kant was strongly in favour of making relations ideal: that is, of treating them as representations existing only in the mind.

It has therefore been shown how the empiricist's conception of the object as a bundle of properties means that some account of the connection holding between these properties is essential, if the unity of the object is to be explained; at the same time, it has just been made clear how Leibniz had a conception of relations in which they are taken to be introduced into our experience by the observing mind. Having examined these two positions in some detail, it should help us see why Kant adopts a conception of the object as reducible to a plurality of simpler elements, while treating the relational unity of these elements in the object as ultimately ideal. Before examining that conception in further detail, however, its place in Kant's more general philosophical project must be explained.

KANT'S COPERNICAN REVOLUTION

In the Preface to the second edition of the *Critique of Pure Reason*, Kant uses the metaphor of the Copernican revolution to characterize his new approach to the problem of knowledge.[22] Just as Copernicus had reversed the assumptions of classical astronomy, so Kant sets out to

reverse the assumptions of Cartesian epistemology, that our representations must conform to an object independent of the mind in order to
constitute knowledge. Rather, Kant argues, we should see any possible
object as having to conform to conditions of our knowledge, before it
can become an object for us. In this way, we are able to investigate the
constitution of the object from the *inside* (so to speak), in so far as it must
reflect the constitution of the cognitive faculties brought to experience
by the subject.

We can get a clear sense of the force of this strategy if we consider it as
an answer to the problem of synthetic *a priori* propositions. In this we are
following Kant, who himself set the problem of synthetic *a priori*
propositions at the head of his inquiry, in order to provide it with a
focus. The problem was important for him, because he felt that any
adequate or successful science (like mathematics, geometry, or natural
science) is based on such propositions; and, furthermore, if philosophy
(or, more particularly, metaphysics) is to be such a science, it too must be
based on synthetic *a priori* propositions. Thus, in asking how synthetic
a priori propositions are possible, and providing an answer, we will also
determine how far metaphysics is possible: in answering our philosophical question, we will be establishing the grounds of metaphysics
itself. In this way, the question unifies both halves of the *Critique*: while
the first half provides an answer to the question, the second draws out
the consequences of what for Kant are the implications of this answer.

First, the problem posed by synthetic *a priori* propositions must be
outlined. The characteristic feature of such propositions is that they are
necessary and universal (because *a priori*) and 'ampliative'[23] (because
synthetic). That is to say, although these propositions apparently
contain universal and necessary truths about objects and the world, they
are not derived empirically or *a posteriori* from our experience of the
objects to which they apply. But, given that they extend our knowledge
of objects, and hence are not analytic, this universality and necessity
cannot derive from a mere analysis of concepts. Kant takes as his
preliminary example of such synthetic *a priori* propositions the judgment: 'Everything which happens has its cause'.[24] This proposition is not
analytic, as the concept of cause is not 'contained in' the concept of
something which happens. Nor can we treat it as a proposition derived
from experience, if it is to be universal and necessary. It is, in short, a
synthetic *a priori* proposition, a proposition which is neither derived
from the empirical world (*qua a priori*), nor from our system of concepts
(*qua* synthetic); but, if is not derived from either of these, how can it have
any validity? It is this puzzle that provokes the questions as to how
synthetic *a priori* propositions are possible.

The answer that Kant gives to this question is to argue that synthetic *a priori* propositions are only possible given what we might call a *framework model*. In general terms, the model is as follows: in order for an object to become an object of experience for me, it must be 'lit up'[25] by being placed within the transcendental framework of sensibility, understanding, and imagination, while outside this framework the object cannot enter into my experience. This framework is not derived *a posteriori* from the object, but brought *a priori* by the subject to experience, as the framework that makes this experience possible. Thus, only in so far as this framework is brought to the cognitive occasion by the subject can the object be realized[26] or come into being as an object of which I am aware. This, then, is the significance of Kant's Copernican revolution:

> Hitherto it has been assumed that all our knowledge must conform to objects. But all attempts to extend our knowledge of objects by establishing something in regard to them *a priori*, by means of concepts, have, on this assumption, ended in failure. We must therefore make trial whether we may not have more success in the tasks of metaphysics, if we suppose that objects must conform to our knowledge. This would agree better with what is desired, namely, that it should be possible to have knowledge of objects *a priori*, determining something in regard to them prior to their being given.
>
> (CPR, Bxvi)

As this passage indicates, given a framework model, synthetic *a priori* propositions lose their mystery. For, in so far as we can establish certain truths about this framework, the truths we establish will be *a priori* and will hold universally and necessarily of objects, as made possible by this framework. Thus, geometry, in determining the properties of space, thereby determines *a priori* the properties of all spatial objects, and it is this that makes geometry a synthetic *a priori* science:

> We have already been able with but little difficulty to explain how the concepts of space and time, although *a priori* modes of knowledge, must necessarily relate to objects, and how independently of all experience they make possible a synthetic knowledge of objects. For since only by means of such pure forms of sensibility can an object appear to us, and so be an object of empirical intuition, space and time are pure intuitions which contain *a priori* the condition of the possibility of objects as appearances, and the synthesis which takes place in them has objective validity.
>
> (CPR A89/B121–2)

Kant's solution to the difficulty posed by synthetic *a priori* propositions is therefore to argue that the only way such *a priori* knowledge is possible is as knowledge of our contribution to the constitution of the object of knowledge; but then, once we start to tell the story of this contribution, we will immediately be involved in something like the framework model, as outlined above.

The framework model is used by Kant at two distinct levels, corresponding to the 'Transcendental Aesthetic' and 'Transcendental Analytic' sections of the *Critique*. The 'Transcendental Aesthetic' deals with the faculty of sensibility, while the 'Metaphysical' and 'Transcendental Deductions', which comprise the first half of the 'Transcendental Analytic', deal with the faculty of understanding. Whilst it is the task of the 'Aesthetic' to establish space and time as the *a priori* forms of intuition, it is the task of the 'Analytic' to establish that experience of objects also requires *a priori* concepts (the categories) contributed by the understanding.

Now, it will be argued in what follows that Kant's way of establishing that this framework of categories must be contributed by *us* is to argue that the *unity* of the object is not given but *constituted* by the experiencing consciousness;[27] and it is this argument that exploits the doubts raised by Locke and Hume over the *intrinsic* unity of the object, and by Leibniz over the objective reality of relations, at what Kant calls the transcendental level. Kant's strategy is to accept the empiricist reduction of the object to a bundle of intuitions on the one hand, while insisting on the other that if the atomistic plurality of intuitions are to represent an object, experience requires relations at the empirical level, at what he calls the level of appearances. Now, given that relations have no reality at the transcendental level, Kant argues that they can only come into being at the empirical level through the introduction of the framework of the categories. Kant therefore allows a role for mind in constructing reality as it is experienced by us at the empirical level, while using the ideality of relations at the transcendental level to introduce that role. For, given the fact that relations are not part of reality at the transcendental level, but given the additional fact that they must be incorporated into the structure of reality at the empirical level, Kant argues that they must be grounded in the framework of the categories which is brought to experience by the cognizing subject. This comes out most clearly in Kant's account of synthesis and the relational unity of objects in the 'Metaphysical' and 'Transcendental Deduction' sections of the *Critique*.

SYNTHESIS AND THE UNITY OF THE OBJECT

In the 'Metaphysical Deduction'[28] Kant puts forward the conditions which he believes must be fulfilled if we are to have consciousness of objects in our experience; then, in the 'Transcendental Deduction' he uses the full force of his Copernican revolution to suggest that these conditions also coincide with what it is to *be* an object at all, in so far as objects form part of our experience. Thus, as Henry Allison has correctly observed, one of the most significant consequences of Kant's Copernican revolution is that 'first-order talk about objects is replaced by second-order talk about the conception of an object, and the conditions of its conception (epistemic conditions). The meaning of "object" is thus to be determined by an analysis of these conditions'.[29] It is therefore Kant's aim in the 'Metaphysical Deduction' to put forward these conditions for the conception of an object, and then in the 'Transcendental Deduction' to argue from this analysis to the conditions for there being objects at all, as we experience them. In what follows I will present what I take to be Kant's central argument in these sections of the *Critique*, concentrating on those parts of the argument that are most directly relevant to my theme, that Kant's transcendental idealism rests on a conception of the object as a plurality of elements related together by the experiencing consciousness.

The starting point of Kant's discussion in the 'Metaphysical Deduction' is that if we are to have conscious awareness of the world, and therefore knowledge, we must be able to *think* about the contents of our experience. Now, according to Kant's transcendental psychology, this ability to think involves more than simply *receiving* representations through the faculty of sensibility; in addition, he insists, 'if this manifold is to be known, the spontaneity of our thought requires that it be gone through in a certain way, taken up, and connected.'[30] Kant claims that this requirement can only be met by the *understanding*, which he therefore describes as 'a faculty of thought'.[31] In addition to sensibility, therefore, Kant insists that we require *understanding* if we are to have consciousness and knowledge of reality.

Why is it that this ability to think stems from the understanding? Kant's answer to this question is as follows: unlike sensibility, which merely contains intuitions, the understanding is a faculty of *concepts*, so that a consciousness that possesses understanding must also possess concepts. Kant insists, however, that 'the only use which the understanding can make of these concepts is to judge by means of them';[32] that is, an intelligence that is capable of having concepts must also be capable of forming judgments *using* these concepts, for, unless it involves making judgments, the notion of 'possessing a concept' cannot mean anything at all.[33] Kant then goes on to suggest that in hereby making judgments, we are in fact unifying and connecting together various representations in a way which (as we have just seen) he takes to be a defining characteristic of thought; it therefore follows that the understanding, as the faculty of concepts and of judgments, must also be the faculty of thought. Kant provides a clear synopsis of this argument in his *Prolegomena to Any Future Metaphysics*:

> The sum of this is as follows. The business of the senses is to intuit; that of the understanding, to think. Now thinking is unifying representations in a consciousness. . . . Unification of representations in a consciousness is judgement. Therefore thinking is the same as judging, or refering representations to judgements in general.
>
> (Prol. pp. 63–4: KW IV p. 304)

From this general account of the relation between thinking, judging, and concepts, Kant's next move is to suggest that if we are to use concepts in order to form judgments, then we must possess certain very general but basic concepts (the categories) which enable us to form judgments in the way that that has been outlined. Kant's insight here is that concepts can be employed in various sorts of judgments; but if we are to use our concepts in these various sorts of judgment (given in the 'Table of Judgements'),[34] we must possess alongside them various sorts of categories (given in the 'Table of Categories'),[35] without which we could not handle the various judgment forms. Thus, to take an example from the *Critique*, if we are to form a universal judgment like 'all bodies are divisible', we must possess the category of unity, without which the notion of *all* bodies being divisible could not be entertained. Similarly, to take an example from the *Prolegomena*, if we are to form a hypothetical judgment like 'If the sun shines on the stone, it grows warm', we must possess the concept of cause. Kant therefore argues that without these (and other) categories it would be impossible for us to form judgments, and thus to bring together various concepts in a thought.

Now, in addition, Kant insists that 'The same function which gives unity to the various representations *in a judgement* also gives unity to the mere synthesis of various representations *in an intuition*':[36] that is, just as we need the categories to unite concepts in the various forms of judgment, so we require these categories to unify our intuitions, and thus the *content* of our experience as it is given to us in sensibility. Thus, to take the categories of unity and cause once again, unless we had the category of unity we would not be able to experience a plurality of intuitions as a whole, and without the category of causality we could not see them as causally interconnected, so that these (and other) concepts are necessary to the synthesis of our intuitions. In giving unity, not just to our concepts in judgments, but *also* to our intuitions in experience, however, these categories have been shown to be part of the framework that determines the *structure* of the manifold as it is given to us, and thus the structure of our experience; for, in order to generate connected experience out of the manifold of intuition, Kant argues, the understanding must contain the *a priori* framework of the categories out of which the unity of that manifold is produced.

In assuming, however, that the unity of intuitions is not given, we begin to see the force of Kant's pluralistic presuppositions; and it is this pluralism which leads him to the doctrine of synthesis, according to which all unity must be subsequent to a relating activity carried out by the thinking subject. Thus, as P. F. Strawson has observed:

> Belief in the occurrence of the process of synthesis as an antecedent condition of experience and belief in the antecedent occurrence of disconnected impressions as materials for the process to work on are beliefs which support each other and are necessary to each other.[37]

Kant's atomistic picture of intuitions, his conception of unity as the relating together of pre-existing elements, and his account of synthesis through the categories are therefore really all of a piece, and they represent a 'package' of doctrines which is characteristic of the outlook associated with transcendental idealism.

Now, having presented this extremely general argument concerning the categories and the unity of intuitions in our experience, Kant then goes on in the 'Transcendental Deduction' to give his whole position an *ontological* twist, by arguing that 'The *a priori* conditions of a possible experience in general are at the same time conditions of the possibility of objects of experience.'[38] Standing behind this move is the insight provided by his Copernican revolution, that the world of objects in space and time do not have a 'transcendental' reality, but rather must be grasped in a way that puts them *inside* our experience, and allows them to be explained within the *conditions* of that experience. By adopting this strategy, however, Kant is able to put forward a redefinition of what it is to be an object: an object can no longer be an item that stands entirely outside our forms of experience, but instead can be nothing more than a centre or focus for the manifold that makes up that experience, a node of unity in what appears to us:

> At this point we must make clear to ourselves what we mean by the expression 'an object of representations'. We have stated above that appearances are themselves nothing but sensible representations, which, as such and in themselves, must not be taken as objects capable of existing outside our power of representation. What, then, is to be understood when we speak of an object corresponding to, and consequently also distinct from, our knowledge? It is easily seen that

this object must be thought only as something in general = x, since outside our knowledge we have nothing which we could set over against this knowledge as corresponding to it.

Now we find that our thought of the relation of all knowledge to its object carries with it an element of necessity; the object is viewed as that which prevents our modes of knowledge from being haphazard or arbitrary, and which determines them *a priori* in some definite fashion. For in so far as they are to relate to an object, they must necessarily agree with one another, that is, must possess that unity which constitutes the concept of an object.

(CPR A104–5)

This characterization of what it is to be an object, of course, fits exactly with Kant's account of the synthesis of representations by the categories, so that his account of how we unify experience, and his account of the nature of the object, coincide. Thus, Kant argues, in bringing unity to our experiences, the framework of the categories *also* makes possible the realization of objects; for objects too are products of unity, and in giving unity to our experience we are also constituting objects as they exist for us.

In this way, Kant's assumptions concerning the structure of experience and representations carry over into his conception of what it is to be an object: just as experience has a fundamentally atomistic structure with a relational unity imposed by the synthesizing activity of the subject, so too does the object. We have therefore seen how Kant's pluralistic account of the object as a product of synthesis evolves.

It may be helpful to outline the position we have now reached. I have dealt with the 'Metaphysical Deduction' section of the *Critique*, and covered some of the arguments in the 'Transcendental Deduction'. According to my interpretation, Kant has argued that objects as they are met with in experience have the structure of complex unities, which can only be realized through the relating together of representations. This relating is the result of an activity of synthesis, which is carried out by the *a priori* categories brought to experience by the understanding. The realization of the object is therefore the result of a synthesizing activity, while the material out of which the object is composed is taken to be an intrinsically unrelated plurality.

This does not complete my analysis of Kant's position, however, as the 'Transcendental Deduction' also contains an important *addition* to this account of the object which we have not yet brought in, and which modifies that account in an important way. The modification, simply put, involves postulating a transcendental unity to ground the relational structure of the object, through which the relatedness of that structure is guaranteed, and from which the unity of the object is then derived. Now, described in this way, Kant's postulation of a transcendental unity grounding the object might appear to signal a return to the traditional conception of an underlying substratum; as we shall see in the next section, however, Kant's position is more complex than this, as *his* substratum is not to be found *in* the world, but only *outside* it, in the merely *formal* unity of the subject. In adopting this position, I will argue, Kant aimed to establish the *necessary* unity of the object on the one hand, while staying as close as possible to the 'bundle' model on the other. In order to see this, we must now examine Kant's account of the transcendental subject.

SYNTHESIS AND THE UNITY OF THE SUBJECT

Kant prefaces his 'Transcendental Deduction' by explaining why a transcendental deduction of the categories is necessary. A transcendental deduction in general is characterized as a *justification* of our employment of *a priori* concepts in relation to the objects of experience. With respect to the categories, therefore, the 'Transcendental Deduction' must justify Kant's contention that they are needed in order to make experience of objects possible. As Kant makes clear, in order for this justification to be successful, it must be able to answer the following challenge: the categories are functions of unity among our representations, through which the complex unity of the object is realized; however, it seems *prima facie* possible that we could have experience that was not unified into objects in this way, but rather consisted of a confused plurality of representations.[39] The claim that experience must display a relational unity must therefore be justified, if the use of the categories is to be shown to be necessary, and this is the task of the 'Transcendental Deduction'. It turns out that representations have to display a relational unity because they must be able to be taken up within the experience of a unified subject; in this way, Kant establishes the necessity of the categories by showing that they generate the kind of connectedness among our representations that is needed if they are to become part of the experience of a single self-consciousness, which is aware of its identity as the subject of distinct perceptions. Kant's argument for this position must now be examined.

In the second edition of the *Critique of Pure Reason*, Kant begins the 'Transcendental Deduction' by discussing the question of synthesis. He re-affirms his view that objects come into being as the result of synthesis, and that this combination of representations accounts for the unity of the object, which it does not possess in itself:

> all combination . . . is an act of the understanding. To this act the general title 'synthesis' may be assigned, as indicating that we cannot

represent to ourselves anything as combined in the object [*Objekt*] which we have not ourselves previously combined, and that of all representations *combination* is the only one which cannot be given through objects. Being an act of the self-activity of the subject, it cannot be executed save by the subject itself.

(CPR B130)[40]

However, Kant now makes an important addition to his position in the 'Metaphysical Deduction', by arguing that this synthesis (or combination) of representations must *itself* rest on a prior unity:

But the concept of combination includes, besides the concept of the manifold and of its synthesis, also the concept of the unity of the manifold. Combination is representation of the *synthetic* unity of the manifold. The representation of this unity cannot, therefore, arise out of the combination. On the contrary, it is what, by adding itself to the representation of the manifold, first makes possible the concept of the combination.

(CPR B130–1)

This gives a fundamentally new twist to Kant's doctrine of synthesis. As in the 'Metaphysical Deduction', Kant claims that the unity of the object rests on the function of relation or synthesis. However, he now adds that this synthesis must itself be grounded in a unity, from which the relation of representations in the object is derived.

The unity in question, however, is not the unity of the object, as some real but unknowable substratum underlying the plurality of our representations. Rather, Kant insists, the unity is the unity of the *subject*:

There can be in us no modes of knowledge, no connection or unity of one mode of knowledge with another, without that unity of consciousness which precedes all data of intuitions, and by relation to which representations of objects [*Vorstellungen von Gegenständen*] is alone possible. This pure original unchangeable consciousness I shall name *transcendental apperception*.

(CPR A107)

It therefore turns out that for Kant the combination of representations is grounded in the unity of the subject; for in so far as the manifold must be taken up within a single consciousness, it must be related together, using the synthesizing categories which that consciousness alone can supply.

In the second-edition version of the 'Transcendental Deduction' Kant's argument for this position begins with his well-known contention that all representations must be owned by a thinking subject, which can claim the representations *as* its own by attaching an 'I think' to them.

This entails the postulation of a transcendental self, to whom the representations belong. Now, as we have seen, Kant argues that this self must constitute a unity, which persists as the same self through a series of different representations. Kant calls this unity the 'analytic unity of apperception'.[41] We are aware of this unity whenever we recognize that the self which had one experience is the *same* self which had a subsequent or different experience: the fact that the experiences are different in no way entails that they are experienced by different selves. The self can persist through a plurality of distinct experiences as a recognizable unity.

However, Kant's next move is to insist that this unity of the subject is only intelligible if the experiences which 'belong' to it have *some* coherent connection with one another. That is to say, representations may only be taken to be the experiences of a recognizably *single* self if they show some relatedness, which enables them to form part of the experience of this persisting unity. If representations themselves exhibited no relation to one another, Kant claims, the very unity of the self would be threatened. As a result, he argues, the representations must undergo the process of synthesis, before they can enter into the unity of the subject:

> As *my* representations (even if I am not conscious of them as such) they must conform to the conditions under which alone they *can* stand together in one universal self-consciousness, because otherwise they would not all without exception belong to me.
>
> (CPR B132–3)[42]

In order to form parts of a unified consciousness, therefore, the manifold must be synthesized into a degree of relatedness that enables it to be incorporated into the unity of the subject. Having argued, in the 'Metaphysical Deduction', that the categories alone are capable of generating that relatedness, the place of the categories as a necessary precondition of experience is now guaranteed.

To sum up: the job of the 'Transcendental Deduction' is to establish that experience is not possible unless we use the categories to bring about the synthesis of the manifold in the complex unity of the object. Kant establishes this by arguing that the manifold must be able to be subsumed in the unity of the subject; for, in order to enter into this unity, the manifold must exhibit a coherent interconnectedness that can only be derived from the synthesizing function of the categories. In this way, Kant's assumption that the categories are necessary for experience is fully justified, and the job of the 'Transcendental Deduction' is complete.

The fundamental point to notice about Kant's position here is that the relational structure of the object turns out to be grounded in the unity of the *subject*, for it is only in so far as the unity of the subject supervenes on the manifold that the complex unity of the object is generated:

> *Understanding* is, to use general terms, *the faculty of knowledge*. This knowledge consists in the determinate relation of given represent-ations to an object; and an *object* is that in the concept of which the manifold of a given intuition is united. Now all unification of representations demands unity of consciousness in the synthesis of them. Consequently it is the unity of consciousness that alone constitutes the relation of representations to an object, and therefore their objective validity and the fact that they are modes of knowledge; and upon it therefore rests the very possibility of the understanding.
>
> (CPR B137)

Kant's doctrine is therefore that the unity of the object rests on the unity of the subject, and that this unified subject is a precondition for the realization of the object. In this way, the relational structure of the object is grounded in the more fundamental unity of the transcendental subject, and Kant has offered the latter as a quasi-substratum in order to account for the structure of the former.

In order to establish the unity of the subject as the basis for the unity of the object, however, Kant had to secure his position *first* against Hume's well-known scepticism over the unity of the self, and *second* against any rival *realist* grounds for the unity of the object.

The first threat to Kant's account is implicit in Hume's doubts over the unity of the self. Basing his argument on the evidence of intro-spection, Hume insists that the self does not constitute any single substance, but is a mere bundle of different perceptions and qualities, which lack any real relation to one another:

> For my part, when I enter most intimately into what I call *myself*, I always stumble on some particular perception or other, of heat or cold, light or shade, love or hatred, pain or pleasure. . . . If any one upon serious and unprejudic'd reflexion, thinks he has a different notion of *himself*, I must confess I can reason no longer with him. All I can allow him is, that he may be in the right as well as I, and that we are essentially different in this particular. He may, perhaps, perceive something simple and continu'd, which he calls *himself*; tho' I am certain there is no such principle in me.
>
> But setting aside metaphysicians of this kind, I may venture to affirm of the rest of mankind, that they are nothing but a bundle or collection of different perceptions, which succeed each other with an inconceivable rapidity, and are in a perpetual flux and movement.[43]

For Kant's strategy to succeed, this Humean argument must be answered, as Kant needs to show that there is more to the unity of the self than a bundle of distinct perceptions, if it is to serve as a basis for the relatedness of the diversified manifold.

In essence, Kant's response to Hume is to distinguish between the *transcendental* unity of apperception (the merely formal 'I') and the *empirical* self of introspection. Given this distinction, Kant then argues that although Hume is right to question the latter's status as a simple substance, he is wrong to question the unity of the former, as that on which the relatedness of experience is grounded. Kant puts this argument very clearly in the following passage from the *Critique*:

> All necessity, without exception, is grounded in a transcendental condition. There must, therefore, be a transcendental ground of the unity of consciousness in the synthesis of the manifold of all our intuitions, and consequently also of the concepts of objects in general, and so of all objects of experience, a ground without which it would be impossible to think any object for our intuitions . . . .
>
> This original and transcendental condition is no other than *transcendental apperception*. Consciousness of self according to the determinations of our state in inner perception is merely empirical, and always changing. No fixed and abiding self can present itself in this flux of inner appearances. Such consciousness is usually named *inner sense*, or *empirical apperception*. What has *necessarily* to be represented as numerically identical cannot be thought as such through empirical data. To render such a transcendental presupposition valid, there must be a condition which precedes all experience, and which makes experience itself possible.
>
> (CPR A106–7)

Only by developing this anti-Humean conception of a unified (transcendental) self could Kant move beyond Hume's atomistic pluralism, and use the subject as a unifying substratum for the diversified manifold of intuition.

The second threat to Kant's position is posed by the postulation of a ground of unity for the object which lies *outside* the experience of the thinking subject, as is envisaged in the substratum model of the object. Kant calls the substratum 'the transcendental object',[44] and using an essentially Lockean argument, insists that it is unknowable as a basis for the unity of the object, and thus of questionable ontological significance. Kant concludes that this substratum is merely a 'shadow' or analogue of the transcendental subject, which is the *real* ground for the unity of the object:

All our representations are, it is true, referred by the understanding to some object; and since appearances are nothing but representations, the understanding refers them to a *something*, as the object of sensible intuition. But this something, thus conceived, is only the transcendental object; and by this is meant a something = X, of which we know, and with the present constitution of our understanding can know, nothing whatsoever, but which, as a correlative of the unity of apperception, can serve only for the unity of the manifold in sensible intuition. By means of this unity the understanding combines the manifold into the concept of an object. This transcendental object cannot be separated from the sensible data, for nothing is then left through which it might be thought. Consequently it is not in itself an object of knowledge, but only the representation of appearances under the concept of an object in general – a concept which is determinable through the manifold of these appearances.

(CPR A250–1)

Following Locke, therefore, Kant uses epistemological difficulties to cast doubt on the intelligibility of any postulation of a material substratum underlying the object, thereby making it possible for him to substitute his own account of the transcendental subject for this realist conception.

However, although Kant constructs his account of the object on the basis of this unified subject, his conception of this subject is extremely formal and etiolated; for the transcendental ego has no real existence as a concrete individual, and it lacks any empirical reality. Kant therefore in no way wishes to introduce the subject into his ontology as some sort of 'simple particular', as he gives it no ontological weight.

This feature of Kant's account of the self is revealed in his treatment of what he calls the 'Paralogisms of Pure Reason'.[45] Here, he goes out of his way to distance his account of the transcendental subject, with its formal view of the self, from the metaphysical conception of the subject as *soul*. He does so, I would argue, in order to distinguish his transcendental account of the subject from those earlier doctrines that had identified the subject with the soul, and which had thereby given the subject some sort of substantial being. Kant wanted to show that these doctrines are guilty of hypostatizing a merely formal unity, and his aim in the 'Paralogisms' is to reveal this mistake; he hopes thereby to replace their concrete subject with his formal conception.[46] This argument will now be examined in more detail.

Kant's account of the paralogisms occurs in the 'Transcendental Dialectic' section of the *Critique*, the aim of which is to expose and explain the various fallacies of pure reason. In general terms, Kant maintains that the fallacies of reason which he identifies are generated through reason's habit of treating merely *systematic* or postulated unities as if there were really existing infinite objects corresponding to them.[47]

In the case of the paralogisms, the synthetic unity in question is that of the analytic unity of apperception, of the pure ego, which (as we have seen) must be taken to underlie all our experience of objects. Kant insists, however, that where reason goes wrong is in postulating a real self or soul as corresponding to this merely formal unity of the ego. Kant's objection to this doctrine of the soul is that the self has no real existence as an object in the world, and we arrive at a conception of the soul by hypostatizing the pure self's merely *formal* unity:

> Nevertheless there is nothing more natural and more misleading than the illusion which leads us to regard the unity in the synthesis of thoughts as a perceived unity in the subject of these thoughts. We might call it the subreption of the hypostatised consciousness [*apperceptionis substantiatae*].
>
> (CPR A402)[48]

Using this argument, Kant therefore distinguishes between the unified synthesizing subject which constitutes experience, and the soul of the rational psychologist, which is treated as if it were a unity *in* experience, while in fact lying outside all the bounds of possible intuition and empirical judgment. Kant insists that the subject *must* lie outside the bounds of the world in this way because it is a merely formal unity, an activity of synthesis and no more, and therefore without any status as a possible object existing in the empirical world:

> We can assign no other basis for this teaching [of rational psychology] than the simple, and in itself completely empty representation 'I'; and we cannot even say that this is a concept, but only that it is a bare consciousness which accompanies all concepts. Through this I or he or it (the thing) which thinks, nothing further is represented than a transcendental subject of the thoughts = X.
>
> (CPR A345–6/B404)

Kant therefore insists on the utterly formal, empty unity of the self, as he rejects any attempt to conceive of it as anything more than an indeterminate X, empty of all reality and content.

Kant's argument here, on the relation between the unity of the transcendental subject and the object that it unifies, should now be fairly clear. Although the subject is a ground for the unity of the object, it constitutes this unity simply as a function of its relating activity, and its *own* unity is merely as a centre or focus for this activity. The subject therefore synthesizes *itself* in the act of synthesizing the object, while both the subject *and* the object have no more than a relational unity, on the pluralistic model.[49] For Kant, therefore, the unity of the transcendental self is purely formal, a mere locus of synthesizing activity, and is thus (so to speak) an extensionless point, on which a coming together of intuitions, and thus the unity of the object is centred. It is only *as* such a centre that it has a unity bestowed on *itself*.

Kant's position in the *Critique of Pure Reason* may therefore be summarized as follows: objects have a relational unity formed out of the atomistic manifold of intuitions by the combining together of these intuitions in the transcendental subject; in this sense, therefore, the object constitutes a unity on the pluralistic model, as it is reducible to a plurality of more basic entities out of which it is constructed. Moreover, although the subject functions as a quasi-substratum on this account, it too has no more than a formal or relational unity, as the subject itself is merely synthesized into a unity through the act of constructing the object; it is in no way a single, irreducible *entity*, in the holistic sense. In this way, Kant manages to give an account of the relational unity of the object on the one hand, without needing to give any content to the formal subject which constitutes that unity on the other. It has been argued, then, that Kant's variety of idealism evolved from a pluralistic conception of the structure of things, and it is on this conception that his doctrine of synthesis relies.

Chapter two

Hegel contra Kant

Kant's model of the object as the product of synthesis, which comes into being through the combination of a plurality of atomistic intuitions, was destined to be rejected by Hegel and other philosophers of his generation, along with the atomistic presuppositions on which it was based. In Hegel's case, the transformation in philosophical outlook that this rejection implied was as profound as it was thoroughgoing: it involved throwing over the empiricist assumption that things are mere congeries of properties, simple ideas or intuitions, and replacing it with an holistic model of individual objects as exemplifying an irreducible substance-universal. Hegel therefore argues, along Aristotelian lines, that in virtue of exemplifying a universal substance-kind (such as 'man', 'cat', or 'rose'), the individual should be treated as an ontologically primary single substance, and not as a combination of more fundamental accidental attributes or sensible properties, as the 'bundle' model adopted by Kant and the empiricists implied. It is this conception of the object, as having an immanent, irreducible unity, that distinguishes Hegel's account from that of Kant, and leads him to reject the latter's picture of the realization of the object.

This chapter will begin by sketching the background to Hegel's dissatisfaction with Kant's pluralistic approach, and will then examine in more detail the treatment Hegel gives of the latter's doctrine of synthesis.

THE NEED OF PHILOSOPHY

Hegel and his contemporaries believed that the main aim of their philosophy should be to overcome the fragmentations and divisions inherent in the philosophical, theoretical, and scientific doctrines of their predecessors, divisions such as those between 'spirit and matter, mind and body, faith and intellect, freedom and necessity, etc.': 'The sole interest of Reason is to suspend [*aufzuheben*] such rigid antitheses.'[1] The picture of the world bequeathed to Hegel's generation by the thinkers of the Enlightenment consisted of a series of oppositions and dichotomies of this sort, and in response they believed that their role as philosophers, poets, reformers, and intellectuals was to overcome these oppositions, and to return to a unified conception in which such divisions were resolved.[2] In an early work, known as the *Differenzschrift*, Hegel states clearly that the overcoming of such dichotomies is the main business of philosophy:

> If we look more closely at the particular form worn by a philosophy we see that it arises, on the one hand, from the living originality of the spirit whose work and spontaneity have reestablished and shaped the harmony that has been rent; and on the other hand, from the particular form of the dichotomy from which the system emerges. Dichotomy is the source of *the need of philosophy*; and as the culture of the era, it is the unfree and given aspect of the whole configuration.
>
> (DFS p. 89: HW II p. 20)[3]

This 'need of philosophy', which was felt so keenly by thinkers of Hegel's period, was thus part of a desire to heal divisions and overcome fragmentation, and to return to a more unified world-view.

As many commentators have correctly pointed out, Hegel's contemporaries characteristically identified the Greeks as having possessed such a unity in their social, religious, and philosophical outlook, so that the ancient world came to represent for them a last but exquisite flowering of this desired unity. All the primary features of this view can be seen in the following passage from Friedrich Schiller's sixth letter *On the Aesthetic Education of Man*:

> At that first fair awakening of the powers of the mind [in Greece], sense and intellect did not as yet rule over strictly separate domains; for no dissension had as yet provoked them into hostile partition and mutual demarcation of their frontiers. Poetry had not as yet coquetted with wit, nor speculation prostituted itself to sophistry. Both of them could, when need arose, exchange functions, since each in its own fashion paid honour to truth. However high the mind might soar, it always drew matter lovingly along with it; and however fine and sharp the distinctions it might make, it never proceeded to mutilate. It did indeed divide human nature into its several aspects, and project these in magnified form into the divinities of its glorious pantheon; but not by tearing it to pieces; rather by combining its aspects in different proportions, for in no single one of their deities was humanity in its entirety ever lacking. How different with us

Moderns! With us too the image of the human species is projected in magnified form into separate individuals – but as fragments, not in different combinations, with the result that one has to go the rounds from one individual to another in order to be able to piece together a complete image of the species. With us, one might almost be tempted to assert, the various faculties appear as separate in practice as they are distinguished by the psychologist in theory, and we see not merely individuals, but whole classes of men, developing but one part of their potentialities, while of the rest, as in stunted growths, only vestigial traces remain.[4]

Schiller is here referring to two different areas of fragmentation suffered by 'us Moderns', in contrast to the unified outlook of the Greeks. First, he is identifying in 'us Moderns' a separation of the faculties of mind, following the distinctions commonly accepted by most eighteenth-century thinkers, between reason and understanding, theoretical and practical reason, thought and desire, sense and intellect, and so on. Schiller's objection to these divisions is that they break up what for the Greeks was a unified conception of the human mind, which overarched this plurality of faculties.[5] Second, Schiller is identifying in 'us Moderns' a separation of the individual from what Ludwig Feuerbach was later to call their 'species-being' (*Gattungswesen*), as individuals have lost touch with their shared humanity, and have taken on a narrower, more specialized form of existence that marks them off from one another;[6] and again, Schiller contrasts this division of humanity in general into particular types with the world of the Greeks, in which individuals could still feel and express their shared nature and be aware of the unity that existed between them. The implication of Schiller's argument is that we as moderns have 'fallen' from the original unity of the Greek world, because the universal species-concept has been lost as a result of the differentiation of individuals into distinct and opposed types.

Not only was the *human* world and consciousness felt to be fragmented and disharmonious in this way: many of the thinkers of Hegel's period lamented the atomistic, mechanistic, and compart-mentalized view of *nature* and natural phenomena which they perceived to be the legacy of modern science from Bacon to Newton. The general objection raised against this atomistic and mechanistic view was that it failed to acknowledge the unity and vitality of *living* nature, and destroyed the harmony that constituted its true character. For many, the *analytical chemist* typified this atomistic approach to nature. This view of chemistry is to be found in the following lines from Goethe's *Faust*, which are quoted with approval by Hegel on two separate occasions:

Wer will was Lebendigs erkennen und beschreiben,
Sucht erst den Geist heraus zu treiben,
Dann hat er die Teile in seiner Hand,
Fehlt leider! nur das geistige Band.
Encheiresin naturae nennt's die Chemie,
Spottet ihrer selbst und weiß nicht wie.[7]

Goethe repeats this criticism of the chemist in *Elective Affinities*, his *Novelle* of 1808; but here he expresses the hope that the analytical procedure of the chemist has been replaced by the more unified vision put forward by *Naturphilosophie*, that mixture of science, *a priori* speculation, and metaphysics which was so enthusiastically championed by the Romantics and Idealists of the period.[8] The passage runs:

> 'To be sure', Eduard replied. 'It even used to be a title of honour to chemists to call them artists in divorcing one thing from another.'
>
> 'Then it is not so any longer', Charlotte said, 'and a very good thing too. Uniting is a greater art and a greater merit. An artist in unification in any subject would be welcomed the world over.'[9]

Schiller expresses a similar condemnation of the method of analysis practised by the chemist, arguing that any philosopher who follows their procedure will miss an understanding of the whole, by reducing the totality to a plurality of atomistic parts:

> Like the analytical chemist, the philosopher can only discover how things are combined by analysing them, only lay bare the workings of spontaneous Nature by subjecting them to the torment of his own techniques. In order to lay hold of the fleeting phenomenon, he must first bind it in the fetters of rule, tear its fair body to pieces by reducing it to concepts, and preserve its living spirit in a sorry skeleton of words. Is it any wonder that natural feeling cannot find itself again in such an image, or that in the account of the analytical thinker truth should appear as paradox?[10]

In the same way as 'us Moderns' have had to suffer the reduction of the human mind to a plurality of faculties, and the division of our shared humanity into particularized types, so here Schiller is suggesting that a similar fragmentation has occurred in our understanding of nature, and a unified conception of the world has been lost.

One other area in which 'us Moderns' are said to have suffered is in the fragmentation of society and the state. Throughout this period, writers contrasted the kind of social and political atomism they found around them with the ideal unity of the Greek city-state or 'polis'.[11] Schiller, once again, gives clear expression to this view:

This disorganization, which was firstly started within man by civilization and learning, was made complete and universal by the new spirit of government. It was scarcely to be expected that the simple organization of the early republics should have survived the simplicity of early manners and conditions; but instead of rising to a higher form of organic existence it degenerated into a crude and clumsy mechanism. That polypoid character of the Greek States, in which every individual enjoyed an independent existence but could, when the need arose, grow into the whole organism, now made way for an ingenious clock-work, in which, out of the piecing together of innumerable but lifeless parts, a mechanical kind of collective life ensued. . . . Everlastingly chained to a single little fragment of the Whole, man himself develops into nothing but a fragment.[12]

In place of an atomistic, mechanical model of the state, Schiller is here arguing for a more organic, holistic conception, in which the community is treated as an irreducible unity: only such a model, Schiller argues, is adequate to a community that has more than the fragmented and atomistic structure of the liberal state.[13]

In one of his contributions to the *Critical Journal of Philosophy*, known as *Natural Law*, we find Hegel arguing along similar lines. At the outset, he rejects the account of society or the state put forward by 'empiricism', on the grounds that this account takes all such communities to be nothing but collections of self-subsistent and independently existing individuals; as a result, he maintains, empiricism can give no satisfactory explanation of how it is that these individuals form unified social groups:

But the unity itself can only proceed, as in empirical physics, according to the principle of an absolute quantitative multiplicity; in place of the many atomic qualities it can only exhibit a multiplicity of parts or relations – once again nothing but multiplex complexities of the presupposedly original simple and separated multiple units, superficial contacts between these qualities which in themselves are indestructible in their particularity and capable of only light and partial interconnections and intermixtures. Insofar as the unity is posited as a whole, it is given the empty name of a formless and external harmony called 'society' and 'state'.

(NL p. 65: HW II p. 447)

As we have just seen, it was exactly this kind of fragmented and atomistic model of social unity that was also criticized by Schiller, as an inadequate picture of the true community to be found in the Greek states. Like Schiller, Hegel aims to replace this model with a more unified conception, which treats the community as an indivisible totality:

> But, as has been shown, absolute ethical life [*die absolute Sittlichkeit*] is so essentially the ethical life of all that we can scarcely say of it that it mirrors itself as such in the individual. For it is of the essence of the individual, just as much as the aether which permeates nature is the inseparable essence of the configurations of nature, and, as space (the ideality of nature's appearances), is not separate at all in any of them.
>
> (NL pp. 112–13: HW II p. 504)

Now, this account of the structure of society foreshadows what was to be Hegel's strategy against 'empiricism' and atomism in all contexts. Along with his contemporaries, he refused to accept that the ultimate structure of any given unity, such as the community or state, could be reduced to a collection of atomistic constituents; rather, he set out to show how this structure is in fact holistic, and to demonstrate that any given totality has an irreducible unity. As a result, he argues that what exists cannot be broken up into self-subsistent and independent units, and aims to provide an account of this unity in his metaphysics.

This is also Hegel's fundamental strategy against Kant, and his rejection of the latter's theory of synthesis must be seen as an attack on the merely pluralistic and atomistic conception of unity on which that theory is based.[14]

HEGEL'S CRITIQUE OF KANT

In his systematic works, Hegel does not often identify the historical sources which lie behind the theoretical position which he attacks. There is no doubt, however, that it is Locke and Kant who should be associated with his discussion of perception (*die Wahrnehmung*) in the *Phenomenology of Spirit* and in the third book of the *Encyclopaedia*, the *Philosophy of Mind*. In fact, in the latter Hegel goes so far as to identify Kant by name, commenting that 'the specific grade of consciousness on which the Kantian philosophy conceives the mind is perception.'[15] Locke, however, is not mentioned explicitly; none the less, it is clear that Hegel had Locke in mind, and that in this section he is attempting to show how Kant's doctrine of synthesis arises out of Locke's etiolated theory of substance on the one hand, and his 'bundle theory' of the object on the other. In the 'Perception' section of the *Phenomenology* and the *Philosophy of Mind*, therefore, we find Hegel presenting in systematic form the historical development from Locke to Kant that we outlined in the first chapter, as part of Hegel's discussion of the dialectical relationship between a thing and its properties. In what follows, I will mainly refer to the more detailed account provided in the *Phenomenology*, merely using the discussion in the *Philosophy of Mind* to supplement my analysis where necessary.

In the 'Perception' section of the *Phenomenology*, Hegel characterizes the object of perceptive consciousness in two related but apparently incompatible ways: as Also (*Auch*) and as One (*Eins*). Conceived of as an Also, the thing is treated as an 'abstract universal medium'[16] or simple substratum, in which various properties subsist, indifferent to each other and to the thing itself. Hegel gives as an example the coincidence of the properties of being white, cubical, and tart in salt:

> The whiteness does not affect the cubical, shape, and neither affects the tart taste, etc.; on the contrary, since each is itself a simple relating of self to self it leaves the others alone, and is connected with them only by the indifferent Also. This Also is thus the pure universal itself, or the medium, the 'thinghood', which holds them together in this way.
>
> (PS pp. 68–9: HW III p. 95)

Next, however, Hegel points out that if the properties of an object are to be determinate, they must be *contrasted* with the properties of other objects, so that the simple substratum that grounds the object must be opposed to other simple substrata; that is, it must be a One in contrast to other Ones:

> the differentiation of the properties, in so far as it is not an indifferent differentiation but is exclusive, each property negating the others, thus falls outside of this simple medium; and the medium, therefore, is not merely an Also, an indifferent unity, but a *One* as well, a unity which *excludes* an other.
>
> (PS p. 69: HW III p. 95)

Hegel therefore maintains that there are *two* ways of characterizing the thing: as an Also and as a One. In the first case, the object is treated as a collection of unrelated properties that come together in an indifferent medium. In the second case, the object is treated as an exclusive unity which achieves a determinateness by being opposed to other objects:

> In these moments, taken together, the Thing as the truth of perception is completed, so far as it is necessary to develop it here. It is (a) an indifferent, passive universality, the Also of the many properties or rather 'matters'; (b) negation, equally simply; or the *One*, which excludes opposite properties; and (c) the many *properties* themselves.
>
> (PS p. 69: HW III p. 96)

This two-fold conception gives rise to a contradiction, however, and perception oscillates between each way of characterizing the object. To begin with, perception views the object as a One, in opposition to other ones; but it is then faced with the problem that the object has universal properties which it shares with *other* ones. Perception then views the object as a community of properties, as Also; but then, the properties that it has are exclusive of other properties, and so the object cannot be an indifferent universal medium, but seems rather to be a One. On the other hand, not *all* properties belonging to the object affect one another, so perhaps the object *is* a community, an Also; but, if the object is an Also, then the properties appear to be unrelated to the substratum, and so are not properties at all. If this is the case, then we are driven back to the indeterminate 'this' of sense-certainty, a level which was meant to have been transcended by the higher level of perception. Clearly, there is something contradictory in perception's understanding of the object.

However, perceptive consciousness is not yet prepared to find fault with its conception of the object, but blames itself for the problems which it has encountered. It now adopts a more subtle approach to the situation, in order to try and overcome these difficulties. While accepting full responsibility for any distortion of the object on itself, it also claims to be able to get round this distortion, and see the object in its truth. So, perception now takes the object to be One *in truth* (we might also say, in itself), but the independent properties that we also perceive in it are in fact the work of the perceiving consciousness. Clearly, there are echoes of Locke in this systematic presentation of perception, in particular of his doctrine of the unknowable real essence on the one hand, and of secondary properties on the other.[17]

However, as Berkeley pointed out, if we separate the secondary properties from the object in this way, it becomes completely indeterminate. The properties must be returned to the thing, and we must revert to thinking of it as a collection of qualities, and thus as an Also. However, we have moved on from our original conception of the thing as an Also, for we have now introduced the activity of perceptive consciousness in the constitution of the object. This, I would suggest, is Hegel's systematic derivation of the Kantian doctrine of synthesis, as it arises from the inevitable collapse of Lockean realism. This comes about as follows.

Having seen the One fall into indeterminacy, perceptive consciousness reverts to a conception of the thing as Also. It will be remembered that the thing as Also is a loose collection of unrelated properties. However, we saw previously that the thing as Also lacks the unity of properties which we would expect to find in an acceptable characterization of the thing: the unrelatedness of the properties leaves it too dispersed. But (and this is the Kantian move) consciousness has now become aware of its own role in the perception of the object. Taking advantage of this insight, consciousness now credits *itself* with giving unity to the plurality of the thing, by postulating itself as a One in which the unrelated properties of the thing (as Also) come to form a unity. It follows that the properties which constitute the thing achieve a kind of relatedness in so far as they are subsumed in the unity of consciousness. Therefore, while the thing in itself is an unrelated Also, it acquires some relatedness through being taken up into the unity of the thinking subject, which is One:

> Now, in perceiving in this way, consciousness is at the same time aware that it is *also* reflected into itself, and that, in perceiving, the opposite moment to the Also turns up. But this moment is the *unity* of the Thing with itself, a unity which excludes difference from itself. Accordingly, it is this unity which consciousness has to take upon itself; for the Thing itself is the *subsistence of the many diverse and independent properties*. Thus we say of the Thing: *it is* white, *also* cubical, and *also* tart, and so on. Positing these properties as a oneness is the work of consciousness alone which, therefore, has to prevent them from collapsing into oneness in the Thing. To this end it brings in the 'in so far', in this way preserving the properties as mutually external, and the Thing as the Also. Quite rightly, consciousness makes itself responsible for the oneness, at first in such a way that what was called a property is represented as 'free matter'. The Thing is in this way raised to the level of a genuine Also, since it becomes a collection of 'matters' and, instead of being a One, becomes merely an enclosing surface.
>
> (PS pp. 73–4: HW III pp. 100–1)

This, then, is Hegel's systematic derivation of Kant's doctrine of synthesis, which (according to Hegel) seeks to make good a conception of the object as an atomistic Also by supplementing the unity of the thing with the synthesizing activity of the subject. Hegel, however, sees no need for this Kantian move, as he rejects the fundamentally atomistic conception of the object on which it is based. He maintains that such an externally unified plurality in fact constitutes no unity at all, commenting in his *Science of Logic* that 'the very expression *synthesis* easily recalls the conception of an *external* unity and a mere *combination* of entities that are *intrinsically separate*.'[18]

In more detail Hegel's argument is as follows. Kant begins with the assumption that the object is constructed out of a plurality of intuitions, and seeks to introduce a degree of relatedness into this plurality using his doctrine of synthesis. The relatedness of intuitions is held to be *necessary* because it must be compatible with the unity of the transcendental self. The fact that the self supervenes on the plurality of intuitions in this way ensures its relatedness: independently of our synthesizing activity, on Kant's doctrine, the structure of reality is intrinsically atomistic, and no object has an irreducible unity. In his *Encyclopaedia Logic* Hegel gives a graphic picture of how it is that Kant's transcendental self introduces unity into the manifold of representations that make up the formless 'given' of our experience:

> Thought or the I occupies a position directly the reverse of the sensible, with its mutual exclusiveness, and its being outside itself. The 'I' is the original identity – at one with itself and all at home in itself [(das) *schlechthin bei sich Seiende*]. The word 'I' expresses the abstract relation to itself, and whatever is posited in this unity is affected by it and transformed by it. The 'I' is as it were the crucible and fire through which the loose plurality of sense is consumed and reduced to unity. This is the process which Kant calls pure apperception in distinction from common apperception, which takes up the manifold as such in itself, whereas pure apperception is to be viewed as the act which makes the manifold 'mine'.
>
> (EL §42Z p. 69; translation modified)

As in the *Phenomenology*, Hegel stresses here how the structure of experience and the object, on which Kant's theory of synthesis relies, is fundamentally atomistic. The object is an 'Also', which requires combining into unity by the subject, which transforms the plurality of the manifold by bringing it into an external relatedness; in this way, the object is realized.

However, Hegel goes on to argue that a central error in Kant's position is his assumption that anything given to us in experience is compounded from a plurality of intuitions; for, Hegel suggests, reality has an intrinsic unity that is free of any activity of synthesis on the part of a Kantian transcendental subject:

> [Kant's] view has at least the merit of giving a correct expression to the nature of all consciousness. The tendency of all man's endeavours is to understand the world, to appropriate and subdue it to himself: and to this end the positive reality of the world must be as it were crushed and pounded, in other words, idealized. At the same time we must note that it is not the mere act of *our* personal self-consciousness which introduces an absolute unity into the variety of sense. Rather,

this identity is itself the absolute. The absolute is, as it were, so kind as to leave individual things to their own enjoyment, and it again draws these back to the absolute unity.

(EL §42Z pp. 69–70)

Against Kant, therefore, Hegel insists that the unity we find in our experience of the world is not constructed *by us* out of a plurality of intuitions; rather, he argues that the proper religious and philosophical standpoint must be one that sees an inherent unity in things, and accepts this as a fundamental feature of reality:

But mind is not satisfied, as *finite* mind, with transposing things by its own ideational activity into its interior space and thus stripping them of their externality in a manner which is still external; on the contrary, as *religious* consciousness, it pierces through the seemingly absolute independence of things to the one, infinite power of God operative in them and holding them all together; and as *philosophical* thinking, it consummates this idealization of things by discerning the specific mode in which the eternal Idea forming their common principle is represented in them.

(EM §381Z pp. 11–12)

According to Hegel, therefore, Kant was led into adopting an essentially pluralistic conception of reality by the atomistic and fragmented nature of our purely sensible experience, and this in turn led him to argue that unified objects can only come into being if some synthesizing activity undertaken by the subject is presupposed. Hegel maintains, however, that Kant's mistake was to assume that things could be reduced to an externally related plurality in this way, instead of acknowledging their intrinsic unity.

Here, then, we come to the crux of the dispute between Kant and Hegel on this issue: Kant's position, as we have seen, depends upon viewing all individual objects as constructions out of a manifold of intuitions; but, according to Hegel, objects are not in fact mere 'combinations' of sensible properties, as the Kantian model suggests, and on which his doctrine of synthesis depends. Instead, as we shall see, Hegel argues that individual objects exist as manifestations of indivisible substance-universals, which cannot be reduced to a set of properties or attributes; he therefore holds that the object should be treated as an ontologically primary whole. As a result Hegel adopts a metaphysical picture which enables him to argue that the object forms an intrinsically unified individual: because the individual is of such and such a kind (a man, a dog, a canary) it cannot be reduced to a plurality of more basic property-universals, while it is the universal that confers this substantiality upon it. In this way, Hegel replaces Kant's 'bundle' model of the object with a more holistic picture, which treats the individual as a unity, in so far as it exemplifies a substance-kind. It is this ontology of substance which lies behind his rejection of the latter's doctrine of synthesis.

It will be the business of subsequent chapters to clarify this central feature of Hegel's philosophy, and to explain how in his ontological scheme a concrete individual is not reducible to a plurality of sensible properties, but rather exemplifies a substance-universal, as a result of which it constitutes a unity. I will argue that because Hegel viewed the object as an exemplification of a substance-universal in this way, he rejected Kant's conception of the object, with its reduction of the individual to a plurality of intuitions. Hegel insisted that Kant's picture of the object as a combination of sensible properties is false, for as the manifestation of a substance-kind the individual is irreducible, and not the product of synthesis as Kant took it to be.

Chapter three
Ontology and structure in Hegel's *Logic*

In the previous chapter it was explained that Hegel rejected Kant's pluralistic model of the object, and so opposed his claim that objects can only be realized through the synthesis of the manifold of intuitions. As my analysis of the 'Perception' section of the *Phenomenology* should have revealed, Hegel held that Kant's view rested on the mistaken assumption that the object is nothing more than a collection of sensible properties, out of which it is compounded by the experiencing subject. In this chapter, it will be argued that Hegel develops an entirely different conception of the individual object, according to which it is the exemplification of an indivisible and irreducible substance-kind or universal essence, as a result of which it constitutes a single, indivisible totality; this enables Hegel to replace Kant's pluralistic account with his own holistic model of the object. In the following chapter it will be shown how Hegel's account of the individual as the exemplification of a substance-kind leads him to reject the atomistic and reductionist approach to nature adopted by the physicist and the chemist, arguing in his *Philosophy of Nature*, as in his *Logic*, that the concrete material object as a whole has an ontologically primary unity that cannot be further reduced. Understanding the metaphysical outlook put forward in the *Logic* is therefore vital if Hegel's subsequent account of nature in the second book of the *Encyclopaedia* is to be properly comprehended.

I will begin by giving an account of how Hegel's analysis of the categories of universal and individual in the *Logic* arises from his account of the *use* consciousness makes of these categories in the *Phenomenology of Spirit*. I will then provide a detailed analysis of the *Logic* itself, which will try to explain how Hegel set about establishing that the individual constitutes an indivisible unity, as a result of its exemplification of a substance-kind.

FROM THE *PHENOMENOLOGY OF SPIRIT* TO THE *LOGIC*

Although the *Phenomenology of Spirit* has a somewhat ambiguous status with respect to Hegel's completed Encyclopaedic system,[1] the clearest and most obvious way of approaching the *Logic* is nonetheless to begin with the *Phenomenology*.

The *Phenomenology* is in essence an account of the development of consciousness from its lowest level of awareness to what Hegel calls 'absolute knowing' (*das absolute Wissen*). The consciousness in question is not just the consciousness of the single individual self, but also that of humanity in general.[2] This movement or evolution goes through various necessary stages, which are plotted out in the *Phenomenology*. At each stage, consciousness has a particular conception of itself and/or the world, and when this conception turns out to be inadequate or incoherent, a higher conception evolves. Hegel compares this movement from partial to absolute knowledge with the Christian account of the journey of spirit through suffering towards redemption and rebirth:

> Now, because it has only phenomenal knowledge for its object, this exposition seems not to be Science, free and self-moving in its own peculiar shape; yet from this standpoint it can be regarded as the path of the natural consciousness which presses forward to true knowledge; or as the way of the Soul which journeys through the series of its own configurations as though they were the stations appointed for it by its own nature, so that it may purify itself for the life of the Spirit, and achieve finally, through a completed experience of itself, the awareness of what it really is in itself.
>
> (PS p. 49: HW III p. 72)[3]

From this, a very general understanding of the *Phenomenology* can be derived: its aim is to trace the practical and theoretical self-education of Spirit (or human consciousness[4]) as it journeys through various inadequate modes of awareness to a fully adequate conception of itself and reality, at which point absolute knowledge will have been attained.

In following Spirit's journey towards absolute knowledge, the *Phenomenology* traces the collapse of each limited theoretical and practical standpoint adopted by consciousness along the way. The *Phenomenology* is therefore peppered with the 'deconstruction' of various inadequate forms of knowledge, such as sense-certainty, perception, empiricism, the scientific understanding of the natural sciences, observing reason, enlightenment rationalism, and so on; it also follows the collapse of various practical standpoints, such as the master–slave relationship, hedonism, virtue, human and divine law, ethical action, and morality. In revealing these theoretical and practical positions as inadequate and incoherent, the *Phenomenology* aims to show why Spirit must move beyond them, and arrive at a form of consciousness (absolute knowing) in which their incoherence is resolved.

Now, Hegel's explanation for the development of consciousness through these various standpoints is not based on some idea of historical necessity or goal-directed evolution, as is sometimes alleged. Rather, consciousness develops in its conception of itself and the world as it comes to see that a certain outlook involves a tension between the categories of *universal* and *individual*, which (as it moves on) it tries to resolve. This tension is generated because consciousness often turns out to be using these two principal categories in an inadequate way, leading it to oppose the universal on the one side to the individual on the other. It is only when this opposition is overcome, and the individual is seen to exemplify the universal, that absolute knowledge is attained. Implicit in the *Phenomenology*, therefore, is an account of the relation between individuality on the one hand and universality on the other, which makes the *Phenomenology* a crucial prolegomenon to the explicit analysis of these categories in the *Logic*, on which Hegel's ontology depends. In what follows I will give a brief account of some of the major episodes in the *Phenomenology*, in order to show that it is the dialectic of universal and individual on which the progress of consciousness turns.

Hegel's starting point in the *Phenomenology* is the most immediate and naive form of consciousness, which he calls 'sense-certainty' (*die sinnliche Gewißheit*). This mode of consciousness holds that what is immediately given in our sensuous experience truly exists, and that this individual sense object, the simple 'This', is the primary sort of being. Hegel suggests, however, that this certainty in sensible experience is shaken when consciousness comes to see that what is here and now is constantly changing, and that the immediately given 'This' passes over into what is *not*. Sense-certainty then comes to understand that what primarily exists is what does not 'vanish' despite the changes in the content of our immediate experiences: the *universal* 'This', 'Now', 'Here', and 'I'. Echoing the Platonic doctrine that particulars are too shifting and changeable to be proper objects of knowledge, Hegel expresses the hope that this dialectic of sense-certainty will have succeeded in undermining the 'astonishing' philosophical proposition 'that the reality or being of external things taken as Thises or sense objects has absolute truth for consciousness'.[5] Consciousness's initial faith in the pure being of the individual sense-object therefore gives way to a preliminary acknowledgement that the true, permanent object of experience is the universal.[6]

In the next section, on perception, the universal appears to consciousness as the manifold of properties belonging to the thing. This leads to the two-fold conception of the object that we analysed in the previous chapter: that is, as a plurality of universal attributes (Also), and as a singular individuality (One). Perception, however, cannot resolve the apparent contradiction between these two moments, and this lies at the heart of its failure to overcome the tension in its conception of the object:

> What the nature of these untrue essences is really trying to get [perceptual] understanding to do is to *bring together*, and thereby supersede, the *thoughts* of those non-entities, the thoughts of that universality and singular being, of 'Also' and 'One'.
>
> (PS p. 78: HW III p. 106)

Thus, the standpoint of perception, like that of sense-certainty, is incoherent according to Hegel because it leaves unresolved the opposition between universality and individuality, and consciousness up to now has failed to bring these two moments together.

This dialectic of universal and individual also lies at the centre of Hegel's critique of the understanding in the next section of the *Phenomenology*. Although this section is extremely opaque, in a general way it is clear that throughout Hegel continues to pursue the dialectic of these two categories, as the understanding moves to a two-tiered view of reality, setting up an essential world of underlying and universal laws behind the atomistic and transitory world of individuals. It therefore distinguishes between the mere appearance of individuals and the world of universal essential laws that govern this realm of appearances. However, the understanding fails to overcome the radical difference between the universal laws and the individual objects of experience, so that in the end the realm of laws becomes an *inversion* of the world of appearances.

Moving on from consciousness to self-consciousness, we find that the dialectic of universal and individual still lies at the heart of Hegel's account. In the well-known section on the master–slave dialectic, self-consciousness is led into contradiction because it cannot recognize that it shares a universal essence with other individuals: instead, it tries to assert its own unique individuality in the face of the other self-consciousness, while at the same time needing the other to acknowledge its own essential nature. Hegel observes in the passage from the *Encyclopaedia* that corresponds to this section of the *Phenomenology*:

> In this determination lies the tremendous contradiction that, on the one hand, the 'I' is wholly universal, absolutely pervasive, and interrupted by no limit, is the universal essence common to all men, the two mutually related selves therefore constituting one identity,

constituting, so to speak, one light; and yet, on the other hand, they are also two selves rigidly and unyieldingly confronting each other, each existing as a reflection-into-self, as absolutely distinct from and impenetrable by the other.

(EM §430Z pp. 170–1)

The aim of the master–slave dialectic is therefore to show that the standpoint of pure individuality is inadequate, and to reveal how self-consciousness must move towards an awareness that others also exist as selves, by recognizing that all share a common universal essence.[7]

However, although this 'resolves' the contradictions inherent in the master–slave dialectic, at this stage this is not properly recognized by the forms of self-consciousness involved, as they are not yet able to take advantage of this insight. Both the master and the slave persist in their inadequate relationship, and seek to compensate for this inadequacy by retreating into various forms of alienated consciousness. These forms of alienated consciousness are identified by Hegel as stoicism, scepticism, and the unhappy consciousness.

Hegel characterizes the stoic consciousness as one that makes up for its lack of real freedom by retreating into the freedom of *thought*:

This consciousness accordingly has a negative attitude towards the lord and bondsman relationship. As lord, it does not have its truth in the bondsman, nor as bondsman is its truth in the lord's will and in his service; on the contrary, whether on the throne or in chains, in the utter dependence of its individual existence, its aim is to be free, and to maintain that lifeless indifference which steadfastly withdraws from the bustle of existence, alike from being active as passive, into the simple essentiality of thought. Self-will is the freedom which entrenches itself in some particularity and is still in bondage, while Stoicism is the freedom which always comes directly out of bondage and returns into the pure universality of thought.

(PS p. 121: HW III p. 157)

Here, again, we find a contradiction between the individual and the universal; for now the contradiction is between individuality and the extreme universality of *thought*, as an *escape* from individuality and the reality of a particular existence. The suggestion is that unless the individual can achieve a *genuine* universality in the social sphere, he will misguidedly seek a *false* universality in the pure abstraction of thought, in which the individual seeks to lose his individuality in the objectivity and universality of ideas.

The abstract nature of this false universality becomes fully explicit in scepticism, which constitutes the next phase of this alienated consciousness. In scepticism, the self-consciousness abstracts not only from the reality of the self, but also from the reality of the object. In doing so, however, it undermines the permanence of the object and reduces it to a confused medley of transient perceptions, while at the same time it seeks to rise above this transience and to grasp itself as permanent and free from this world of appearances.

Finally, in the unhappy consciousness (*das unglückliche Bewußtsein*) this sceptical sense of transience and unreality infects even consciousness's conception of *itself*, so that the unhappy consciousness takes itself to be an equally transient and inessential being. At the same time, it projects an unchangeable reality *outside* itself, with which it contrasts its own impermanence. As unhappy consciousness, therefore, self-consciousness once more re-enacts the dialectic of universal and individual, this time by contrasting the transience and finitude of itself as individual with the permanence and infinitude of the universal. Although it sees that the universal and individual can come together (for example, in the incarnation), it is not able at this stage to fully comprehend this fact, and insists on an ultimate separation between these two categories. Thus, although it tries to think together the universal and the individual, it cannot do so without feeling a contradiction:

> [Unhappy consciousness] brings and holds together pure thinking and particular individuality, but has not yet risen to that thinking where consciousness as a particular individuality is reconciled with pure thought itself.
>
> (PS p. 130: HW III p. 168)

The unhappy consciousness tries to overcome this contradiction by denying its own individuality, by surrendering its finite bodily form, and seeking to rise to universality. However, Hegel insists that this strategy also fails:

> But this unity is at the same time affected with division, is again broken within itself, and from it there emerges once more the antithesis of the universal and the individual.
>
> (PS p. 134: HW III p. 172)

In the end, unhappy consciousness can only overcome the separation of individual and universal by putting in place a mediator or priest, who can mediate between these two extremes. However, although the individual can achieve a step towards universality by putting himself under the sway of the priest, this is more a *negative* loss of self than a *positive* acceptance of certain universal principles as his own, and so does not really signal the synthesis of individual and universal:

This positive meaning of the negatively posited particular will is taken by this consciousness to be the will of the other extreme, the will which, precisely because it is an 'other' for consciousness, becomes actual for it, not through the Unhappy Consciousness itself, but through a Third, the mediator as counsellor. Hence, for consciousness, its will does indeed become universal and essential will, but consciousness itself does not take itself to be this essential will. The surrender of its own will, as a *particular* will, is not taken by it to be in principle the positive aspect of universal will. Similarly, its giving up of possessions and enjoyment has only the same negative meaning, and the universal which therefore comes to be for it, is not regarded as its *own doing*.

(PS p. 138: HW III pp. 176–7)

Thus, though the unhappy consciousness has surrendered itself to some extent to the universal and altruistic concerns of the 'good life' enjoined by the priest, it has not properly 'internalized' this universality, and so the opposition between its own individuality and the universal ethical realm remains unresolved.

In the following chapter of the *Phenomenology*, on Reason, we find a similar tension between these categories. In the first section, Hegel begins with what he calls Observing Reason, which is a theoretical form of consciousness that claims to arrive at universal categories and laws to cover its observations of the world and of human beings in that world. It turns out, however, that all the universal categories and laws that it constructs are too abstract and arbitrary. The difficulty Reason faces lies in its attempt to form universal laws that can plausibly be said to govern organic nature and the behaviour of human beings. Reason's attempts turn out to be self-refuting because neither organic nature nor self-conscious human beings are in any genuine sense governed by the kind of universal laws it puts forward.[8] In all cases, the individual that is meant to be subsumed under these laws is too complex, protean, and self-determining to be governed by such laws. If the individual is to be subsumed under universal laws, they must be far more profound than the superficial correlations put forward by Reason in this section of the *Phenomenology*: the individual's sense of freedom at this stage makes a nonsense of all attempts by Reason to determine the nature of individuality through supposedly necessary universal correlations.

In the next section of this chapter on reason, entitled 'The Actualization of Rational Self-Consciousness Through Its Own Activity', Hegel considers this clash between the individual and universal laws as it occurs in the ethical domain. At this stage, the individual sets himself outside the universality of ethical laws, and gives primary significance to his own individual nature.[9]

This emphasis on the independence of the individual from all ethical laws first emerges in the pursuit of pleasure as the satisfaction of the individual's desires, which Hegel characterizes as being earthly, rather than heavenly. Modelling his analysis of this form of consciousness on the Faust legend, Hegel suggests that this utterly free hedonistic individualism collapses into the fated death of the individual, who in death gives up his individuality to universality.[10]

The individual then tries to incorporate the universal and necessary laws which determined his death, and arrives at what Hegel calls 'the law of the heart'. This section is important, because here we get a further clash between individual and universal, but this time between the individual's own law, his own moral prescriptions by which he pursues the good, and the universal law that prescribes the good for all. The clash arises because on the one hand the individual tries to impose his own law on the rest of mankind, while it is in fact too tied to his own personality to be truly universal; on the other hand the clash arises because the individual is not able to recognize any law other than that derived from his own moral feeling, and so cannot recognize the true universal law that stands above him. When the individual feels this tension with the universal law, he descends into a raving self-conceit, denouncing the universal law as an intolerable constriction upon the individuality of the law of the heart.

In order to overcome this deranged form of consciousness, the individual then takes up the opposite position, for instead of insisting on the supreme importance of his own individuality against the universal law, he now sinks his individuality into the pursuit of purely universal aims and aspirations. This state of consciousness is said by Hegel to constitute *virtue*, which sets itself up against the pleasure-seeking individuality of the 'way of the world'. As Hegel puts it:

> It is from virtue now that the universal is to receive its true reality by nullifying individuality, the principle of perversion. Virtue's purpose is, by so doing, to reverse again the perverted 'way of the world' and to make manifest its true essence.
>
> (PS p. 230: HW III p. 285)

However, Hegel insists that virtue's attempts to transcend individuality are life-denying and invalid, as only individuality can bring the abstract good of virtue into existence. The result, therefore, is a re-emergence of individuality as a valid principle, of an individuality that can in fact realize the universal:

> The individuality of the 'way of the world' may well imagine that it
> acts for *itself* or in its own interest. It is better than it thinks, for its
> action is at the same time an implicitly universal action.
>
> (PS p. 235: HW III p. 291)

In the last section of this chapter on Reason, finally, we come to forms of
consciousness in which the individual sees himself as united with the
universal. This last section is therefore entitled: 'Individuality Which
Takes Itself To Be Real In And For Itself'.[11]

In the first subsection of this section, Hegel considers the relation
between the acting individual and individuality as it is expressed in action.
He contrasts those individuals whose primary concern is that they alone
should achieve an end through their own action, and those whose primary
concern is that the end should be achieved, regardless of who gets the
credit. In so far as consciousness arrives at this disinterested desire
simply to see the end achieved, it has risen above the egoism of wanting
to take the individual credit, and so attained a degree of universality.

In the following subsection, Hegel returns to the question of the
relation between the individual and the universal ethical laws. Here, the
individual is said to immediately recognize and acknowledge the
universal law, such as the injunction that 'Everyone ought to speak the
truth.' Difficulties arise, however, as such injunctions are not straight-
forwardly universal, as they only cover those people (for example) who
actually *know* the truth which is to be spoken. Hegel's point is that even if
the individual wishes to set himself under universal ethical laws, there
are considerable difficulties in arriving at these laws in abstraction from
an ethical community, which has not yet been introduced.

In the final subsection of this section, and thus in the conclusion to this
chapter, Hegel uses this difficulty to attack the Kantian position,
according to which universal ethical laws are supposed to be arrived at
simply through testing various maxims for their formal universality and
self-consistency. Hegel makes the not unfamiliar point that almost any
maxim can be shown to fulfil these formal criteria. He argues that it is a
nonsense to treat and test laws formally in this way: they must emerge
from the life of a spiritual community, a community that only comes on
the scene in the following chapter on Spirit.

In this chapter on Spirit, the tension between the universal and the
individual once again centres on the ethical realm, although the tension
is beginning to be overcome.[12] The clash here is between the individual
conscience with its own ethical law, supported by personal religious
conviction, and the universal ethical law of the community, backed by
the authority of the state:

Confronting this clearly manifest ethical power [of the state] there is, however, another power, the Divine Law. For the ethical power of the state, being the movement of self-conscious action, finds its antithesis in the simple and immediate essence of the ethical sphere; as *actual* universality it is a force actively opposed to individual being-for-self; and as actuality in general it finds in that *inner* essence something other than the ethical power of the state.

(PS p. 268: HW III p. 330)

This tension can only be resolved when the individual gives up a one-sided allegiance to the divine law and individuality, and comes to see himself as part of the more unified totality of the just state with its ethical laws.

However, the synthesis at this stage is still unstable, and a conflict between individuality and universality re-emerges, as a clash between the close individual allegiances represented by woman and the family, and the more impersonal and universal relations represented by man and the state. The state therefore tries to *suppress* this individuality, feeling it to be a threat. In doing so, it destroys its own unity and universality, collapsing into a plurality of individuals. The state now merely becomes an atomistic community of *persons*, defined merely by their legal status and lacking any sense of their shared universal essence:

> But with the vanishing of this determinateness . . . the life of Spirit and this Substance, which is self-conscious in everyone, is lost. The substance emerges as a formal universality in them, no longer dwelling in them as a living Spirit; on the contrary, the simple compactness of their individuality has been shattered into a multitude of separate atoms [*Punkte*].
>
> The universal unity into which the living immediate unity of individuality and substance withdraws is the soulless community which has ceased to be the substance – itself unconscious – of individuals, and in which they now have the value of selves and substances, possessing a separate being-for-self. The universal being thus split up into a mere multiplicity of individuals, this lifeless Spirit is an equality, in which all count the same, i.e. as *persons*.

(PS pp. 289–90: HW III pp. 354–5)

Having arrived at this extreme of individuality, the person takes his selfhood to be supreme, becoming a 'titanic self-consciousness that thinks of itself as being an actual living god'.[13]

As yet, however, this pure selfhood is free of any *content*, which the individual now tries to acquire in the realm of *culture* (*Bildung*). In giving himself a content, the individual is once more faced with the antithesis of individuality and universality, as he must choose between an allegiance to self and an altruistic allegiance to the universal good. As in his previous account of virtue, Hegel insists that the latter course is in fact not valid, as at this stage it merely involves the loss of self to some utterly abstract universal concept of 'the general good'.[14] This antithesis leads the individual into hypocrisy, for on the one hand he mouths allegiance to this universal good, while on the other hand he is only serving his own interests. The result is the collapse of moral categories, and a nihilistic confusion that no longer takes seriously any conception of right or wrong.

In reaction to this collapse of the moral world, consciousness now retreats into the tranquillity and certainty of faith. Opposed to such superstitious religiosity is the secular culture of the Enlightenment, which then gives way to the revolutionary claims of absolute freedom. At this standpoint, each individual claims to represent the universal, and to speak for the totality; as such, all differentiation among individuals is abolished, as each speaks for all: 'its purpose is the general purpose, its language universal law, its work the universal work.'[15] However, once again Hegel insists that this claim to absolute universality means a loss of all determination on the part of the individual, and leads to empty abstractness. Individuals cannot persist in this empty abstractness, but will begin to differentiate themselves from other individuals into different classes and groups: the only way the rigid uniformity of abstract universality can then be preserved is through the Terror.

Consciousness now moves to the standpoint of morality, and the moral view of the world. Here the individual now subsumes his actions under the demands of duty and a universal ethical law, while at the same time hoping to find in that law a proper expression of his own individuality. However, that this is not the case becomes immediately apparent in the dialectic of *action*, where the individual's conduct is inevitably tied to his specific individual aims, which conflict with the purely universal outlook of duty.[16] In so far as duty cannot in fact be carried out by the individual, it becomes a mere postulate, as something that only *ought* to be.

This contradiction is apparently resolved in the emergence of *conscience*: for now, the individual uses his conscience to tell him what is his duty, while each person's conscience is directly related to his own individuality:

> Conscience, on the other hand, is awareness of the fact that, when the moral consciousness declares *pure duty* to be the essence of its action, this pure purpose is a dissemblance of the truth of the matter; for the fact is that pure duty consists in the empty abstraction of pure

thought, and has its reality and its content only in a specific reality, in a reality which is the reality of consciousness itself, and consciousness not as a mere 'thought-thing' but as an individual. As for consciousness itself, this knows that it has its truth in the *immediate certainty* of itself. This *immediate* concrete self-certainty is the essence [of the action]; looking at this certainty from the point of view of the antitheses of consciousness, the content of the moral action is the doer's own immediate *individuality*; and the *form* of that content is just this self as a pure movement, viz. as [the individual's] knowing or his *own conviction*.

(PS pp. 386–7: HW III p. 468)

With the emergence of conscience, therefore, the antithesis of universal and individual is seemingly resolved, as each individual is positively committed to some definite universal moral law that has a determinate content, while at the same time avoiding the exclusive egoism and inwardness of pure individuality.

However, conscience itself quickly loses the concrete individuality that had enabled it to give a content to the pure moral law; for, as it becomes too highly developed, conscience collapses into the 'beautiful soul', which is too fine to commit itself to anything, and once again can only attain an empty universality. Again, the individual faces the contradiction between its own particular motivations in acting, and the desire to abstract from this concrete individuality and attain a purely universal standpoint:

[Conscience's] pure self, as an empty knowing, is something devoid of content and determination. The content which it gives to that knowing is taken from its own self, as *this specific* self, is taken from itself as a natural individuality. And, in speaking of the conscientiousness of its action, it may well be aware of its pure self, but in the *purpose* of its action, a purpose with an actual content, it is aware of itself as this particular individual, and is conscious of the antithesis between what it is for itself and what it is for others, of the antithesis of universality or duty and its reflection out of universality into itself.

(PS pp. 400–1: HW III pp. 484–5)

This clash between individual motivation and the universal standpoint results in a clash between two types of moral outlook, one that insists on the validity of acting from one's own desires and conscience, and another that insists that the only good deed is the deed done from purely abstract, universal motives.[17] However, this latter consciousness is in fact hypocritical, as it is afraid to act, and pretends its cowardice is really high morality. In the end, however, both the moralist and individual agent must achieve a reconciliation, and so recognize the synthesis of universality and individuality within consciousness. It is this reconciliation of universal and individual that characterizes *absolute* Spirit:

> The word of reconciliation is the *objectively* existent Spirit, which beholds the pure knowledge of itself *qua universal* essence, in its opposition, in the pure knowledge of itself *qua* absolutely self-contained and exclusive *individuality* – a reciprocal recognition which is *absolute* Spirit.
>
> (PS p. 408: HW III p. 493)

Looking back over the ground covered by consciousness in these chapters, I hope it has emerged to what extent consciousness was propelled forward by the tension it felt between the categories of universal and individual.[18] In its journey through the various inadequate standpoints covered in the *Phenomenology*, failure to overcome the antithesis of universal and individual undermined one form of consciousness after another; only once this antithesis was resolved could consciousness overcome its contradictions and reach the level of absolute spirit.

In the *Phenomenology*, however, this dialectic of universal and individual is only treated *implicitly*, in the context of the general development of consciousness through various stages of experience; in the *Logic*, however, these categories are given a more explicit analysis, and it is to that analysis that we must now proceed.

NOTION, JUDGMENT, AND SYLLOGISM

In the account of the *Phenomenology of Spirit* put forward in the previous section it was shown how a tension between the categories of universal and individual plagued consciousness's conception of itself and the world; only once a standpoint was reached in which consciousness succeeded in bringing together *both* these categories could it avoid a felt contradiction in its experience. As it is presented in the *Phenomenology*, however, consciousness is not *itself* aware that it is this dialectic of universal and individual which lies at the root of the difficulties which Hegel describes: rather, only we, as privileged phenomenological observers, have seen that the true cause of consciousness's problems has been its failure to overcome the tension between these two categories. In short, while consciousness has been implicitly thinking in terms of universality on the one hand and individuality on the other, it has not yet subjected these categories themselves to an explicit examination, for it has merely been using them in an unreflective way.

Once it has attained the standpoint of absolute knowledge, however, consciousness is able to give these categories *explicit* treatment, and it is this that we find in the *Logic*:

> In life, the categories are *used*; from the honour of being contemplated for their own sakes they are degraded to the position where they *serve* in the creation and exchange of ideas involved in intellectual exercise on a living content . . . ./ As impulses [*als Triebe*] the categories are only instinctively active. At first they enter consciousness separately and so are variable and mutually confusing; consequently they afford to mind only a fragmentary and uncertain actuality; the loftier business of logic therefore is to clarify [*zu reinigen*] these categories and in them to raise mind to freedom and truth.
>
> (SL p. 34, p. 37: HW V p. 24, p. 27)[19]

Now, in 'clarifying these categories' in the first book of the *Encyclopaedia*, Hegel is led towards a particular philosophical ontology of his own, as he tries to develop a metaphysics in which the unity of these categories can be conceived. In so doing, I will suggest, Hegel puts forward a distinctive account of universal and individual, from which his model of the object is then derived. It is therefore essential to examine Hegel's explicit treatment of these categories as it is set out in the *Logic*.

Prior to his account of universal and individual, Hegel examines the dialectical relationship between other categories of thought, such as Being and Nothing, Quality and Quantity, Identity and Difference, Whole and Part, Inner and Outer, and so on. Hegel's analysis of these and other categories is designed to show how none of these terms is fully intelligible taken *singly*, as each can only make sense when correlated with its other; only once this relation between the categories has been acknowledged, Hegel argues, will consciousness have achieved a properly *rational* mode of thinking. Now, reason (*die Vernunft*) has a very definite meaning for Hegel, which must be explained if the structure of the *Logic* is to be made comprehensible.

Hegel's account of reason both stems from and is a critique of Kant's conception of it, as developed by the latter in his *Critique of Pure Reason*. Like Kant, Hegel draws a definite contrast between reason and the understanding (*der Verstand*), and Hegel himself acknowledges his debt to Kant in drawing this distinction.[20] However, while Kant had a dim view of reason as leading into metaphysical error, and put forward the understanding as yielding the only possible form of (albeit limited) knowledge, in Hegel the order of priority is reversed: Hegel argues (contra Kant) that reason *can* attain knowledge of ultimate reality, and that as a consequence reason stands above the understanding, which has only a limited range.

Furthermore, Hegel's account of *why* the understanding is limited also differs from Kant's. For the latter, the understanding was limited because it must work within the bounds of possible experience; certain infinite objects (such as God, the extent of the world, the soul) lie outside possible experience, however, and so cannot be known through the understanding. For Hegel, by contrast, the understanding is more crucially limited than that: for Hegel, the understanding is limited because the categories with which it conceives the world are *finite*, and cannot be used to think about infinite objects such as God or the world as a whole. In more general terms, Hegel's point is as follows: the understanding is limited because the categories it uses in its conception of the world are one-sided and opposed to their 'opposite', while an infinite object (such as God or the soul) is apparently contradictory for the understanding because it is *not* one-sided in this way, but seems to *encompass* opposites, by being *both* finite *and* infinite, one *and* many, limited *and* unlimited, and so on. This criticism of the understanding, for operating with one-sided and limited categories, comes out clearly in the following passage:

> The metaphysic of the understanding is dogmatic, because it maintains half-truths in their isolation: whereas the idealism of speculative philosophy carries out the principle of totality and shows that it can reach beyond the inadequate formularies of abstract thought. Thus idealism would say: The soul is neither finite only, nor infinite only; it is really the one just as much as the other, and in that way neither the one nor the other . . . . We show more obstinacy in dealing with the categories of the understanding. These are terms which we believe to be somewhat firmer – or even absolutely firm and fast. We look upon them as separated from each other by an infinite chasm, so that opposite categories can never get at each other. The battle of reason is their struggle to break up the rigidity to which understanding has reduced everything.
>
> (EL §32Z pp. 52–3)

As this last sentence indicates, whereas understanding operates with a firm distinction between its categories, reason for Hegel reveals that these distinctions are not tenable, and so forces thought to move beyond the opposed categories of the understanding, to a higher category in which such oppositions are resolved.

This unKantian account of the understanding and reason means that Hegel has a reading of the antinomies that differs from that put forward by Kant in the *Critique of Pure Reason*. For, whereas Kant had diagnosed the antinomies as being caused by our attempt to know about something beyond experience,[21] Hegel argues that the antinomies are generated by understanding's insistence on thinking in terms of one-sided and mutually exclusive categories, so that it cannot settle on the correctness of either one or the other of them, but instead oscillates between them both. As Hegel puts it:

> Kant . . . never penetrated to the discovery of what the antinomies really and positively mean. That true and positive meaning of the antinomies is this: that every actual thing involves a coexistence of opposed elements. Consequently to know, or, in other words, to comprehend an object is equivalent to being conscious of it as a concrete unity of opposed determinations.

> (EL §48Z p. 78)

The understanding is therefore led into contradictions and is limited for Hegel because the concepts or categories with which it operates are treated as mutually exclusive opposites, whereas in fact they entail one another, and should be unified in a higher mode of thought.

According to Hegel, this higher mode of thought is *reason*, which is able to see how the apparently opposed categories of understanding can in fact be brought together in this way. Thus, while the understanding insists in using categories that divide the world up into mutually exclusive aspects, reason is able to see how these aspects cannot be divided and separated from one another, but must be brought together and viewed as interdependent.

This account of understanding and reason comes out clearly in Chapter VI of the *Encyclopaedia Logic*, entitled 'Logic Further Defined and Divided'. In this short chapter, Hegel distinguishes three stages in the development of thought, which he identifies as '(a) the Abstract side, or that of understanding; (b) the Dialectical, or that of negative reason; (c) the Speculative, or that of positive reason'.[22] The first stage, or understanding, is characterized as that faculty of thought which treats categories *not* as unified and mutually inclusive, but rather as apparently discrete and finite; it thereby 'sticks to fixed determinations [*Bestimmtheit*] and the distinctness of one determination from another: every such limited abstraction it treats as having a subsistence and being of its own'.[23] Hegel insists, however, that the categories or concepts cannot be kept apart in this way, but are essentially connected to one another. This leads to the second or *dialectical* stage, which is 'the inherent self-sublation [*Sichaufheben*] of these finite determinations and their transition into their opposites'.[24] As a result of this dialectic, therefore, the understanding's attempts to treat its categories as mutually exclusive are undermined, as such categories are shown to pass over into their opposite, thereby making a nonsense of understanding's efforts to keep them apart. This then leads on to the third and final stage of *reason*, which 'apprehends the unity of the determinations in their opposition – the affirmation, which is embodied in their disintegration and their transition [*Übergehen*]'.[25] Thus, after the dialectical stage, in which each finite category passes over into its opposite, they are then taken up by reason, and brought together in a unity. We can therefore summarize Hegel's position by saying that for him, to think rationally is to set aside the distinctions imposed on things by the understanding, and to see the various determinations of reality as dialectically interrelated.

It is important to notice, however, that as the *Logic* proceeds the dialectical movement of the categories undergoes a transformation:[26] whereas at the level of Being (the first subdivision of the *Logic*) the movement is characterized as one of 'transition' (*Übergehen*), this becomes 'appearance in the other' (*Scheinen in dem Entgegengesetzten*) or 'reflexion' (*Reflexion*) at the next level of Essence, and 'development' (*Entwicklung*) at the final level of the Notion (*Begriff*). The *Logic* reaches its highest point once this close interrelation of the categories is attained:

> The onwards movement [*das Fortgehen*] of the notion is no longer either a going-over [*Übergehen*] or appearance in the other [*Scheinen in Anderem*], but development [*Entwicklung*], in that the distinguished elements are without more ado at the same time posited as identical with one another and with the whole, and the specific character of each is a free being of the whole notion.
>
> (EL §161 p. 224; translation modified)

Now, the categories of the notion, which are said to constitute a unity in this way, are precisely those that have been identified as being central to Hegel's metaphysics:

> The Notion as such contains the moments of *universality*, as the free equality with itself in its determinateness – of *particularity*, the determinateness, in which the universal continues serenely equal to itself, and *individuality*, as the reflexion-in-itself of the determinateness of universality and particularity, which negative unity has determinateness in and for itself and at the same time is identical with itself or the universal.
>
> (EL §163 p. 226; translation modified)

The categories of universal and individual therefore enter Hegel's *Logic* as the highest determinations in his philosophical ontology, and most closely represent the rational forms of thought. As such, Hegel's metaphysical system is founded on these categories, and in what follows I will argue that it is from his treatment of these categories that his account of the object, as the exemplification of a substance-universal, is derived.

Hegel begins his analysis with a frankly realist and essentialist account of universality, stating that the universal constitutes the '*essential being*' and '*substance* of its determinations':[27] 'it is the soul [*Seele*] of the concrete which it indwells, unimpeded and equal to itself in the manifoldness and diversity of the concrete.'[28] Hegel defends the view that it is the universal that constitutes the real nature of the particular individual by claiming that the universal determines what *sort* of being each individual is; and unless it exemplified a substance-kind the individual could not exist. Hegel puts this point very clearly in one of the introductory chapters of the *Encyclopaedia Logic*:

> Now, the animal, *qua* animal, cannot be shown; nothing can be pointed out excepting some special animal. Animal, *qua* animal, does not exist: it is merely the universal nature of the individual animals, while each existing animal is a more concretely defined and particularised thing. But to be an animal – the law of the kind which is the universal in this case – is the property of the particular animal, and constitutes its definite essence. Take away from the dog its animality, and it becomes impossible to say what it is. All things have a permanent inward nature, as well as an outward existence. They live and die, arise and pass away; but their essential and universal part is the kind; and this means much more than something *common* to them all.
>
> (EL §24Z p. 37)

As can be seen from this passage, Hegel does not want to defend a Platonic view of universals as *ante res*; rather, he accepts the Aristotelian view that every universal must be exemplified in an individual. At the same time, he rejects the attempt to treat all universals as quality-predicates (like 'red', 'hot', 'round', and so on), which are only accidentally attached to an independently identifiable individual; such universals, he argues, are merely *abstract*, and are arrived at by *dividing up* the individual into isolated attributes: 'Abstraction, therefore, is a *sundering* of the concrete and an *isolating* of its determinations; through it only single properties and moments are seized.'[29] Against this, Hegel argues that *concrete* universals (such as 'man' or 'dog') constitute the nature of the individual *as a whole*, in so far as they represent the essence of the thing *per se*:

But if the truth of the matter is what we have already stated and also is generally admitted, namely that the nature, the peculiar essence, that which is genuinely permanent and substantial in the complexity and contingency of appearance and fleeting manifestation, is the *notion* of the thing, the *immanent universal*, and that each human being though infinitely unique is so primarily because he is a *man*, and each individual animal is such an individual primarily because he is an animal: if this is true, then it would be impossible to say what such an individual could be if this foundation were removed, no matter how richly endowed the individual might be with other predicates, if, that is, this foundation can equally be called a predicate like the others.

(SL pp. 36–7: HW V pp. 26–7)

Hegel therefore draws a crucial distinction between the universal considered as an accidental quality, of which the individual may have many, and the universal as a substance-kind or species-form, of which the individual exemplifies *one*, and which constitutes the essence of the individual *as a whole*. This distinction is central to Hegel's ontology, and without it any understanding of his metaphysics will be lost.

For, by treating the individual as the exemplification of a universal from the category of substance (like 'man', 'dog', or 'rose'), Hegel was able to reject the substratum theory, which treats the individual as 'bare'; on the contrary, Hegel claims, the individual must always exemplify *some* universal, and so is not to be treated as an unintelligible 'somewhat'. At the same time, Hegel was also able to reject the 'bundle' model of the object, which conceives of the object as a mere collection of *particular* qualities, and thereby reduces the substance-universal to a set of simpler terms. Hegel hopes to show that while the object can be analysed into many such qualities, this does not mean it can be broken up or reduced to a plurality of mutually independent and self-subsistent components; rather, he argues, these qualities should be treated as interdependent aspects of its nature as a *whole*, which is correctly characterizable only by an irreducible substance-universal. The substance-kind account of universals therefore enables Hegel to avoid both the substratum and the bundle models of the individual object, as an examination of his account of the judgment and syllogism will now make clear.

Hegel's analysis of the forms of judgment follows directly from the account of the categories of the notion that we have just examined. In many ways, this is to be expected: there is a clear connection between the category of individual and the idea of a logical subject, and between universality and predication. Hegel explains the transition as follows: we have seen that at the level of the Notion the universal is held to be the 'essential being' of the individual. However, the dialectic does not stop there:

the individual now comes to be treated as a self-subsistent and immediate being, and the universal is reduced to the status of a common property:

> The individual, therefore, as self-related negativity is the immediate identity of the negative with itself; it is a *being-for-self.* Or it is the abstraction that determines the Notion according to its ideal moment of *being* as an *immediate.* In this way, the individual is a qualitative *one* or *this* . . . . Universality, when related to these individuals as indifferent ones – and related to them it must be because it is a moment of the Notion of individuality – is merely their *common element.* When one understands by the universal, what is *common* to several individuals, one is starting from the *indifferent* subsistence of these individuals and confounding the immediacy of *being* with the determination of the Notion. The lowest conception one can have of the universal in its connexion with the individual is this external relation of it as merely a *common element.*
>
> (SL p. 621: HW VI pp. 299–300)

Thus, according to Hegel, the individual now emerges as a self-subsistent 'this', which is only externally related to the universal. Drawing on the etymology of *Urteil* ('original division'),[30] Hegel suggests that this separation between the categories is made explicit in the nature of judgment.

Hegel sets out to argue, however, that no form of judgment can be coherent which treats the universal as a mere property-universal in this way, and that we must proceed to a variety of judgment which predicates a substance-universal of the subject. He therefore presents an analysis of the main types of judgment which is meant to show that only when we treat the universal as 'the soul of the subject' will we be able to use the judgment as a 'vehicle for truth', as a way of expressing genuine knowledge. In this way, Hegel's account of the types of judgment in this section of the *Logic* must be seen against the background of the essentialist and realist account of universals which he presented in the previous section.

The first form of judgment, in which the division between individual and universal is most extreme, is what Hegel calls the judgment of *existence* (*Dasein*) or *quality*, which simply predicates an accidental property of a particular individual (e.g. 'Gaius is learned' or 'This rose is red'). The universal at this stage appears to be ontologically dependent on the subject, in which it inheres. In so far as the universal is merely an accidental property, it is only one of a manifold of attributes that can be truly predicated of the individual; the individual is therefore conceived of as a bundle of properties, out of which it is composed:

The subject, which in the first instance is the *immediate individual*, is related in the judgement itself to its *other*, namely, the universal; consequently it is posited as the *concrete*; in the sphere of being as a something of *many qualities*, or as the concrete of reflection, *a thing of manifold properties*, an *actuality of manifold possibilities*, a *substance* of such and such accidents.

(SL p. 633: HW VI pp. 313–14)

Hegel suggests, however, that this kind of merely qualitative predication is not a vehicle for truth; by which he means, that while the judgment may be factually *correct*, it tells us nothing regarding the *nature* of the individual, nothing about what the individual *is*, or *ought* to be. As he makes clear, this is because a mere predicate-universal does not constitute the substantial form of the subject:

We may add that the untruth of immediate judgement lies in the incongruity between its form and content. To say 'This rose is red' involves (in virtue of the copula 'is') the coincidence of subject and predicate. The rose however is a concrete thing, and so is not red only: it has also an odour, a specific form, and many other features not implied in the predicate red. The predicate on its part is an abstract universal and does not apply to the rose alone. There are other flowers and other objects which are red too. The subject and predicate in the immediate judgement touch, as it were, only in a single point, but do not cover each other. The case is different with the notional judgement . . . . In the judgement of the notion the predicate is, as it were, the soul of the subject, by which the subject, as the body of the soul, is characterised through and through.

(EL §172Z p. 237)

Hegel's doctrine of 'truth' here is clearly tied in with his essentialism and his account of the universal as species-form: this will emerge even more clearly in what follows.

What should be obvious already, however, is that Hegel's aim is to undermine all those forms of judgment which treat the predicate-term as a mere sensible property or simple idea, on the grounds that such forms of judgment reduce the individual subject to a collection of predicates. Hegel's argument is that in these judgments the predicate is merely one of a plurality of accidents that are externally connected to the subject, so that (as we have seen) the unity of the subject comes to depend on the synthesizing activity of a Kantian transcendental consciousness:

The Subject is assumed as a fixed point to which, as their support, the predicates are affixed by a movement belonging to the knower of the

Subject, and which is not regarded as belonging to the fixed point itself.

(PS p. 13: HW III p. 27)

In criticizing these forms of judgment, therefore, Hegel's aim is to undermine the bundle model of the object on which they rely, and to replace this pluralistic ontology with his own holistic model of the object, by treating the latter as the exemplification of a substance-universal. The suggestion is that once we treat the predicate-term in the judgment as a substance-universal in this way, the subject will no longer be seen as a collection of atomistic attributes, but as constituting a single, unified whole.

The second form of judgment Hegel discusses is termed the judgment of *reflection*, which he distinguishes from the previous form of judgment on the grounds that 'its predication is not an immediate or abstract quality, but of such a kind as to exhibit the subject as in relation to something else'.[31] He gives as an example the judgment 'This plant is medicinal', which involves relating the plant to the sickness which it cures. Reflection then goes on to apply such predicates to *all* individuals of the same class, which are collected together in universal judgments. However, Hegel makes clear that reflection has not yet arrived at the conception of a substance-universal, as it treats the individual as if it belonged to a kind in a merely *accidental* way:

> It is as 'all' that the universal is in the first instance generally encountered by reflection. The individuals form for reflection the foundation, and it is only our subjective action which collects and describes them as 'all'. So far the universal has the aspect of an external fastening, that holds together a number of independent individuals, which have not the least affinity towards it.
>
> (EL §175Z p. 240)

Hegel insists that the mistake reflection is making here lies in treating substance-kinds, such as 'man', as if they were merely inessential, abstract universals, which arise from *our* comparison of self-subsistent individuals; he argues, however, that it is wrong to treat the substance-kind as a product of external classification in the nominalistic manner:

> the universal is the ground and foundation, the root and substance of the individual. If e.g. we take Caius, Titus, Sempronius, and the other inhabitants of a town or country, the fact that all of them are men is not merely something which they have in common, but their universal or kind, without which these individuals would not be at all. The case is very different with that superficial generality falsely so called,

which really means only what attaches, or is common, to all the individuals . . . . The individual man is what he is in particular, only in so far as he is before all things a man as man and in general. And that generality is not merely external to, or something in addition to, other abstract qualities, or to mere features discovered by reflection. It is what permeates and includes in it everything particular.

(EL §175Z p. 240)

It is clear that Hegel's target here is the conceptualist account of universals, which holds that universals are no more than the concepts *we* use to classify individuals and subsume them under general terms.[32] Hegel insists, however, that universals exist *in re*, and form the essential nature of the individual in which they are exemplified.

Once this is accepted, the dialectic moves on to the judgments of *necessity*, the first stage of which is the categorial judgment. This form of judgment has the species or genus for its predicate, which represents 'the Universal inner nature of the subject':[33]

The Categorial judgement (such as 'Gold is a metal', 'The rose is a plant') is the unmediated judgement of necessity, and finds within the sphere of Essence its parallel in the relation of substance. All things are a Categorial judgement. In other words, they have their substantial nature, forming their fixed and unchangeable substratum. It is only when things are studied from the point of view of their kind, and as with necessity determined by the kind, that the judgement first begins to be real.

(EL §177Z pp. 241–2)

Hegel is making the essentially Aristotelian point,[34] that the species-universal is a predicate in the category of substance, which tells us *what* the subject is. As such, he holds, it is paradoxical to separate the subject from the predicate, or to think of them in a merely external relation; instead, the universal here must be thought of as inseparable from the individual.

In the second stage of the judgment of necessity, the hypothetical judgment, this necessary connection between subject and predicate is explicitly asserted, in the form of a causal relation between the two terms. Finally, in the third stage, the dogmatic judgment, we specify the particular species under which the individual, *qua* member of a genus, can actually fall.

From judgments of necessity, Hegel then passes on to judgments of value ('This house is good', 'This action is good'), which Hegel calls judgments of the *notion*. Implicit in any judgment of value, Hegel argues, is a comparison between how a thing is, and how it ought to be; but in making such comparisons, he suggests, the individual is set alongside its universal essence or substantial nature, and an assessment is made as to whether or not it realizes or actualizes this substantial nature in an adequate way. At first, this comparison is only implicit, and the judgment is merely *assertoric*; it can then be met with another contrary assertion, whereby it becomes *problematic*. We cannot make the element of comparison fully explicit without moving beyond the judgmental form of subject and predicate, and moving to the inferential form, to the *syllogism*: for only the syllogistic form allows a comparison between the particular nature of the individual and its universal essence, thereby allowing us to judge as to its value.

It should now be clear that Hegel's analysis of the forms of judgment has shown how we must move progressively towards an account of the universal as a substance-kind. His aim throughout has been to show that only the most inadequate judgments predicate a property-universal of the individual, and that consciousness only comes to be aware of the 'essential nature' of things when it grasps the species-form that the individual exemplifies.[35] According to this doctrine, therefore, the individual is not merely constituted out of a bundle of properties, but exists as the actualization of a substance-universal; it is this doctrine which underlies Hegel's account of the structure of the object. Before summarizing this account, however, it is necessary to look at Hegel's treatment of the syllogism.

Hegel's treatment of the syllogism, like his account of the judgment that preceded it, must be understood against the background of his conception of the universal as a substance-kind. For, just as he criticizes those judgments as inadequate which fail to express the universal substance-form which constitutes the 'soul of the subject', so in his treatment of the syllogism he claims that the argument must be based on a proposition which states the universal essence of the individual. In tracing the collapse of various types of syllogism, therefore, he is in fact offering an argument for his conception of universality, and his treatment of the latter as the substantial form of the individual.

In arriving at the syllogism we are faced with Hegel's curious-looking claim that we are dealing with the form of the rational: 'The syllogism is the *rational* and everything rational'; 'Therefore, not only is the syllogism rational, but *everything rational is a syllogism*'.[36] These are hard sayings, but it is of great importance that we try to make them intelligible; for, unless we take these dicta seriously, we ignore or make incomprehensible some of Hegel's other characteristic insights, and in particular his claim to have united individual and universal through his account of these categories in the *Logic*. For, the short answer as to why

Hegel associates the syllogism with the rational is that reason alone is capable of bringing together the separated moments of universal, particular, and individual, and this unity is reflected in the form of the syllogism. Let us look at this in more detail.

In order to understand Hegel's account of reason and the syllogism, it is first necessary to have grasped his conception of understanding and judgment. As has already been shown, according to Hegel the judgment form breaks up the notion into separate determinations, and so distinguishes the three moments of universal, particular, and individual. As I have also explained,[37] Hegel took this division of the categories to be the work of the understanding, in so far as the latter misconceives the nature of these determinations, and thereby sets them apart from one another. More especially, Hegel emphasizes that the understanding treats the universal as being *abstracted* from the particular, with the result that it sets these two categories in opposition to one another, as the universal is no longer 'the soul of the subject':

> The action of Understanding may be in general described as investing its subject-matter with the form of universality. But this universal is an abstract universal: that is to say, its opposition to the particular is so rigorously maintained, that it is at the same time also reduced to the character of a particular again.
>
> (EL §80 p. 113)

The understanding is therefore guilty of treating these categories as opposed determinations, and this is reflected in the structure of the judgment, in which the categories are only externally related.

By contrast, Hegel insists that reason returns to a conception of the universal which constitutes the essential form of the particular, and so returns us to the Notional unity of these moments:

> Only on the third stage of pure thinking [that is, of reason] is the Notion as such known. Therefore, this stage represents comprehension in the strict sense of the word. Here the universal is known as self-particularizing, and from the particularization gathering itself together into individuality; or, what is the same thing, the particular loses its self-subsistence to become a moment of the Notion. Accordingly, the universal is here no longer a form external to the content, but the true form which produces the content from itself, the self-developing Notion of the thing.
>
> (EM §467Z p. 227)

Only this idealistic conception of the universal, as the essence of the particular individual, can unite these two categories; and only by insisting on the unity of these two categories can Hegel develop his model of the object.

Thus, whereas the judgment form reflected the separation of these categories by the understanding in its thinking about the world, the syllogistic form is inherently rational, in bringing these moments together again:

> Thus the syllogism is the completely posited Notion; it is therefore the *rational*. The understanding is regarded as the faculty of the *determinate* Notion which is held fast *in isolation* by abstraction and the form of universality. But in reason the *determinate* Notions are posited in their *totality* and *unity*. Therefore, not only is the syllogism rational, but *everything rational is a syllogism*.
>
> (SL p. 664: HW VI pp. 351–2)

In making his claim that the syllogism is the form of the rational, therefore, Hegel is referring to the fact that reason restores the unity of the Notional categories of universal, particular, and individual, and this is reflected in the syllogistic form.

In the terms of the system, the syllogism is the unity of the notion and the judgment. It is the judgment because the moments of universality, particularity, and individuality are distinguished in it; but it is the notion, in that these moments are returned to unity:

> The actual is one: but it is also the divergence from each other of the constituent elements of the notion; and the Syllogism represents the orbit of intermediation of its elements, by which it realizes its unity.
>
> (EL §181 p. 245)[38]

The syllogism therefore makes explicit the unity of these categories that we saw in the notion, yet in a more developed form.

However, though the structure of the syllogism will ultimately enable us to express the true unity of the universal and individual, its initial forms are not fully rational as they stand. Its termini persist in an external relation to each other; the two extremes of individual and universal are only partially linked via the mediation of particularity. The three moments do not therefore achieve their rational unity straight away.

The first inadequate syllogism is the qualitative syllogism, in which the moments of individual, particular, and universal are connected in a causal and external fashion. It thus has the form I–P–U: a subject as individual is coupled with a universal by means of a particular quality. Hegel gives the following as an example of this sort of syllogism:[39]

	(1) This rose is red	I
	(2) Red is a colour	P
Therefore	(3) This rose is a coloured object	U

Hegel points out the inherent inadequacy of this form of syllogistic deduction: since its middle term is only contingently connected with its two extremes, it can yield only a contingent, externally connected conclusion, the contrary of which could just as easily have been arrived at by employing some different, just as loosely connected, middle term. For, first, the subject has many other qualities besides redness, and so could be coupled with many other universals. Second, the particular in the middle term *also* has other characteristics, which would also connect the subject with *different* universals. Lastly, in a genuine syllogism, the two extremes should be completely united in the middle term – but this is not the case here. And, syllogisms stating non-essential connections readily lead to the 'bad infinite', as we have to provide further syllogisms to prove our premises.

But of course, in order to prove the premises of this first-figure syllogism, we must devise other syllogistic forms, the conclusions of which are I and P. The positive aspect of this infinite progression of proofs is that it shows that the form I–P–U is defective as it stands:

> The truth of the infinite progression consists, on the contrary, in the sublation of the progression itself and the form which is already determined by it as defective. This form is that of mediation as I–P–U.
>
> (SL p. 673: HW VI p. 363)

The trouble with the form I–P–U as a qualitative syllogism is that because the premises involve merely qualitative predicates, the two transitions involved (I–P and P–U) are inadequate. For instance, in the case of the transition from P to U, because colouredness is an inessential aspect of the rose, to move from talk of colouredness (P) to talk of the *rose* as a coloured object (U) seems arbitrary: why not post-boxes, sunsets, etc., rather than a rose? However, in the later forms of the syllogism, in which we are talking of essential aspects, the particular determination (e.g. manhood) is an essential aspect of the individual (e.g. Gaius as a man), so that the move from mortality in relation to manhood, to *Gaius'* mortality constitutes an internally coherent transition.

In order to overcome the artificiality of the transitions from P–U and I–P these transitions must *themselves* be mediated, by the individual in the first case, and by the universal in the second: this leads to the second-figure (P–I–U) and the third-figure (I–U–P) syllogisms. Each of these three figures relies on the others to justify itself: thus, whilst the first and third figures rely on the transition I–U, this transition is itself justified by the second figure. Further, whilst the first figure relies on the transition I–P, this is justified by the third figure, and so on. The need for these three figures arises because, in the first figure, the three moments were only immediately related and not fully interconnected: we therefore need the other two figures to achieve this mediation. Thus, Hegel says of the third-figure syllogism (I–U–P):

> The objective significance of the syllogism in which the universal is the middle term, is that the mediating element, as unity of the extremes, is *essentially a universal*. But since the universality is in the first instance only qualitative or abstract universality, it does not contain the determinateness of the extremes; their conjunction, if it is to be effected, must similarly have its ground in a mediation lying outside this syllogism and is in respect of this latter just as contingent as in the case of the preceding forms of the syllogism. But now since the universal is determined as the middle term, and the determinateness of the extremes is not contained in it, this middle term is posited as a wholly indifferent and external one.
>
> (SL p. 679: HW VI p. 371)

This passage explains clearly how Hegel takes the inadequacy of the qualitative syllogism to rest on the fact that the universal employed here is merely an accidental property of the individual: as such, he argues, the syllogistic form is incoherent and the conclusion reached is not necessary. As with his analysis of the forms of judgment, therefore, Hegel's aim is to show that no syllogistic form can be adequate which merely conceives of the object in terms of property-universals or accidental qualities; he hopes to show that only when the object is treated as the exemplification of a substance-universal can a fully coherent type of syllogism be reached.

Now, we have seen that the inadequacy of the qualitative syllogism as it stands lies in the contingency and externality of the connection of its terms. In the next class of syllogism, the syllogism of reflection, this externality is overcome, as the Notional moments are more closely related.

> The course of the qualitative syllogism has sublated what was *abstract* in its terms with the result that the term has posited itself as a determinateness in which the other determinateness is also *reflected*. Besides the abstract terms, the syllogism also contains their *relation*, and in the conclusion this relation is posited as mediated and necessary; therefore each determinateness is in truth posited not as an individual, separate one, but as a relation to the other, as a *concrete* determinateness.
>
> (SL p. 686: HW VI p. 380)

We must therefore pay particular attention to the structure of mediation in this syllogism, in which the different categories of universal, particular, and individual are said to be more adequately treated. A better mediation is found when individuality is used to mediate between particularity and universality, where the individuals concerned are grouped into a *class*, and the inference concerns the whole of the class.

Hegel calls the first syllogism of reflection the Syllogism of Allness. He gives as an example of this form of syllogism:

	(1) All men are mortal
	(2) Gaius is a man
Therefore	(3) Gaius is mortal

This syllogism differs from the corresponding qualitative syllogism in that being a man is not a contingent property that Gaius may or may not have: Gaius with all his properties is contained in the class of men, and the connection of humanity with mortality is taken to be established for the *whole* of this class. But in fact the syllogism is not unproblematic: we can conclude that Gaius is mortal because he is a man, on the grounds that all men are mortal; but, the universal proposition that all men are mortal is only itself arrived at because we have observed empirically and on its own account that those individuals that are men are also always mortal. This proposition – that because Gaius is a man he is mortal – is the truly immediate proposition, while the universal proposition that all men are mortal is mediated by it. Thus, the individual (Gaius) is not in fact connected with the universal (mortality) by way of the particular (humanity) (I–P–U); but rather, the particular (humanity) only comes to be connected with the universal (mortality) through the countless individuals who are *both* human *and* mortal (i.e. U–I–P). For, the truth of the premiss that all men are mortal presupposes the truth of the inference that if Gaius is a man, he is mortal; and this inference is established *inductively* in the second syllogism of reflection, the inductive syllogism.

Hegel gives the following as the schematic representation of the syllogism of induction:

$$
\begin{array}{c}
\text{I} \\
\text{P} - \text{I} - \text{U} \\
\text{I} \\
\cdot \\
\cdot
\end{array}
$$

The mediation between P and U now consists of a complete list of individuals. However, the list is only arrived at by means of external reflection or experience, and no *internal* relation is yet posited between the individuals as collected. This makes it impossible to arrive at a principle of completeness for the list, and a tension thus arises between the middle term and the universality of the conclusion. The conclusion of the syllogism of induction therefore remains *problematic*. However, the search for a principle of completeness leads to the postulation of certain similarities between the individuals, so that individuals with one sufficiently essential property in common might be taken to have others in common.

This is the reasoning behind the syllogism of analogy, in which we conclude from the fact that an individual possesses a certain quality that the same quality is possessed by other individuals of the same kind. Thus, we reason from the fact that all planets hitherto discovered have been subject to the laws of motion, to the conclusion that anything in the future that we admit to being a planet (perhaps on grounds *other* than obeying the laws of motion) will be subject to these laws. But, the problem with the syllogism of analogy is that it will only work with respect to *essential* properties: that is, one can only infer that one member of a genus will have the property (or properties) of all other members of the genus if the property (or properties) in question are essential to members of that genus. And, of course, one way of deciding (at least at this level) whether a property is essential is to see whether it is possessed by all members of that genus. The success of the inference therefore seems to depend on the *prior* subsumption of the individual under the universal, a subsumption that itself depends on the success of the inference.

The breakdown of the syllogism of analogy leads us out of the syllogism of reflection, in which the individual acted as the mediating element, and into the syllogism of necessity, in which the universal is the middle term. Thus the middle term is no longer a class or collection (as it was in the syllogism of reflection), but rather is the essence, the specific or generic nature of the individuals concerned.

The first form of the syllogism of necessity is the categorial syllogism, in which some essential property is predicated of an individual, as a result of its exemplification of a universal from the category of substance:

The categorial syllogism in its substantial significance is the *first syllogism of necessity*, in which a subject is united with a predicate through *its substance*. But substance raised into the sphere of the Notion is the universal, posited as being in and for itself in such a manner that it has for the form or mode of its being, not accidentality, which is the relationship peculiar to substance, but the Notion-determination. Its differences are therefore the extremes of the syllogism and, precisely, universality and individuality.

(SL p. 696: HW VI p. 392)

An example of this type of syllogism might be:

	(1)	Gaius is a man
	(2)	A man is mortal
Therefore	(3)	Gaius is mortal

Here, manhood is part of the essence of the individual, and so the subject is no longer contingently united through the syllogism with *any* quality through *any* middle term. This categorial syllogism thus avoids the problems that faced the qualitative syllogism. Equally the syllogism does not presuppose its conclusion for the truth of its premises, for the proposition 'A man is mortal' is not based on inductive evidence, but is a necessary truth. This syllogism thus avoids the problems faced by the syllogism of reflection.

But, Hegel claims, the categorial syllogism still faces difficulties.[40] In the first place, there are an indefinite number of *other* individuals who could *also* be subsumed under the *same* genus: it is therefore arbitrary that this one is chosen. Further, the individual also has a number of *unique* determinations, specific qualities which are *not* covered by the genus. The individual is thus contingently placed in the syllogism, introducing an element of uncertainty which is reflected in the hypothetical syllogism, which has the form:

	(1)	If A is, then B is
	(2)	But A is
Therefore	(3)	B is

Lastly, in the disjunctive syllogism, we arrive at a universal genus that makes good the limitations of the categorial syllogism, in so far as it is a universal genus that contains within itself the full particularization of the species, a particularization that leads to the determination of the individuals: A that is B or C or D. In determining which of the possible determinations A is, we particularize it (A is neither C nor D), thereby determining it as an individual (A is B).

An example may help here. Let us assume that all states are either monarchies, oligarchies, or democracies. Thus, we begin with the state as a universal genus, which we determine into species:

(1) The state is either a monarchy, oligarchy, or democracy

We then particularise the kind of state we are considering by distinguishing it from other members of the genus:

(2) The state is neither a monarchy, nor an oligarchy

This enables us to determine the state as an individual:

(3) The state is a democracy

Thus, the state has moved through the three moments of universal, particular, and individual. However, the important point to note is that this form of syllogism is only workable if the concept in question is a self-determining universal: that is, if the genus 'state' is a universal concept that can be exhaustively specified with respect to its species. It follows, then, that the universal as subject of the first premiss must be a universal notion, which contains the particular and individual in itself as their essential nature. The structure of the disjunctive syllogism therefore brings us full circle, returning us to the Notion from which we began.

THE SUBSTANCE-KIND MODEL OF THE OBJECT

The aim of Hegel's discussion of the notion, judgment, and syllogism, and the associated categories of universal, particular, and individual, is to modify the way in which we think of these categories, and thus to transform our metaphysics. In an extremely Kuhnian-sounding passage from the introduction to his *Philosophy of Nature*, Hegel stresses the importance of this conceptual revolution:

> metaphysics is nothing but the range of universal thought-determinations, and is as it were the diamond-net into which we bring everything in order to make it intelligible. Every cultural consciousness [*gebildetes Bewußtsein*] has its metaphysics, its instinctive way of thinking. This is the absolute power within us, and we shall only master it if we make it the object of our knowledge. Philosophy in general, as philosophy, has different categories from those of ordinary consciousness. All cultural change reduces itself to a difference of categories. All revolutions, whether in the sciences or world history, occur merely because spirit has changed its categories in order to understand and examine what belongs to it, in order to possess and grasp itself in a truer, deeper, more intimate and unified manner.

(EN §246Z, I p. 202)

As was explained in my account of the *Phenomenology*, Hegel holds that the way we use categories like universal and individual will determine our ontology, and thus the view we have of ourselves and our world; he also holds that various wrong-headed conceptions of these categories must be overcome, and this revision of our categories will enable us to understand reality in a new way.

Now, as we have also seen, there is a particular picture of reality that Hegel wishes to undermine by offering his revised conception of the categories of universal and individual. This picture is one which treats all things as reducible to a plurality of distinct ideas, intuitions, or properties, and thus as atomistic in structure. This is an account of objects which he traces back to empiricism:

> In order to form experiences, Empiricism makes especial use of the form of Analysis. In the impression of sense we have a concrete of many elements [*ein mannigfach Konkretes*], the several attributes [*Bestimmungen*] of which we are expected to peel off one by one, like the coats of an onion. In thus dismembering the thing, it is understood that we disintegrate and take to pieces these attributes which have coalesced, and add nothing but our own act of disintegration. Yet analysis is the process from the immediacy of sensation to thought: those attributes, which the object analysed contains in union, acquire the form of universality by being separated. Empiricism therefore labours under a delusion, if it supposes that, while analysing the objects, it leaves them as they were: it really transforms the concrete into something abstract. And as a consequence of this change the living thing is killed: life can exist only in the concrete and the one.
>
> (EL §38Z pp. 62–3)

It is Hegel's aim in the *Logic* to show that this reductionist ontology rests on the mistaken assumption that all individuals can be analysed into a plurality of property-universals. His analysis of the notion, judgment, and syllogism is designed to establish that in fact a *substance* universal forms the essential nature of the individual *as a whole*, and that this universal cannot be reduced to a collection of universals of another type. It can therefore be seen that in adopting his realist and essentialist theory of universals in the *Logic*, Hegel hoped to show that the conception of this category adopted by the empiricist is mistaken, with the result that the pluralistic ontology associated with it must be overturned.[41]

It has also been explained how far Kant's doctrine of synthesis can be taken to arise out of the empiricist's account of the object as a plurality of sensible properties; for this bundle model clearly lies behind the latter's account of the combination of the manifold by the transcendental consciousness. In adopting his anti-reductionist metaphysics of the substance-universal, therefore, Hegel was also explicitly challenging the assumptions of Kant's account of synthesis.

One way of casting light on the dispute here is by showing how it compares to a debate that has gone on in more recent philosophy over the ontological structure of things. This debate was sparked off by Bertrand Russell's theory of descriptions, which gave new life to the suggestion that objects can be reduced to a bundle of qualities,[42] as it was supposed to reveal how proper names and definite descriptions can be replaced by variables and purely predicative general terms: by appearing to show how it is possible to talk (in logic, if not in language[43]) without using expressions that denote things, Russell's theory is said to have demonstrated the dispensability of any doctrine of substance.

Now, while the value of Russell's account for logic has not been denied, doubts have been raised over this supposed ontological implication of his theory. Against those like A. J. Ayer, who have sought to re-introduce the bundle model of the object as a result of the eliminability of singular terms, it has been pointed out that Russell's theory does not in fact license this reduction of the object to a collection of qualities; for, the predicate-letter 'F' in the expression $(\exists x)(Fx)$ can be a substance-universal as well as a quality-universal, and in predicating a substance-universal we are in no way committed to treating the object as a collection of qualities, as the bundle model implies.[44] Moreover, it has been argued that if in using a substantive we are merely saying that a plurality of properties is instantiated, we would not be talking about a real *thing* unless it was also taken that these properties constituted a genuine unity, and *this* could not be expressed unless we introduced substance-universals (like 'man', 'rose', etc.) into our description of the world.[45]

These objections to the reduction of objects to a collection of predicates capture the force of Hegel's dissatisfaction with Kant, and in many ways mirror his strategy in arguing against the latter. Hegel rejects the idea that the object is nothing more than a synthetic unity of a manifold of predicates,[46] and argues that as an individual substance, it constitutes an irreducible thing. It is this insight, I have argued, that causes him to treat the predicative element in the judgment as a *substance*-universal, and which leads him towards his non-reductive ontology of the object.

To sum up: according to Hegel, both Kant and the empiricists are mistaken in treating the object as reducible to a plurality of distinct property-universals, as the object is primarily an exemplification of a substance-universal (such as man, dog, or whatever), and as such it constitutes an irreducible unity. In treating the object as manifesting a substantial form that is not further divisible in this way, Hegel arrives at an holistic conception of the object, using an account of the categories that is meant to overturn the limited view of individuality and universality that led Kant and the empiricists into atomistic pluralism.

In adopting this model of the object, therefore, Hegel's aim was to undermine the reductionist and atomistic metaphysics of the empiricist; as will emerge in the next chapter, his critique of the latter also led him to condemn the reductionist, atomistic metaphysics of some of the natural sciences, with which Hegel associated it. It is therefore necessary to follow Hegel as he develops his ontological position in the context of his *Philosophy of Nature*.

Chapter four

Unity and structure in Hegel's *Philosophy of Nature*

In the account of the *Logic* given in the previous chapter, it was shown that Hegel adopts an ontological model of concrete individuals which treats them as indivisible primary substances, by virtue of exemplifying a substance-universal, which cannot be reduced to a plurality of attributes. He therefore defends a metaphysical account of things which is undeniably *holistic*, and rejects the model adopted by the empiricists and by Kant, who had treated the object as a plurality of property-universals, intuitions, or simple ideas, and thereby reduced the object to a manifold of ontologically self-subsistent elements, which can exist outside and prior to their instantiation in the whole. Hegel's claim, therefore, is that because individuals exemplify a substance-universal, they must be treated as irreducible wholes, or substantial unities, and he cannot accept the empiricist reduction of things to a plurality, arguing that it is wrong to treat the object in this atomistic way.

However, there is an obvious difficulty for Hegel's model of the object, as there is for any account that tries to treat the individual as an irreducible unity, on the grounds that it exemplifies a substance-universal:[1] those entities which Hegel wants to treat as unified substances are all *material* things, and so must be divisible into the kinds of atomistic entity which the physicist tells us are constituents of any ordinary object. It would therefore seem that the individuals which exist must be taken as mere complexes after all, at this physical level. This might suggest that it is the ontological model of the object put forward by Kant and the empiricists that best fits this picture offered to us by science of the way things are, and that Hegel's account runs counter to this immensely valuable explanation of the nature of reality, as the complex unity of atomistic elements.

Now, by examining his *Philosophy of Nature*, we will come to see that Hegel was not unaware of this difficulty, for in this work he set out to answer it, precisely by setting up limits to this atomistic picture of the world put forward by Newtonian science, and by trying to show how nature overcomes what he call its 'asunderness'.[2] In so far as his metaphysical model of the object is holistic and anti-reductionist, as a result of his conception of the substance-universal, so he aims to show in the second book of the *Encyclopaedia* that the material world has a unity that makes it possible to treat certain entities as irreducible substances, in line with his metaphysical model of things. In the introduction to his *Philosophy of Nature*, he insists that this model alone will save us from falling for a bogus atomism and reductionism in our scientific inquiries:

> The inadequacy of the thought-determinations used in physics may be traced to two very closely connected points. (a) The universal of physics is abstract or simply formal; its determination is not immanent within it, and does not pass over into particularity. (b) This is precisely the reason why its determinate content is external to the universal, and is therefore split up, dismembered, particularized, separated and lacking in any necessary connection within itself; why it is in fact merely finite. Take a flower, for example. The under-standing can note its particular qualities, and chemistry can break it down and analyse it. Its colour, the shape of its leaves, citric acid, volatile oil, carbon, hydrogen etc. , can be distinguished; and we then say that the flower is made up of all these parts . . . . [But] Intuition has to be submitted to thought, so that what has been dismembered may be restored to simple universality through thought. This contemplated unity is the Notion, which contains the determinate differences simply as an immanent and self-moving unity. Philo-sophic universality is not indifferent to the determinations; it is the self-fulfilling universality, the diamantine identity, which at the same time holds difference within itself.

(EN §246Z, I pp. 202–3)[3]

Hegel here states clearly that on his view the empiricist conception of the object as a collection of 'particular qualities' and the scientific con-ception of the object as a plurality of chemical and physical parts, are two sides of the same coin, and his holistic and anti-reductionist model of the object means that he can accept neither. It is now necessary to examine Hegel's *Philosophy of Nature* in this light, to show how it should be read as an attempted vindication of his metaphysics from a scientific perspective,[4] aimed at defeating those who might support their atomistic and reductionist ontology by adopting just such an atomistic and reductionist picture of the natural world.

NATURE AND OBJECTIVITY

It is the substance of my interpretation of Hegel's philosophy that he develops a model of unity using the metaphysical categories of the Notion, and uses this model as the background to his account of various natural phenomena. In some ways, on this interpretation, it is to be expected that Hegel move straight from his discussion of the formal Notion as it appears in the *Logic*, to an account of how this model is realized in nature. However, he does not do this, but interposes two further sections, which he entitles 'The Object' (*Das Objekt*) and 'The Idea' (*Die Idee*).

Far from being a problem for my interpretation, however, these sections provide a detailed support for it. For, in these sections, Hegel gives a general account of how the categories of the Notion apply to the natural world, though at the abstract level of the *Logic*. That is, Hegel does not make his descent from the metaphysical abstractness of the Notion to the concrete realities of nature *immediately*, but rather provides a re-interpretation of the formal Notion in terms of the less formal categories of nature, while none the less remaining at the abstract level of the *Logic*. In this way, we can view the sections on the Object and the Idea as important transitional passages from the purely metaphysical categories of the subjective Notion to the objective categories that apply to the concrete reality of nature; this enables Hegel to show how the formal Notion can provide a basis for these objective categories, without as yet having to deal with the empirical detail that we find in the full account as given in the *Philosophy of Nature*.

Much of the philosophical substance of Hegel's discussion of nature is therefore prefigured in his analysis of Mechanism, Chemism, Teleology, and Life, as given in the *Logic*. We will therefore examine Hegel's account of Mechanism and Chemism here in more detail, postponing a discussion of Teleology, and Life until we reach the final section of the *Philosophy of Nature*, to which these categories correspond.

Hegel's complaint against mechanism is that the object considered mechanically lacks any *intrinsic* unity, in so far as each part of the object is only externally related to each other part. The mechanical object is therefore characterized as having no real substantial form, for its unity is only that of an external aggregation:

> The determinatenesses, therefore, that [the mechanical object] contains, do indeed belong to it, but the *form* that constitutes their difference and combines them into a unity is an external, indifferent one; whether it be a *mixture*, or again an *order*, a certain *arrangement*

of parts and sides, all these are combinations that are indifferent to what is so related.

(SL p. 713: HW VI p. 412)[5]

Hegel accepts, of course, that in the case of certain natural phenomena, the mechanical way of viewing things is absolutely justified; he warns, however, that it would be a mistake to extend the categories of mechanics to the investigation of more intrinsically unified phenomena, such as the soul, which should not be regarded as 'a mere group of forces and faculties, subsisting independently side by side'.[6] As we shall see, Hegel treats the soul as a substance-universal, which cannot be reduced to a plurality of self-subsistent parts in the way that mechanistic thinking prescribes.

Not only is the structure of the mechanical object itself a merely external unity; mechanics also views the relation *between* objects as equally external, so that they form an ununified plurality:

In so far as [objectivity] has the Notion immanent in it, it contains the difference of the Notion, but on account of the objective totality, the differentiated moments are *complete* and *self-subsistent objects* which consequently, even in their relation, stand to one another only as *self-subsistent* things and remain *external* to one another in every combination. This is what constitutes the character of *mechanism*, namely, that whatever relation obtains between the things combined, their nature is one *extraneous* to them that does not concern their nature at all, and even if it is accompanied by a semblance of unity it remains nothing more than *composition*, *mixture*, *aggregation* and the like.

(SL p. 711: HW VI p. 409)

As A. N. Whitehead observed, 'Newtonian physics is based upon the independent individuality of each bit of matter',[7] and it is precisely this external relatedness that Hegel identifies as characteristic of mechanism. Only in Absolute Mechanics, as realized in the solar system, is matter bound together in a way that represents a more genuine unity, based on the unifying function of the central body, which constitutes 'the permanently underlying universal substance'[8] through which the various bodies in the solar system are brought together:

Its determinateness is essentially different from a mere *order* or *arrangement* and *external connexion* of parts; as determinateness in and for itself it is an *immanent* form, a self-determining principle in which the objects inhere and by which they are bound together into a genuine One.

(SL p. 723: HW VI p. 424)

By treating the central body of the solar system as a universal, and by identifying it as the ground of unity for the planetary bodies, Hegel is here clearly referring us back to his account of the universal in the *Logic*, and using this to explain the unity of the system as a whole.

However, although the solar system constitutes a totality, still masses do not really combine, and the world considered mechanically remains an aggregate of independent elements. Hegel therefore passes on to the level of *chemism*, where objects, far from being indifferent to one another, are related by virtue of their own intrinsic qualities:

> The chemical object is distinguished from the mechanical by the fact that the latter is a totality indifferent to determinateness, whereas in the case of the chemical object the *determinateness*, and consequently the *relation to other* and the kind and manner of this relation, belong to its nature.
>
> (SL p. 727: HW VI p. 429)

The phenomenon of chemical combination clearly impressed Hegel, on the grounds that such an affinity between material substances was an indication of the evolving unity of the natural world.

The explanation Hegel offers of the chemical process is that different substances are one-sided particularizations of the same universal, and therefore combine together in order to overcome this one-sidedness, and realize the universal as a whole:

> [The chemical process] begins with the presupposition that the objects in tension, tensed as they are against themselves, are in the first instance by that very fact just as much tensed against one another – a relationship that is called their *affinity*. Since each through its Notion stands in contradiction to the one-sidedness of its own existence and consequently strives to sublate it, there is immediately posited in this fact the striving to sublate the one-sidedness of the other object; and through this reciprocal adjustment and combination to posit a reality conformable to the Notion, which contains both moments.
>
> (SL p. 728: HW VI p. 430)

What Hegel is doing here, I would argue, is taking the explanation of affinity offered by Schelling and other *Naturphilosophen*, who talked in terms of a polarity of forces that are reconciled through combination, and transposing this explanation into his own metaphysical terminology.[9] Thus, where Schelling had explained chemical affinity through the chemical equilibrium of opposed forces that are encompassed in an original One, so Hegel explains this phenomenon by treating the chemical objects as opposed particularizations of the same universal, in which their difference from one another is overcome:

> The relationship of the objects, as a mere communication in this element, is on the one hand a quiescent coming-together, but on the other hand it is no less a *negative bearing* of each to the other; for in combination the concrete Notion which is their nature is posited as a reality, with the result that the *real differences* of the object are reduced to *its* unity. Their previous self-subsistent *determinateness* is thus sublated in the union that conforms to the Notion, which is one and the same in both, and thereby their opposition and tension are weakened, with the result that in this reciprocal integration the striving reaches its quiescent *neutrality*.

(SL p. 729: HW VI p. 431)

Hegel's position here is inexplicable unless it is taken that he is trying to show how chemical combination represents a partial overcoming of the external relatedness of mechanism, and reveals the intrinsic overarching unity of the universal form inherent in each of the chemical substances.

However, chemism too is flawed. For, though the differentiated moments in a chemical reaction come to form a unity in the neutral product, with this neutral product the process comes to an end: chemical substances do not undergo a *continuous* movement of integration. The unity that was implicit in this process is made explicit at the next level, of Teleology; but I will present my account of Hegel's analysis of Teleology and Life later in this chapter.

What is important to stress here is that this account of mechanism and chemism is designed to show how nature displays a greater degree of unity and integration as it advances through these levels, and that this should be remembered as providing the background to the treatment of mechanism and chemism in the *Philosophy of Nature*. It is to Hegel's account of mechanics given there that I now turn.

STRUCTURE AND NATURE

Mechanics

It has been pointed out that Newtonian mechanics rests on the assumption that 'the material world is composed of equal particles, whose essential properties would belong to each and every particle even as a single particle in empty space'.[10] In this section of the *Philosophy of Nature*, Hegel is concerned to show how this mechanical world-view is inadequate, in so far as it treats reality as if it were made up of self-subsistent atomistic units in this way. Against this, Hegel wants to show that the systematic unity of things cannot be reduced to a plurality of distinct and independently existing elements. Mechanism, by itself, cannot do justice to this fundamental insight of his metaphysical system, and Hegel's insistence that we pass on to a less atomistic outlook should be seen as part of his attempt to show that the structure of things is holistic in character.

Drawing on his prior account of space as 'self-externality' (*Außersichsein*),[11] Hegel begins by describing matter in space as an atomistic plurality of many ones that stand outside one another. As in the *Logic*, Hegel argues that this plurality is upheld by *repulsion*, which acts between the many ones, and thereby keeps them apart. The fact that all units of matter repel each other in this way is the result of matter's tendency towards absolute difference.

However, Hegel also insists that this tendency towards absolute difference is opposed by a tendency towards absolute unity, as the many seek to come together in the one. Hegel accounts for this tendency on the grounds that though spatially separated from each other, the units of matter are in fact qualitatively identical, and so try to realize this identity by forming a continuous unity and thereby overcoming their spatial separateness. In this way, repulsion gives way to attraction:

> Matter maintains itself against its self-identity and in a state of extrinsicality, through its moment of negativity, its abstract *singularization* [*Vereinzelung*], and it is this that constitutes the *repulsion* of matter. As these different singularities are one and the same however, the negative unity of the juxtaposed being of this being-for-self is just as essential, and constitutes their *attraction*, or the continuity of matter. Matter is inseparable from both these moments, and constitutes their negative unity, i.e. singularity.
>
> (EN §262, I p. 241)

As Hegel had argued in the *Logic*, therefore, the dialectic of the one and the many gives rise to the seemingly opposed moments of attraction and repulsion, which tend towards continuity and discreteness respectively.[12] However, Hegel argues in the *Logic* that these two moments in fact actually *require* one another, and so cannot be in complete opposition. Attraction requires repulsion, he argues, because without the many generated by repulsion there could be no corresponding drive towards oneness, and thus no attraction.[13] Conversely, repulsion requires attraction, as otherwise the many would disperse into infinite space and lose any relation to one another, including the relation of repulsion.[14] The upshot of this is that repulsion and attraction turn out to be correlative concepts, and both moments must be balanced in a unity.

In the *Philosophy of Nature*, Hegel argues that the unity of attraction and repulsion constitutes *gravity*:

> Matter is spatial separation. By offering resistance it repels itself from itself, and so constitutes repulsion, through which it posits its reality and fills space. The singularities, which are repelled from another, all merely constitute a unit of many units; they are identical with each other. The unit only repels itself from itself, and it is this which constitutes the sublation of the separation of being-for-itself, or attraction. Together, attraction and repulsion constitute gravity, which is the Notion of matter. Gravity is the predicate of matter, which constitutes the substance of this subject.
>
> (PN §262Z, I p. 243)

Hegel makes clear that gravity involves a unity of attraction and repulsion because gravity entails a *balance* between these two apparently opposed moments. For, while on the one hand the units of matter remain ultimately distinct and self-subsistent, on the other hand they are attracted towards a common centre of gravitational attraction, in which they would unite into one;[15] and conversely, while matter is drawn towards a centre in which it would converge, on the other hand the moment of repulsion keeps it from ever reaching this centre.[16] Gravitation thus involves a compromise between attraction and repulsion, and between the opposed tendencies of matter towards the many and the one.

Once Hegel has explained how the forces of attraction and repulsion achieve a balance in gravitation, he then proceeds to give an account of the solar system in which the different bodies are interrelated in an external way. Hegel compares this structure of the solar system to that of the syllogism, in which the moments of universal, particular, and individual form a unity:

> In the syllogism which contains the *Idea* of gravity, this Idea is the Notion disclosing itself in external reality in the particularity of bodies, and at the same time in the ideality and intro-reflection [*Reflexion-in-sich*] of these bodies, displaying its integration into itself in motion. This contains the rational identity and inseparability of the moments which are otherwise taken to be independent. In general, motion as such only has significance and existence when there is a system of *several* bodies, which are variously *determined*, and so stand in a certain relationship to one another. The closer determination of

this syllogism of totality, which is in itself a system of three syllogisms, is given in the Notion of objectivity.

(EN §269, I p. 261)

Using this model of the syllogism, Hegel therefore compares the three moments of universal, particular, and individual with the three elements of the solar system, characterized as the central body, the dependent bodies, and the relative central bodies.[17] In real terms, these are the sun, the comets and satellites and moon, and the planets. These bodies make up the completed totality of the solar system, and Hegel insists that they correspond to the moments of the Notion:

> As it constitutes the third sphere, the planet concludes and completes the whole. This quadruplicity of celestial bodies forms the completed system of rational corporeality. It is necessary to a solar system, and is the developed disjunction of the Notion. These four spheres between them show forth the moments of the Notion within the heavens.

(EN §270Z, I p. 279)

In this way, Hegel refers back to the abstract relationship of the categories in the *Logic* while giving his account of absolute mechanics.

Now, one commentator has recently dismissed Hegel's attempts to draw an analogy between the structure of the syllogism and objective structures (such as the solar system and the state) as 'simply elaborate nonsense'.[18] At one level, of course, the drawing of such analogies was just part of the programme begun by Plato in his *Timaeus*, of showing how various natural phenomena correspond to some rational ordering; for Plato that ordering was based on the forms, while for Hegel it is based on the categories. Thus, in the *Timaeus* Plato tried to establish the rationality of there being five elements on the grounds that there are five regular solids to which these elements correspond;[19] likewise, Hegel here attempts to establish the rationality of there being three components of the solar system (the central body, the dependent bodies, and the relative central bodies) on the grounds that the Notion has three components (the universal, particular, and individual) to which they can be correlated. In this way, Hegel thinks, he can establish that there is some kind of rational pattern and 'order of things'.[20]

At the same time, however, it should not be thought that the tracing of such patterns is *all* that Hegel is doing here. At a deeper level, I would argue, Hegel's aim in referring back to the categories of the *Logic* is to suggest that only those natural phenomena which display an indivisible unity in fact correspond to the structure of the notion, and his account of the solar system in syllogistic terms reflects his preoccupation with the notional model. As we have seen, this model treats the individual as an irreducible totality, in so far as it exemplifies a universal substantial form that cannot be broken up into a plurality of mutually independent qualities. Hegel's point here, however, is that the solar system consists of no more than a plurality of externally related elements, and so represents a mere collection or compound of different entities which fail to manifest any such universal substantial form.[21] As a result, Hegel argues that the overarching unity of the universal is missing in the structure of the solar system, and the sun (which corresponds to this moment of universality) is merely the centre of an externally related plurality, which fails to display a substantial unity. It follows, therefore, that Hegel treats the relatedness of material bodies as only the first intimation of how the universal realizes itself in nature, and how unity is exemplified within the natural world: this emergence of form within matter becomes more explicit in the next section, on physics.[22]

Physics

After Absolute Mechanics and his discussion of the solar system, Hegel leaves the level of mechanics and passes on to physics. At this level, we have moved on from the quantitative to the *qualitative* consideration of matter, and to an investigation of how these qualities change, culminating in the chemical process.

At first, Hegel claims, matter manifests itself as a pure self-identical universal, that lacks any specific determination, and so has nothing but an abstract mode of existence. This abstract universality is *light*, which corresponds to the universal moment of the sun in the solar system:

> Gravity, acidity, and sound, are also manifestations of matter, but they do not have the purity of light, and they are not manifested without inherent and determinate modification. We can not hear sound as such, we merely hear a determinate sound, a certain pitch; it is always a determinate acid which we taste, never acidity as such. Only light exists as this pure manifestation, this abstract and unindividualised universality.
>
> (EN §276Z, II p. 19)

Hegel insists that in so far as light is an abstract universality, it is an 'immaterial matter',[23] which should not be treated by the physicist as if it were compounded out of light-rays or particles; for, as utterly ideal, it cannot be broken up into concrete material entities.[24] By virtue of its universality, therefore, Hegel takes light to be an absolute identity, that cannot be divided up into parts.

However, Hegel insists that this utterly abstract, indeterminate universality is incoherent, as it lacks any specific qualities: that is, it only exists as light as such, without existing in any more determinate manner. In line with Spinoza's dictum 'omnis determinatio est negatio', Hegel suggests that only in so far as it is limited in some way can light become determinate, by being marked off from what it is *not*. This occurs, Hegel argues, when the passage of light is 'interrupted' by some opaque material body, which once illuminated reveals various determinate qualities that set it apart from the abstract universality of light. Having identified light with the sun, Hegel identifies these opaque bodies with the moon and comets which stand 'in opposition to' the former.

Finally, Hegel comes to the third syllogistic moment of individuality, which is represented in the solar system by the earth. The earth, Hegel claims, has within it the four elements (air, water, fire, and earth) that correspond to the heavenly bodies, and which form 'moments' of its individuality. As such, he argues, they are not to be viewed as distinct constituents of a chemically analysable compound, for the earth is a 'universal individual' which has a concrete unity that cannot be broken up into a plurality along atomistic lines:

> Chemistry assumes the individuality of bodies, and then attempts to break down this individuality and the point of unity in which the differences are contained, and to free these differentiae from the force which constrains them . . . . If the body is merely the neutrality of its differences, we shall be able to point out its aspects when we break it down. These aspects are not universal elements and original principles, however, they are merely qualitatively, i.e. specifically determined constituents. The individuality of a body is much more than mere neutrality of these aspects however; *it is infinite form which is the main thing*, particularly in living existence . . . . In dealing with the physical elements, we are not in the least concerned with elements in the chemical sense. The chemical standpoint is certainly not the only one, it is merely one particular sphere, with no right whatever to impose itself upon other forms, as if it were their essence.
>
> (EN §281Z, II pp. 34–5; my emphasis)

Now, I would not wish to deny that aspects of Hegel's discussion here are nothing short of fanciful. It is important to remember, however, what he is setting out to do: he is trying to show how his categories of the Notion, which imply an holistic and anti-reductionist picture of the nature of things, are to be preferred to the 'barbarous categories' of Newtonian physics and the new French chemistry, which reduce everything to unchanging and externally related particles. This attack on the basic premisses of atomistic physics lies at the centre of the section of the *Philosophy of Nature* we have just discussed, and is unintelligible unless the metaphysical background that was uncovered in the *Logic* is taken into account.

This attack on atomism continues in the next section, which deals with the meteorological process. Here Hegel argues that, although the four elements of air, water, fire, and earth can be distinguished, they can none the less undergo processes of transformation in which each passes over into the other. Hegel contrasts his understanding of this process with that offered by finite physics, which views all things as made up of permanent material particles with connate properties, that can only be broken up and combined, but cannot undergo any process of coming to be or passing away:[25]

> The physical process is determined by the transmutation [*Verwandlung*] of the elements into one another. This transmutation is quite unknown to finite physics, in which the understanding always holds fast to the persistence of abstract identity, whereby the elements, being composite, are merely dispersed and separated, not really transmuted. Water, air, fire, and earth, are in conflict within this elementary process.
>
> (EN §286Z, II p. 44)

Hegel takes the formation of rain to be a particular example of transmutation, in this case of air into water. The formation of rain is misunderstood by finite physics, Hegel claims, because it cannot accept that air is able to change into water, and must instead explain this phenomenon by postulating the presence of water in air even *prior* to its manifestation as rainfall. Hegel, however, scornfully rejects 'nebulous ideas'[26] of this kind, and makes three objections to such a theory of rainfall: first, rain can come out of apparently dry air; second, in the summer, when humidity ought to be at its highest, the air is most dry; and third, it is not clear 'where the water stays'.[27] Hegel takes these three (rather feeble) points to refute the view opposed to his own, which is that air turns into water *directly*.

Hegel now moves from a discussion of the earth and the four elements to an account of the structure and qualitative determination of individual bodies. He begins his account with a discussion of specific gravity and cohesion. As a result of its cohesion, a particular body forms a relatively stable unity, which then (Hegel argues) is given expression in *sound*, in so far as sound involves the oscillation of parts throughout the body. Sound then gives way to *heat*, through which the structure of the body is reduced to formlessness, as its rigidity is undermined.

In the next chapter, entitled 'Physics of Total Individuality', Hegel moves from a study of the spatial determination of particular bodies, via the relation between the properties of bodies and the elements, to chemical process as it occurs between bodies.

Hegel's account of the spatial configuration of matter is discussed under the heading of *shape* (*Gestalt*). The particular spatial determinations in question are those of point, line, and surface (*Oberfläche*). Hegel suggests that these determinations are appropriate for inorganic being, which cannot yet attain the asymmetry and irregularity of organic forms.[28] Hegel then associates *magnetism* with the line, and the structure of the *crystal* with the spatial determination of the plane.

Hegel begins his discussion of magnetism by referring to the way in which this phenomenon had been taken up so eagerly by Schelling and the other *Naturphilosophen*. He attributes this to the apparently Notional structure of the magnetic body, in which opposed poles form a unity:

> Magnetism is one of the determinations which inevitably became prominent when the *Notion* began to be aware of itself in determinate nature, and grasped the Idea of a *philosophy of nature*. This came about because the magnet exhibits the nature of the Notion, both in a simple straightforward way, and in its developed form as syllogism.
>
> (EN §312, II p. 99)

As we have seen throughout, Hegel associates the Notional model with a structure of unity-in-difference, in which different determinations none the less form a unity; the phenomenon of magnetism corresponds to such a structure in so far as the opposed poles are contained in a single body. However, Hegel makes clear that the poles are only connected as mutually determining polar opposites, while the magnetic body itself lacks any substantial form in which its unity is grounded.

Hegel stresses that in the case of the crystal, by contrast, there is an inner unity of form, according to which each part shares a common structure, as a result of which the crystalline body constitutes a totality:

> Iceland spar is rhomboid; if it is fractured, its parts are found to be perfectly regular, and if the fracture takes place in accordance with its inner texture, all the planes are mirrorlike. No matter how often it is fractured, it will always display the same features; the ideal nature of its form is soul-like and omnipresent in its permeation of the whole.
>
> (EN §315Z, II p. 115)[29]

This metaphor of the 'soul' as the form which 'permeates' the whole recalls Hegel's description of the universal as the 'soul of the subject'; it also foreshadows his account of the soul as the 'substantial essence' of the organic totality.

The discussion then moves abruptly, from a consideration of the spatial form of material bodies to the *properties* of these bodies, as they arise from the interaction between a body and the universal elements of light, air, fire, and water. Of particular interest to us is the first part of this discussion, in which Hegel considers the property of *colour*, as it arises (according to Hegel) from the interaction of the material body with light. As will emerge, Hegel's account of colour rests on his Notional model, and thus has a direct bearing on my analysis of his system.

Hegel's account of colour is one of the most notorious sections of the *Philosophy of Nature*, as in it Hegel sets himself against the Newtonian conception of this phenomenon, and instead aligns himself with Goethe's account. In brief, on Newton's theory white light is said to be compounded of all the primary colours, into which it may then be decomposed. As Newton puts it in the *Opticks*:

> Whiteness, and all grey Colours between white and black, may be compounded of Colours, and the whiteness of the Sun's Light is compounded of all the primary Colours mix'd in a due Proportion.[30]

By contrast, Goethe argues against Newton that the colours are not the constituents of white light; rather, white light contains no such constituents, but is instead a simple unity, and colours are generated only when it is *dimmed* by coming into contact with darkness. As Petry has put it: 'Instead of taking the colours of the spectrum to be the constituents of white light, [Goethe] takes light and darkness to be the constituents of colour.'[31] Thus, Goethe's theory reverses the direction of Newton's account: while Newton had derived white light from the combination of the colours, Goethe set out to derive the colours from light, in so far as the pure whiteness of light is dimmed by coming into contact with darkness.

Hegel is outspoken in his support for Goethe's account, and biting in his attacks on Newton. Leaving aside the personal and nationalistic reasons behind this partisanship, in what follows I will consider the *philosophical* arguments Hegel gives for favouring Goethe's account, as they rest on his general conception of the categories of the Notion.

Hegel's main philosophical reason for supporting Goethe's theory of colour is that it recognizes the abstract universality of light, and thus its simplicity, and so does justice to its ideality and 'purity of form'.[32] According to Goethe, light itself is undifferentiated and homogeneous, and colour is generated by the combination of light and darkness. By contrast, Newton's theory treats white light as a *compound* of different colours, that are nothing more than externally related heterogeneous elements. As A. I. Sabra has pointed out, this account of the heterogeneity of light stemmed from Newton's predisposition towards atomism;[33] and it is in order to oppose this atomism that Hegel defended Goethe's theory of colours:

> There are *two* prevailing *ideas* about colours; the one with which *we* concur recognises the simplicity of light, the other maintains that light is composite, which is the crudest of metaphysical propositions, and stands in direct contradiction to every Notion. It is pernicious, because it is symptomatic of the whole way in which things are treated. It is with light that we put aside the contemplation of separateness and plurality, and have to raise ourselves to the abstraction of existent identity. It is therefore necessary to think in an ideal manner when thinking about light, although the coarsening influence of the Newtonian doctrine has tended to make this impossible. Under no circumstances is composition the concern of philosophy therefore. Philosophy has to do with the Notion, and with the unity of differences, and this is immanent, not external or superficial.
>
> (EN §320Z, II p. 141)

As our examination of the *Logic* revealed, Hegel takes unity to be immanent in the Notion because in it the category of universality is treated as a substance-form which is embodied in the individual; Hegel's claim is that light is just such a moment of universality, and so cannot be broken up into a plurality of colours along Newtonian lines. Thus Newton's theory of colours went against Hegel's holistic account of the structure of this phenomenon, and so was opposed by the latter on philosophical grounds.

After this account of colour, Hegel moves on to give an account of how fire, air, and water relate to material bodies. He then proceeds to give his analysis of *electricity*, which, like magnetism, had excited the interest of Schelling and other *Naturphilosophen*. According to Hegel, the phenomenon of electricity is to be explained as the attempt by bodies to overcome their difference:

> This electrical relationship is activity, but as it is not yet product, it is an abstract activity; it is only present where the contradiction of the tension is not yet resolved, so that each term, while maintaining its independence, contains its opposite.
>
> (EN §324Z, II p. 168)

In Hegel's view, the two separated and individual bodies are seeking to become one, while at the same time they want to maintain their independence from each other; he argues that the spark and flow of electricity between them is the result of this contradictory relationship:

> In the electrical process, each of the two distinct bodies has a differentiated determination which is only posited through the other, but in the face of which the further individuality of the body remains free and distinct. Consequently, the two electricities could not exist unless each had its own individual body . . . . Its tensioned extremities do not yet constitute the actuality of a total process, they are still independent, so that their process is still their abstract self. Their physical differentiation does not constitute the whole of corporeality, and electricity is therefore only the abstract totality of the physical sphere.
>
> (EN §324Z, II pp. 174–5)

From electricity, which (according to the Hegelian Georg Friederich Pohl) 'is really no more than the faint stirring of an incipient chemical process',[34] Hegel passes to the chemical process proper. In his account of the chemical process we will find him arguing that different chemical terms are internally related, and that in the chemical process the qualitative difference of substances is overcome as they form a homogeneous unity in the neutral product. In more detail, the account of chemism offered in the *Philosophy of Nature* runs as follows.

Hegel introduces his discussion of the chemical process by characterizing it as the unity of magnetism and electricity.[35] In magnetism, though there was a relation between two opposed poles, these moments had no real difference, as they existed immediately in one body. On the other hand, in electricity, the opposed moments did exist as separate bodies; but they never overcame their opposition, as they remained differently charged. In the chemical process, both these limitations will be avoided, as chemically opposed bodies are none the less brought together in the neutral product.[36] The chemical process therefore exhibits a Notional structure for Hegel, as in a chemical reaction different elements come to lose their difference, and are transformed into a unified neutrality. This means that chemism approaches the Notional model more fully than mechanism, even when the latter reaches the level of the solar system; for, although the moments of the solar system (the heavenly bodies) are related to one another, they do not lose their intrinsic difference, as occurs in the chemical process:

> The process of the heavenly bodies is on the contrary still abstract, because these bodies preserve their independence. Consequently, the

individual chemical process is more profound, for the truth of particular bodies is actualized as they seek and attain their unity within it.

(EN §326Z, II p. 181)[37]

As we shall see, in so far as the chemical process involves the transformation of different elements into a unified neutrality, the chemical process is taken by Hegel to represent the overcoming of difference by unity, and thus the beginning of the true realization of the Notion.

Hegel opens his account, however, with a brief discussion of the formal chemical process, which (following J. J. Winterl) he calls 'synsomation' (*Synsomatien*). By this process, Hegel simply means the combination of bodies that are chemically inactive with regard to each other, so that while they may undergo some purely physical changes (for example, in their density or cohesion), no real transformation occurs. As a result, the elements have not lost their difference from one another, and remain externally mixed or compounded: 'They are combined or separated in an immediate manner, and the properties of their existence are preserved'.[38] Hegel therefore argues that we have not yet encountered true chemical interaction or change.

The chemical process proper has a tripartite syllogistic structure, in which the mediating term consists of the elements of air or water. In the process itself, the moments characteristically undergo either combination (*Vereinigung*) or separation (*Scheidung*), while the process as a whole involves both these moments. Thus, 'as a totality, the general nature of the chemical process is that of the double activity of parting, and of the reduction of that which is parted to unity.'[39] The chemical process therefore involves an oscillation between unity and difference, as some substances are analysed into a plurality, while others are synthesized into a unified neutrality. As a result, the process as a whole reflects the dialectical tension between these two categories, and the continual transition between these two states of being:

> The moments of the developed totality of individuality are themselves determined as individual totalities, as wholly particular bodies, and are at the same time only moments, related to one another as differentials. As the identity of non-identical independent bodies, this relation is a contradiction. It is therefore essentially a *process*, the determination of which conforms to the Notion, in that it posits that which is different as identical and undifferentiated, and that which is identical as differentiated, activated and separated.

(EN §326, II p. 178)

The first chemical process Hegel considers is *galvanism*, which provides a good transitional step from electricity to chemistry, for it involves both electrical and chemical episodes. Thus, while on the one hand Hegel continues to explain the production of electric shocks and sparks in terms of a 'tension' between the metal ends of the pile, on the other hand he explains the electrical tension by pointing to the chemical reaction that occurs between the metal plates and the mediating element of water in the pile.

By arguing that the operation of the pile depends on the chemical interaction between the plates and the moist electrolyte, Hegel was opposing the 'contact theory' of Alessandro Volta, and agreeing with the 'chemical theory' of Humphrey Davy and J. W. Ritter. According to Volta's contact theory, the source of the 'electric force' lies solely in the contact of the two metals in the cell, and not from any chemical reaction of these with the moist electrolyte between them. As explained by Volta, the only role of the electrolyte is therefore as a conductor, to connect the metal plates, and 'to impel the electric fluid in one direction, and to make this connection so that there shall be no action in a contrary direction'.[40] As early as 1796, however, Giovanni Fabroni had observed that chemical changes do occur in the pile, and in 1800 Davy showed that the electrical effects of the pile depend upon the oxidizing of the zinc plates. Though Davy later attempted a compromise between the contact and chemical theories,[41] the chemical theory of the pile was supported by William Hyde Wollaston and William Nicholson, and also by the *Naturphilosoph* Ritter.

Now, for our purposes one important feature of Hegel's discussion of galvanism is his account of the differentiation of water into hydrogen and oxygen that occurs in the pile. Hegel insists that this differentiation is not simply the breaking up of an externally related compound, and rejects the analytical view of the chemist, according to which water is simply the external combination of these two self-subsistent component parts. By contrast, Hegel suggests that *prior* to the chemical reaction in the pile water is simply a homogeneous substance which is undifferentiated until oxygen and hydrogen come into being, and is not just a compound made up of these distinct elements.[42] As we have noted before, Hegel objects to any conception of a material substance as simply a *compound* of pre-existing elements that are ontologically independent of each other and the whole; for Hegel, a substance like water cannot be such an external unity, but must constitute a totality in which no parts can be isolated, until it undergoes a process of 'separation' or division. Of course, as an account of the structure of chemical compounds Hegel's position is unhelpful; but in showing how he thought his model of substances might differ from the reductionist and atomistic accounts implied by the new French chemistry, this part of Hegel's argument is revealing.

After a brief discussion of the process of fire, which he associates with the production of acidity and alkalinity,[43] Hegel now passes on to a discussion of neutralization or salt formation. The only method of salt formation that he analyses is that in which a base is neutralized by an acid. Here, the two sides are posited in opposition, and each wants to overcome the difference of the other in neutralization. The result of the chemical combination of acid and base is a neutral salt, which is the topic of the next section.

As neutral bodies, salts do not immediately fall into a chemical process, but must be mediated by some other substance, such as water. Salts mainly enter into a process of elective affinity (*Wahlverwandt-schaften*), a process that interested Goethe enough to inspire him to use it as a model for human relations in his *Novelle* of the same name.[44] In double affinity, two salts exchange radicals, so that the original two salts give rise to two new salts.[45] With this process, the two reacting salts achieve a more stable form, and we return to the kind of undifferentiated substance we had in the metal poles of the galvanic process.

Hegel has therefore traced a sequence of combination and separation, whereby difference gives rise to unity and unity gives way to difference. However, the chemical outlook retains a conception of the object according to which it is no more than a compound of self-subsistent elements, which are ontologically prior to and independent of the substances in which they are combined. Though Hegel objects that even at this level this outlook is mistaken, it is only really at the level of *organic being* that this merely synthetic view of unity is transcended. As he puts it:

> *Animal* and *vegetable* substances . . . should principally serve to counteract the sort of metaphysics which prevails in both chemistry and physics however, and which employs thoughts or rather confused concepts such as the *immutability of substances* in all circumstances, and categories such as composition and *subsistence*, on the stength of which bodies are supposed to be formed from such substances.
>
> (EN §334, II pp. 214–15)[46]

With organic being, therefore, nature finally attains a form of existence that corresponds to Hegel's notional model of unity, and his holistic account of the structure of the object at last becomes clear.

Organics

Hegel's Romantic contemporary, the philosopher and poet Friedrich Schlegel, expressed a hope that 'after the chemical epoch an organic one would follow'.[47] In treating the organism as the climax of his account of nature, therefore, Hegel may appear to be doing nothing more than following the fashion of his time.[48] However, I shall argue in this section that his account of the organism is more than just a vogueish excursion into natural philosophy; rather, Hegel's interest in the organism stems from its approximation to the Notional model of the object, from which his account of nature derives. It is as an exemplification of this model that the organism gains its significance for Hegel, and a proper study of this section of the *Philosophy of Nature* will therefore help in coming to grips with the metaphysical abstractions of the *Logic*.

In the introduction to the third part of the *Encyclopaedia*, the *Philosophy of Mind*, Hegel briefly summarizes the development he has traced in nature, from mechanism to organics. He argues that nature to begin with is 'the element of asunderness', in which all bodies and elements are self-subsistent and distinct from one another. Hegel suggests that the planets and the four elements display exactly this kind of externality.[49] However, the organism marks a decisive break from such mechanical structures, because in the organism the differentiation of parts is grounded and pervaded by 'the same one universal', as a result of which it has the structure of a genuine substantial unity:

> An even more complete triumph over externality is exhibited in the animal organism; in this not only does each member generate the other, is its cause and effect, its means and end, so that it is at the same time itself and its Other, but the whole is so pervaded by its unity that nothing in it appears as independent, every determinateness is at once ideal, the animal remaining in every determinateness the same one universal, so that in the animal body the complete untruth of asunderness is revealed.

> (EM §381Z p. 10)

In Hegel's terms, this structure of the organism may be compared to the structure of the Notion, in which the individual none the less embodies a substance-universal, as a result of which it comes to form a unity; in this way, the organism turns out to be the highest realization of the Notion that we will encounter at the level of nature.

In order to see how Hegel arrives at this account of the organism, it is necessary to begin with the important transitional category of *Teleology*, which comes between Chemism and Life in the *Logic*. Teleology is the final stage of Objectivity, because in the teleological mode of thought we have begun to break away from the mechanical and chemical conception of the world as made up of externally related units, and begun to conceive these units as parts of organized wholes, thereby moving towards an organic conception of reality. This comes about as follows.

Teleological explanation (explanation in terms of ends) is characteristically introduced into our account of the world in order to explain the existence and structure of *organized wholes*. As Kant himself declared: 'In fact, if we desire to pursue the investigation of nature with diligent observation, be it only in its organized products, we cannot get rid of the necessity of adopting the conception of a design as basal.'[50] The case for teleological explanation is therefore that we cannot account for the nature and existence of an organized whole unless we take it to have some purpose or end. Only if we add a final cause to any account in terms of efficient cause will our explanation of the organized whole be complete.

Conversely, if we are willing to adopt the method of teleological explanation with respect to those totalities that we find in Nature, we will come to see these totalities *not* as a random coming together of indifferent elements, but as organized wholes in which the elements that make up the whole all play a determinate and important part. As Charles Taylor has put it: 'Teleological explanation is explanation out of totality. The partial processes are explained by their role in the whole.'[51] Once we accept that a whole exists in order to fulfil a particular end, we will be led to view the elements that make up that whole as more closely interrelated with one another, in so far as they are explained primarily in terms of their contribution to the workings of the totality. The teleological approach is therefore used by Hegel to get us from the atomistic thinking of mechanics and chemistry to the holistic thinking of organics.

In the *Logic* Hegel's account of teleology is therefore succeeded by an account of *Life*. This discussion in the *Logic* foreshadows the account given of the organism in the *Philosophy of Nature*, in the same way as the account of mechanics and chemistry given in the latter was also foreshadowed in the former. It is therefore first necessary to consider the treatment Hegel gives of life in the *Logic*, before we turn to his more detailed account in the *Philosophy of Nature*.

While Teleology constitutes the final stage of Objectivity in the *Logic*, life constitutes the first stage of the Idea. Hegel describes the Idea as 'the absolute unity of notion and objectivity'.[52] In other words, at the level of the Idea the Notion is finally adequately realized in reality, so that reality properly exemplifies this rational structure; and life, as the first level of the Idea, is the first stage of this realization.

Let us briefly reconsider the structure of the Notion, as Hegel presents it using the categories of the *Logic*. The Notion, as defined by him, is the unity of universal, particular, and individual, such that none of these moments stand outside one another, but are dialectically interrelated. He treats the universal as a substantial form, which is embodied in each determinate particular individual; this individual therefore has a fundamental unity by virtue of exemplifying this substance-kind. The structure of the Notion therefore involves the interpenetration of the two aspects of unity (universality) and difference (particularity), and the Notional totality is said to embody both these moments, as the differentiated individual none the less exemplifies a unified substance-form.

Now, Hegel argues that the living individual exemplifies this Notional structure of unity-in-difference. He identifies the moment of unity or universality with the *soul*, which is the substantial form exemplified by the organism as a whole. As a result of embodying this substantial form the material plurality of the body is said to be overcome, as each apparently distinct part is none the less permeated and structured by this overarching universality, as a result of which the individual constitutes an irreducible unity. Hegel also comments that only a mode of thinking capable of grasping this interpenetration of unity *in* difference will be capable of making sense of how the organism comes to form a totality in this way:

Life, considered now more closely in its Idea, is in and for itself absolute *universality*; the objectivity that it possesses is permeated throughout by the Notion and has the Notion alone for substance. What is distinguished as part, or in accordance with some other external reflection, has within itself the whole Notion; the Notion is the *omnipresent* soul in it, which remains simple self-relation and remains a one in the multiplicity belonging to objective being. This multiplicity, as self-external objectivity, has an indifferent subsistence, which in space and time, if these could already be mentioned here, is a mutual externality of wholly diverse and self-subsistent elements. But in life externality is at the same time present as the *simple determinateness* of its Notion; thus the soul is an omnipresent outpouring of itself into this multiplicity and at the same time remains absolutely the simple oneness of the concrete Notion with itself. The thinking that clings to the determinations of the relationships of reflection and of the formal Notion, when it comes to consider life, this unity of the Notion in the externality of objectivity, in the absolute multiplicity of atomistic matter, finds all thoughts without exception are of no avail; the omnipresence of the simple in manifold externality is for reflection an absolute contradiction, and as reflection must at the same time apprehend this omnipresence for its perception of life and therefore admit the actuality of this Idea, it is an *incomprehensible mystery* for it, because it does not grasp the Notion, and the Notion is the substance of life.

(SL p. 763: HW VI pp. 472–3)

In the structure of the organism, therefore, externality is overcome, as the universal form of the soul permeates the whole, and constitutes a unity underlying the plurality of parts within the totality of the body. Thus, Hegel argues, although the various parts of the organism may be distinguishable from one another, they should not be treated as ontologically independent entities into which the whole can be *reduced*, as this would be to overlook its fundamental unity.

None the less, although the living individual is itself a unity, a division is now introduced between the living individual on the one hand, and the inorganic world on the other. Finally, in the genus process the individual faces a similar opposition between itself and other members of the same genus, to which, as instances of the same universal, it is none the less related. The relation individuals achieve, however, is only the external one of copulation, and not, for example, the real unity achieved by citizens in the state. It therefore follows that the genus is not a Notional totality, but merely an external unity in which the individual cannot properly overcome its difference from other individuals. In the genus process, therefore, individuals in fact produce *another* individual through the sex-relation, which in turn stands opposed to them. This contradiction between the individual and the universal genus leads to the death of the former, and with this Hegel moves from the concrete reality of nature to the level of consciousness, and the Idea of Cognition.

Having sketched the background to Hegel's account as it appears in the *Logic*, it should now be possible to trace the main outlines of his argument in the *Philosophy of Nature*.

After giving an account of the 'terrestrial organism' (the earth) which forms the 'ground and basis of life',[53] but which is itself lacking in animation, Hegel passes on to a discussion of the vegetable organism, which is a truly living being; as such, it is 'the shape which has substantial form dwelling within it'.[54] None the less, putting forward an idea that is now familiar from systems theory,[55] Hegel suggests that the plant cannot form a genuine unity, as each part is too easily capable of becoming a self-subsistent individual in its own right; as such, it can always be removed from the integrated system, making the system itself unstable. On these grounds, Hegel denies that the plant represents a genuine substantial unity, and does not allow that it truly embodies a universal substance-form:

> The members of the plant are only particular in relation to one another therefore, not in relation to the whole. These members are wholes in their own right . . . . /[The growth of the plant] is not the individual coming to itself, it is a *mulitiplication of individuality*, in which the single individuality is merely the superficial unity of the many. The singularities remain a mutually indifferent and separated plurality; the substance from which they proceed is not a common essence.
>
> (EN §343Z, III p. 46 and p. 47)

Only when the parts are ontologically subordinate to the whole can the totality be treated as a substance, therefore, and thus as a realization of the Notion.

This subordination occurs in the animal organism, and it is the animal organism that best fits the model of the object which Hegel had put forward in his doctrine of the Notion. In contrast to the external relatedness of bodies in the solar system, the animal embodies an ideal moment, which constitutes its unity. This moment of unity is the soul:

> The Sun and the members of the solar system are independent, and present us with spatial and temporal interrelatedness, not one which accords with the physical nature of these bodies . . . . The unity which is produced has being for the implicit unity of the animal. This implicit unity is the soul or Notion, which is present in the body in so far as the body constitutes the process of idealization. The subsistence of the mutual externality of spatiality has no significance for the soul. The soul is incomposite and finer than any point, but incongrously enough, attempts have been made to locate it. There are millions of points in which the soul is omnipresent, yet it is precisely because the extrinsicality of space has no significance for it, that the soul is not present in any of them. This point of subjectivity is to be firmly adhered to; the other points are mere predicates of life.
>
> (EN §350Z, III p. 103)

The animal organism therefore displays a Notional structure, in which the unity of the individual is constituted by the universality and identity of the soul, which forms its essential nature. This understanding of the structure of the animal organism is a crucial feature of Hegel's account.

Hegel first discusses the organism in terms of the three functions of sensibility, irritability, and reproduction, and in this he was following the lead of the other *Naturphilosophen*.[56] The first two functions were brought to prominence by the biological speculations of Albrecht von Haller, who defined those parts of the body as irritable which contracted when touched, and those parts as sensible whose stimulation is consciously noticed by the subject:

> I call that part of the human body irritable, which becomes shorter upon being touched; very irritable if it contracts upon a slight touch, and the contrary if by a violent touch it contracts but little.
>
> I call that a sensible part of the human body, which upon being touched transmits the impression of it to the soul; and in brutes, in whom the existence of a soul is not so clear, I call those parts sensible, the irritation of which occasions evident signs of pain and disquiet in the animal.[57]

Haller argued that only those parts of the body that are supplied with nerves possess sensibility, while irritability is a property of muscular fibres. In this way he clearly distinguished sensibility and irritability, and argued that they should be identified with distinct parts of the body.[58] However, Haller's account gave rise to controversy, and it was argued by biologists like Robert Whytt that the two functions should not be so definitely distinguished from one another.[59]

Given his holistic account of the animal organism, and his hostility to the division of such a Notional unity into self-subsistent component parts, it is not very surprising to find that Hegel supports this criticism of Haller. In particular, he argues against Haller that no *one* part of the organism can be exclusively identified with *one* of the functions of life, but rather that sensibility and irritability are found in each part of the whole. So, while he accepts a basic identification of sensibility with the nervous system, irritability with the circulatory system, and reproduction with the digestive system, he none the less insists that this identification be made more complicated, so that each of these systems also contains within itself a *further* determination into moments of sensibility, irritability, and reproduction. So, for example, though we may associate the nervous system with sensibility, it also involves a moment of irritability, whereby the nervous system reacts to an external impulse.[60] We therefore see how no *one* corporeal system or shape is exclusively related, in a lawlike way, with any *one* function of life, but rather that each function interpenetrates the others and is present throughout the system. Thus, in response to Gottfried Reinhold Treviranus's observation that 'all animal bodies may be analysed into three different constituents of which all their organs are compounded, i.e. cellular tissue, muscular fibre, and nerve pulp',[61] Hegel comments:

These are the simple abstract elements of the three systems. However, as these systems are equally undivided, so that each point contains all three in an immediate unity, they do not constitute universality, particularity and singularity, which are the abstract moments of the Notion. On the contrary, each of these moments exhibits the totality of the Notion in its determinateness, the other systems being present as existences in each of them.

(EN §354Z, III pp. 112–13)

Once again, therefore, Hegel's Notional model has led him to reject any talk of analysis and composition, and to insist that any proper account of the organism as a totality must recognize that its parts are *not* ontologically independent of one another and prior to the whole.

From the claim that the organs and limbs of the body must comprise elements of all three functions of sensibility, irritability, and reproduction, Hegel goes on to argue that in a developed organism the regions of the body, as well as its organs, cannot be exclusively identified with any one function, but in fact each displays them all. Thus, while in the case of the insect (for example) we may be able to distinguish the head, thorax, and abdomen, on the grounds that they are centres of sensibility, irritability, and reproduction respectively, in the case of a more developed organism these functions all involve one another, and the associated organs can be found *throughout* the body:

As each abstract system permeates them all, and is connected with them, and each exhibits the whole shape, the systems of nerves, veins, blood, bones, muscles, skin, glands etc. each constitute a whole skeleton. This establishes the contexture of the organsim, for at the same time as each system is interlaced into the domain of the other, it maintains the connexion within itself. In the head and brain there are organs of sensibility, bones, and nerves; but all the parts of the other systems, blood, veins, glands, skin, also belong there. It is the same with the thorax, which has nerves, glands, skin etc.

(EN §355Z, III p. 127)

Once again, Hegel is here taking his Notional account of the organism to imply that the organic whole cannot be broken down into self-subsistent and distinct parts, but must be treated as a systematic unity.

Finally, Hegel turns from his discussion of the relation between the functions and shapes of the body to the process of formation itself, as it occurs in the animal organism. Given that each bodily organ is essentially interpenetrated by all three functions of life, none of these organs can maintain any of those functions without the others. As a result, the parts of the organic being are essentially related to the system as a whole, and cannot function when separated from that system.

From the process of formation, Hegel passes to the second of the three processes of life, the process of assimilation. Hegel argues here that chemistry alone cannot explain how nutriments are transformed in the process of digestion, and insists that the process involves more than simply decomposition of food into its chemical elements: for, Hegel argues, in being broken down, the nutriments are changed completely, and do not remain the same as they were when they formed a unity. Likewise, the organism itself should not be thought of as simply compounded from these self-subsistent chemical substances, as it has a greater unity than that to be found in any such compound. Hegel comments as follows regarding the production of the blood:

> It is on this immediate transition and transformation that all chemical and mechanical explanations of the organism founder and find their limit . . . . Try as they will, neither chemistry nor mechanics can trace empirically the transformation of the nutriment into blood. Chemistry certainly displays something similar in both of them; albumen perhaps, and certainly iron and suchlike, as well as oxygen, hydrogen, nitrogen etc. It will certainly extract matters from the plant that are also present in water. Wood, blood and flesh do not remain the same thing as these matters however, because, quite simply, both sides are at the same time something else. Blood which has been broken down into such constituents is no longer living blood.
>
> (EN §365Z, III pp. 156–57)[62]

Hegel's point is that it is a mistake to treat an organic substance like blood as nothing more than a compound of unchanging chemical elements, that can be separated and united without being fundamentally altered: blood is more of an organic unity, and cannot be understood as just an external composition of the sort of distinct substances that were discussed at the level of chemistry.

From the assimilative process, Hegel passes to the generic process, in which each individual attempts to overcome the opposition between self and other that was implicit in the assimilative process. However, whereas in the latter, the other was inorganic nature, in the generic process the other is another organic individual. Each individual feels itself to share a common universal essence with other individuals, and so they come together in the sex-relationship:

> The relation of one individual to another of its kind is the substantial relationship of the genus. The nature of each permeates both, and

both find themselves within the sphere of this universality. Both are implicitly a single genus, the same subjective vitality, and in the process they also posit this as being so.

(EN §368Z, III p. 173)

However, at this stage the individuals cannot reconcile this unity with the sense of their particular difference from one another, and this contradiction explains their finitude and consequent deaths.

Before discussing the death of the individual, however, Hegel briefly puts forward an account of illness and its cure, in which he argues that illness essentially involves the destruction of the unity of the organism, as one of the organs sets itself up in opposition to the whole:

> The organism is in a *diseased* state when one of its systems or organs is *stimulated* into conflict with the inorganic potency of the organism. Through this conflict, the system or organ establishes itself in isolation, and by persisting in its particular activity in opposition to the activity of the whole, obstructs the fluidity of this activity, as well as the process by which it pervades all the moments of the whole.

(EN §371, III p. 193)

Hegel suggests that this stage of illness is the most dangerous, as at this stage the very *unity* of the organic whole is threatened by the isolation of the diseased organ.

However, at the next stage of the illness, the disease becomes a fever, which passes through the *whole* body, and infects the entire organism. Hegel argues that at this stage a cure is relatively straightforward, as the original site of the disease no longer stands outside the unity of the body, in that the whole of the organism is now affected. Fever therefore makes possible a return to the original organic unity, and thus restores the body to health. [63]

Hegel's account of nature concludes with 'the death of the individual of its own accord', which occurs when the body finally breaks down into a plurality of merely chemical substances and processes, and the unity of the soul is no longer present in the organism. With the collapse of natural being Hegel makes the transition to spirit, thereby concluding his account of how the Notion is realized in nature. In what follows, the significance of this account will be examined.

NATURE AND UNITY

At *Metaphysics* Z 16 Aristotle faces the difficulty that the part–whole constitution of living things seems to pose for his claim that plants and animals are substances: the fact that organic bodies are divisible into parts appears to threaten their unity as individuals, on which his account of them as substances depends. Aristotle answers this difficulty by pointing out that none of the parts of the organism can exist as living entities on their own, so that the elements of the body lack the ontological independence necessary if they are to be treated as substances in their own right, to which the individual is reducible; it is therefore justifiable to treat the individual as an indivisible totality, and not as a complex of self-subsistent parts.

Now, in the previous chapter it was shown that, like Aristotle, Hegel adopts a metaphysical model of the individual as an irreducible unity: because he treats the object as an exemplification of a substance-universal, he argues that it cannot be broken down into a plurality of sensible properties or attributes, but must constitute an indivisible substance, by virtue of being of such and such a kind. In this chapter we have seen that, also like Aristotle, Hegel must show how this model can be defended against the reductionist and atomistic account of material objects, which treats them as complex unities composed of distinct and self-subsistent parts. Hegel argues, along Aristotelian lines, that in the case of genuine substances like the animal organism, the parts cannot exist as living entities independently of the whole, which must therefore be treated as an irreducible unity:

> If animal being is now also a sun, then the stars are after all interrelated within it in accordance with their physical nature; they are taken back into the sun, which holds them within itself in a single individuality. In so far as the animal's members are simply moments of its form, and are perpetually negating their independence, and withdrawing into a unity which is the reality of the Notion, and is for the Notion, the animal is the existent Idea. If a finger is cut off, a process of chemical decomposition sets in, and it is no longer a finger. The unity which is produced has being for the implicit unity of the animal. This implicit unity is the soul or Notion.
>
> (EN §350Z, III p. 103)[64]

In this way, Hegel's rejection of atomism and reductionism at the metaphysical level, in his ontological model of the object, leads him towards an account of natural phenomena that emphasizes their holistic structure. He therefore comes to oppose the pluralistic conception of things, as being divisible into stable and independent units, and it is the dominance of this conception that his *Philosophy of Nature* is designed to counter. In this second part of the *Encyclopaedia*, as we have seen, Hegel argues that nature contains certain concrete individuals (such as animal organisms) which cannot be explained as the combination of independently existing elements, but must be treated as irreducible wholes, in a way that only his ontological model of the object allows.

Now, I would not wish to deny that often Hegel's attempts to claim that natural phenomena have a holistic structure are ineffective, and that many of his attempts to justify his position using evidence from the science of his period have a merely historical interest. None the less, it has been pointed out[65] that Hegel's ideas have found an echo in the principle of 'organicism' adopted by many biologists and philosophers of biology in the first half of the twentieth century, leading to the development of systems theory. [66] The systems view treats the organism *as a whole* as the ontologically primary entity, and argues that it cannot be reduced to a plurality of self-subsistent parts. In consequence, this approach holds that the parts of the organism cannot be understood outside the context of the totality in which they exist, and it is a mistake to subject the totality to a reductionist analysis. As the noted biologist Paul Weiss has observed:

> we can assert definitely and incontrovertibly, on the basis of strictly empirical investigation, that the sheer reversal of our prior analytic dissection of the Universe by *putting the pieces together* again, whether in reality or just in our minds, *can yield no complete explanation of the behaviour of even the most elementary living system.*[67]

This conception of things is one with which Hegel's metaphysics, as we have seen, is very much in accord, and is one that appears to be increasingly influential in modern biology, as well as in some of the other sciences.

Of course, I do not wish to make the absurd claim that Hegel is in some way the 'father' of systems theory, or for that matter that he somehow 'prefigured' the more holistic outlook that has emerged in the 'new physics'. [68] All I wish to suggest is that modern science has independently given us an account of reality that is congenial to his metaphysical thinking, in a way that he would surely have found most appealing; at the same time, this picture seems to be at odds with the atomism and reductionism of the position he was opposing. That science itself would seem to confirm the validity of Hegel's holistic and non-reductionist metaphysical paradigm therefore supplements the programme of the *Philosophy of Nature* in an unexpected way, and may serve to make the claims of the latter more compelling.

Chapter five

The unity of the object and the unity of the subject

Throughout his *Philosophy of Nature*, Hegel sets the holistic model of the object that he adopted in the *Logic* against the reductionist and atomistic picture of reality offered by physics and chemistry. His claim is that the individual is the embodiment of a substance-universal; he therefore develops an ontology in which objects are taken to have an intrinsic unity that cannot be reduced to the plurality of atomistic entities which are treated as fundamental by Newtonian science. In this way, as we have seen, it is important to contrast Hegel's metaphysics to the pluralistic view, which takes all things to be constituted out of a manifold of distinct and self-subsistent elements.

Now, this pluralistic view was precisely that adopted by Kant, who, as we showed, treated the object as a 'combination' of atomistic intuitions brought together by the synthesizing subject. Kant's fundamentally atomistic conception of the object is therefore in contrast to the holistic model developed by Hegel in his *Logic* and *Philosophy of Nature*, and the aim of this chapter is to examine this difference in further detail. It will be argued that the break between Kant's subjective idealism and Hegel's absolute idealism can be traced back to this divergence in their accounts of the structure and realization of the external world.

UNITY AND SYNTHESIS

In an early essay, entitled *Faith and Knowledge*, Hegel offers the following concise account of Kant's doctrine of synthesis:

> From this exposition we may gather briefly what transcendental knowledge is in this philosophy. The deduction of the categories, setting out from the organic Idea of productive imagination, loses itself in the mechanical relation of a unity of self-consciousness which stands in antithesis to the empirical manifold, either determining it or reflecting on it. Thus transcendental knowledge transforms itself into

formal knowledge. The unity of self-consciousness is at the same time objective unity, category, formal identity. However, something that is not determined by this identity must supervene to it in an incomprehensible fashion; there must be an addition, a *plus* of something empirical, something alien. This supervening of a B to the pure Ego-concept is called experience, while the supervening of A to B, where B is posited first, is called rational action, A:A + B. The A in A + B is the objective unity of self-consciousness, B is the empirical, the content of experience, a manifold bound together through the unity A. But B is something foreign to A, something not contained in it. And the *plus* itself, i. e. the bond between the unifying activity, and the manifold, is what is incomprehensible.

(FK pp. 92–3:HW II pp. 328–9)

This schematic outline nicely illustrates Kant's picture of the realisation of the object, as Hegel saw it: in itself, the manifold is an unstructured atomistic plurality. The unity of the object must therefore lie in the categorial framework located in the cognizing subject. The manifold must be transformed in this way if it is to enter into the unity of the I, and thus be brought to consciousness. The fact that the I forms a unity therefore entails the relational structure of the realized object. Or, taking the argument in the opposite direction: the object must be taken into the experience of the self-conscious subject, which forms a unity. The pre-realizational object is an unstructured manifold, however. Therefore the manifold must be related together (synthesized) by the categorial framework brought to experience by the cognizing subject.

Now, Kant's picture gains what persuasive force it has from the assumption that all things can be reduced to a plurality of intrinsically unrelated intuitions, which require synthesizing by the subject if they are to form a unity, as a result of which the object comes into being. It was precisely this assumption that Hegel rejected, however. He argued, as we have seen, that individual substances exist as the exemplification of a universal substance-form, which cannot be analysed into a plurality of sensible properties or intuitions;[1] this irreducibility implies that the framework of synthesis is incoherent as an account of the existence of such entities, and that it must be set aside.

In conceiving of the object as the exemplification of a substance-universal, therefore, Hegel set out to challenge the pluralistic model on which Kant's doctrine of synthesis was based. In the introduction to his *Philosophy of Mind*, Hegel states clearly the way in which his own variety of idealism runs counter to this pluralism:

We have said that mind negates the externality [*Äußerlichkeit*] of Nature, assimilates Nature to itself and thereby idealizes it. In finite mind which places Nature outside of it, this idealisation has a one-sided shape; here the activity of our willing, as of our thinking, is confronted by an external material which is indifferent to the alteration which we impose on it and suffers quite passively the idealization which thus falls to its lot.... [But] philosophical thinking knows that Nature is idealized not merely by us, that Nature's asunderness [*Außereinander*] is not an insuperable barrier for Nature itself, for its Notion; but that the eternal Idea is immanent in Nature or, what is the same thing, the essence of mind itself at work within Nature brings about the idealization, the triumph over asunderness, because this form of mind's existence conflicts with the inwardness of its essence. Therefore philosophy has, as it were, only to watch how Nature itself overcomes its externality, how it takes back what is self-external into the centre of the Idea, or causes this centre to show forth in the external, how it liberates the Notion concealed in Nature from the covering of externality and thereby overcomes external necessity. This transition from necessity to freedom is not a simple transition but a progression through many stages, whose exposition constitutes the Philosophy of Nature.

(EM §381Z p. 13)

As this passage makes plain, Hegel took the doctrine of synthesis, which treats the structure of reality as 'imposed on it', to rest on Kant's atomism and reductionism; he argues, however, that this atomism and reductionism is based on a failure to acknowledge the overarching Idea which constitutes the immanent unity inherent in the structure of things.[2] That unity, as we saw in the *Logic*, is the moment of universality or the substance-universal, which constitutes the essential form of the individual as a whole, as an irreducible totality. Once the object is viewed as possessing this *intrinsic* unity, this frees the external world from having its structure *imposed* on it by the finite mind; for this unity no longer depends on the external relating together or combination of sensible properties, and so no longer fits in with any Kantian doctrine of synthesis.

Thus, given this holistic conception of the structure of the object, Hegel treats the *realization* of the object in a different way. That is, rather than seeing it as the result of an activity of synthesis by the transcendental subject, he views the unity of the individual (as we have seen) as being derived from its manifestation of some universal substance-kind: and it is just this realist account of universals that distinguishes his absolute idealism from Kant's merely subjective idealism.

ABSOLUTE AND SUBJECTIVE IDEALISM

In his own accounts of his relation to Kant, Hegel insists that whereas the former adopted a merely subjective idealism, his own philosophy is an *absolute* idealism. The force of this distinction is not immediately clear, and many commentators, in misunderstanding the nature of the distinction, have misunderstoood Hegel's critique of Kant; as a result, they have misidentified the vital difference between the Kantian and Hegelian systems. In what follows, I will argue that in labelling Kant's idealism 'subjective', Hegel's point was not that Kant is a 'phenomenal-ist' or 'Berkeleyean', and neither is his own 'objective idealism' merely a claim to be able to know 'things-in-themselves'.[3] Rather, I will claim that Kant's idealism is subjective for Hegel in employing the activity of the synthesizing subject to explain the genesis and structure of the object, while Hegel's idealism is objective in treating the substance-universal which it exemplifies as constituting the unity of the individual. As a result, whereas Kant's philosophy is idealistic because it treats the unity of the object as dependent on the structure imposed on experience by the transcendental subject, Hegel's philosophy is idealistic because it operates with a realist theory of universals, which have a fundamental place in his ontology. Ultimately, therefore, the distinction between subjective and absolute idealism turns out to depend on the different ways in which Kant and Hegel account for the unity and realization of the object, and the nature of the distinction will be misunderstood if this is overlooked.

In the account of Kant's philosophy given in the first chapter, it was shown how in the latter's system the structure of the object depends upon the *a priori* categories brought to experience by the cognizing subject, through which the manifold of intuitions is unified. The decisive point to notice is that the object is only realized in this way when it is part of the experience of a transcendental *subject*: for, only this subject can introduce 'combination' into the plurality of the manifold. It follows from this that Kant's conception of the transcendental ego (the analytic unity of apperception) plays a vital role in determining the structure of the object as a complex unity. Kant's entire account of how the object is realized through the combination of the manifold rests on his conception of the synthesizing activity of the subject: without the subject to act as this central focus for the plurality of intuitions, this plurality would never achieve a unity, and thus never be formed into an object.[4] To use Hegel's image, in Kant's account, the subject acts as a crucible (*Schmelztiegel*)[5] in which the atomistic manifold is formed into the unity of the object. The fact that Kant gives the transcendental consciousness this central role in realizing the object is what leads Hegel to call his system a subjective idealism: for, only by virtue of the synthesizing activity of the subject can the unity of the object be guaranteed.[6] It is therefore clear that for Kant the subject has a vital *ontological* role to play in bringing the object into being.

Now, some commentators have attempted to establish a connection between this Kantian conception of the transcendental ego and Hegel's conception of *Geist*. Of recent commentators, R. C. Solomon has perhaps been most forthright in seeking to establish this connection. In brief, Solomon argues that Hegel differs from Kant only in so far as he 'depersonalises' the ego, so that *Geist* represents a more general and universal consciousness; none the less, he insists that this consciousness has the same unifying function as Kant's transcendental ego:

> The subject of philosophy is not a person, is not an individual, but must be referred to *simpliciter* as *subject*, without any pretense toward identification or individuation with persons. But the notion of *subject* is precisely Hegel's notion of *Geist*. For Hegel, the *Transcendental Ego*, as *Geist*, is a literally general or universal consciousness, as it *ought* to have been for Kant. Hegel's *Geist* is Kant's Ego without the unwarranted claim that there is one Ego per person. *Geist* is simply the underlying unifying principle of consciousness.[7]

According to Solomon, therefore, Hegel's *Geist* is merely Kant's 'subject-writ-large',[8] and it too constitutes a central unity around which the manifold of experience is organized. Given this account of *Geist*, Solomon then goes on to stress the essential similarity of Kantian and Hegelian idealism, on the grounds that both treat subjective consciousness as the starting point of their philosophical systems. In this way, Hegel's idealism turns out to be as mentalistic and subjective as Kant's, and both are said to stand in a tradition which began with Descartes' 'Cogito'.[9]

Following my detailed analysis of Hegel's *Logic* and *Philosophy of Nature*, however, it should be clear that this view of Hegel's idealism is profoundly mistaken. In the previous chapter, I showed how Hegel's model of the realization of the object does not depend on any synthesizing subject, but rather on a universal substance-form that underlies the 'externality' of nature. It follows from this that in so far as natural phenomena can be shown to exemplify such moments of universality they are *inherently* unified, and so not in *need* of 'combination' by any Kantian transcendental subject, whether that subject be an individual ego or *Geist*. It follows that according to Hegel's *absolute* idealism, the unity of the object is derived from the embodiment of a universal substance-form, and is *not* grounded in the unity of the subject. Absolute idealism therefore arrives at a realist account of universals, according to which objects are structured by concepts; but (in contrast to Kant) both the concepts and the objects exist *independently* of the activity of the subject. As a result, Hegel's metaphysics is rightly called idealist because universals are used to account for the structure of the object; but it is opposed to *Kantian* idealism because this structure is not tied in with the synthesizing activity of any *subject*. Let me explore this distinction in more detail.

In one of the introductory chapters to the *Encyclopaedia Logic*, Hegel comments that 'thought is the constitutive substance of external things';[10] and it is this characteristic insistence of the fundamental reality of thought (or the Idea) that renders Hegel's philosophy *idealistic*. In opposition to materialism, Hegel argues that the world of sensible existents is in fact grounded in an intelligible realm of thought, which confers a more permanent and unified reality on the transient world of finite and apparently divisible things: this is the full extent of his metaphysical idealism.

Hegel's view of materialism is that it is merely a variety of empiricism, which takes reality to be what is given to us by the senses. According to Hegel, however, empiricism is mistaken in that it accepts as fundamental what is merely the initial appearance of things, as a world of atomistic, self-subsistent existents, that have a merely external unity. As he puts it:

> the essential feature of the sensible is individuality, and as the individual (which, reduced to its simplest terms, is the atom) also stands in a connection, sensible existents present a number of mutually exclusive units (*ein Außereinander*) – of units, to speak in more definite and abstract formulae, which exist side by side with, and after, one another.
>
> (EL §20 pp. 29–30; translation modified)

By basing its conception of the world on the testimony of the senses, and by viewing reality as made up of a plurality of material units, empiricism is confined to a standpoint which takes objects to be fragmented, merely compound, entities; in insisting on the primacy of sense, this is the only conception of reality that empiricism can consistently achieve.

Now, Hegel's fundamental objection to Kant is that his subjective idealism begins from this empiricist standpoint, *not* in the sense that Kant accepted the representationalism and phenomenalism of the latter, but rather in the sense that he accepted its *reductionist atomism*; Hegel argues that Kant failed to see that the individual exists as the exemplification of a substance-universal, and began with the assumption that the object is reducible to a plurality of sensible properties that are combined together by the experiencing subject. Against this, Hegel argues that idealism is capable of grasping the substance-universal that underlies the plurality given to us by the senses, and thus of transcending empiricism's reductionist and atomistic account of reality:

> Nature shows us a countless number of individual forms and phenomena. Into this variety we feel the need of introducing unity: we compare, consequently, and try to find the universal of each single case . . . In thus characterizing the universal, we become aware of its antithesis to something else. This something else is the merely immediate, outward and individual, as opposed to the mediate, inward, and universal. The universal does not exist externally to the outward eye as a universal. The kind as kind cannot be perceived: the laws of celestial motion are not written in the sky. The universal is neither seen nor heard, its existence is only for the mind. Religion leads us to a universal, which embraces all else within itself, to an Absolute by which all else is brought into being: and this Absolute is an object not of the senses but of the mind and of thought.
>
> (EL §21Z p. 34)

According to Hegel, therefore, we are driven towards idealism and a realist account of universals if we seek to escape from the fragmented and confused world of sense,[11] and wish to treat the individual as a whole as the ontologically primary entity; for, it is in acknowledging that the object exemplifies a substance-universal that we come to see the individual as a single, irreducible thing (a man, a dog, a horse), and to realize that its various other qualities are merely aspects or moments in this unity:

> Intuition has to be submitted to thought, so that what has been dismembered may be restored to simple universality through thought. This contemplated unity is the Notion, which contains the determinate differences simply as an immanent and self-moving unity. Philosophic universality is not indifferent to the determinations; it is the self-fulfilling universality, the diamantine identity, which at the same time holds difference within itself.
>
> (EN §246Z, I p. 203)

It is clear, therefore, that Hegel was led towards a realist account of universals as a result of his conviction that they constitute the substantial form of individual objects, which determine and make possible their unity: this explains the central place such universals have in his ontology. Hegel is explicit in comparing his own position here to that of ancient idealism:

> This universality of things is not something subjective and belonging to us; it is, rather, the noumenon as opposed to the transient phenomenon, the truth, objectivity, and actual being of the things themselves. It resembles the platonic ideas, which do not have their being somewhere in the beyond, but which exist in individual things as substantial genera.
>
> (EN §246Z, I p. 200)[12]

In this way, the moment of universality is treated as the substance-form which constitutes the essence of the whole, and thought becomes the basis for the world of things.

In contrast to Kant's subjective idealism, therefore, Hegel argues that unity is *inherent* in the object as the embodiment of an irreducible substance-kind; the object is therefore not brought into being by any synthesizing subject. In opposition to this latter idealism – which treats concepts as 'ours merely and not also characteristics of the objects'[13] – Hegel insists that universals must be considered as subsisting *outside* the subject mind,[14] as moments of unity located *in things* independently of the experiencing consciousness. In this way, Hegel avoids the subjectivist turn, according to which all concepts can only be contained in a thinking mind; by contrast, he insists that the universal is *prior to* and *independent of* the conscious subject, and present in the object, not just in the mind. Hegel therefore arrives at an *absolute* or *objective* idealism, according to which the world is indeed informed and constituted by concepts (and in this sense fully rational), but by concepts that structure the object in a way that frees both from any dependence on the constituting activity of the mind.[15]

ABSOLUTE IDEA AND ABSOLUTE SPIRIT

The question now arises as to the place of consciousness and *Geist*[16] in Hegel's system. If, as I have suggested, mind for Hegel has nothing like the role of Kant's synthesizing subject in structuring empirical reality, it might seem odd that Spirit has such obvious importance in Hegel's philosophy. If the Idea alone constitutes the world, what then (it might be asked) is the function of Absolute Spirit? Surely it is an indication of Hegel's essential Kantianism that *Geist* looms so large and with such evident authority in Hegel's system? It is this challenge to my understanding of Hegel's absolute idealism that I aim to answer in this section.

A vital indication of the role of Spirit in Hegel's system is given at the end of his *Encyclopaedia*, at the climax of *The Philosophy of Mind*.[17] There, in a sequence of three syllogisms, Hegel sketches what he takes to be the logical interrelation of the three parts of his system: that is, Logic, Nature, and Spirit. A careful study of these three syllogisms will provide us with a crucial insight into the connection between Logic, Nature, and Spirit, and help us assess the role of the latter within Hegel's idealism.[18]

In the first syllogism, the three parts of the system appear as they are located in the *Encyclopaedia* itself: that is, Logic and Spirit constitute the two termini, with Nature as the mediating element:

> The first appearance is formed by the syllogism, which is based on the Logical system as starting-point, with Nature as the middle term which couples the Mind with it. The Logical principle turns to Nature and Nature to Mind.
>
> (EM §575, p. 314)

The form of this syllogism, and the form of the *Encyclopaedia* itself, is clearly difficult to reconcile with Hegel's putative subjective idealism. For, if we accept Hegel's insistence that Nature must act as the mediating element between Logic and Spirit, the implication is first that Idea and Mind cannot be *simply* identical, and second that Nature must be distinct from Mind if it is to act as this mediating element.

I have already stressed the consequences of this first point for Hegel's idealism. For, as I argued in the previous section, the characteristic feature of Hegel's absolute idealism is his freeing of the Idea from Mind and from the thinking subject; by contrast, any such distinction between Idea and Mind was impossible for Kant's merely subjective idealism.[19] Given this separation of these elements, the first syllogism requires mediation by the third element of Nature.

Second, although Nature constitutes the mediating element, it still remains distinct from Logic and Spirit, and cannot be reduced to either: indeed, if we follow the movement of the *Encyclopaedia* itself, Nature comes into existence *before* Spirit, making it difficult to accept the view that for Hegel 'there is no reality apart from consciousness'.[20] Further, despite the fact that the logical structures are reflected in Hegel's treatment of Nature, Hegel maintains that the latter is ultimately distinct from Logic, and cannot be reduced to pure thought: recall his repeated assertion that Nature is the Idea in its otherness. As Emil Fackenheim has pointed out, this first syllogism is testimony to the realist assumptions behind Hegel's philosophy.[21]

It is perhaps due to this irreducible realism that Hegel characterizes the mediation in this form of syllogism as merely an external *transition* (*übergehen*). For, although Nature is implicitly the Idea, it remains different in character from both Logic and Mind, and the mediation between them can therefore only be external:

> Nature, standing between Mind and its essence, sunders itself, not indeed to extremes of finite abstraction, nor itself to something away from them and independent – which, as other than they, only serves as a link between them: for the syllogism is *in the Idea* and Nature is essentially defined as a transition-point and negative factor, and as implicitly the Idea. Still the mediation of the notion has the external form of *transition*, and the science of Nature presents itself as the course of necessity, so that it is only in one extreme that the liberty of the notion is explicit as a self-amalgamation.
>
> (EM §575, p. 314)

The 'otherness' of Nature makes it an awkward mediating element, as its own relation to the two opposed termini is itself problematic, and must itself be mediated.

In the second syllogism, the relation between Nature and Logic is mediated by Mind, thereby resolving the merely external transition of the first syllogism:

> In the second syllogism this appearance is so far superseded, that that syllogism is the standpoint of the Mind itself, which – as the mediating element in the process – presupposes Nature and couples it with the Logical principle. It is the syllogism where Mind reflects on itself in the Idea: philosophy appears as a subjective cognition, of which liberty is the aim, and which is itself the way to produce it.
>
> (EM §576, p. 314)

Now, at first blush it might appear from the form of this syllogism that it confirms Hegel as a merely subjective or Kantian idealist: Spirit brings together Logic and Nature, so that the intelligibility of Nature turns out to rest on the activity of Mind. As with Kant, it seems that with Hegel also the Mind has a central role in establishing the ideal within the real, and in imposing the structure of the Idea on the otherness of Nature.

However, such an interpretation of the second syllogism would be profoundly mistaken in its understanding of the role of Spirit as *mediator*. Hegel makes this role clearer in his account of the syllogism given in the *Logic*:

> Then, in the second place, Mind, which we know as the principle of individuality, or as the actualizing principle, is the mean; and Nature and the Logical Idea are the extremes. It is Mind which discerns

(*erkennt*) the Logical Idea in Nature and which thus raises Nature to its essence.

(EL §187Z, p. 251; translation modified)

In this passage, Hegel states clearly that the role of Spirit as mediator is *not* to determine or structure Nature through the Idea *itself*, but merely to *recognize* or *discern* (*erkennen*) this structure as it *already exists* in Nature. For, as Hegel stated in the first syllogism, Nature is '*in itself* the Idea': the task of Spirit as mediator is to make this implicit structure *explicit*, and thereby enable Nature to mediate between itself and Logic.

It follows from this that the place of Spirit in Hegel's system is not to determine Nature itself, but rather to bring to light the extent to which Nature is already determined by the Idea.[22] Unlike in Kant's idealism, therefore, Mind for Hegel is not *ontologically* active, in structuring and determining Nature, although it *is* active in discerning the structure of the Idea in its otherness.[23] In short, Mind brings out the presence of the Idea, even as it exists in its other, and in recognizing the structure of the Idea in this way, it establishes the implicit existence of the Idea in Nature.

In order to be able to discern the Idea in Nature, Spirit must have undergone considerable development, both in itself and in its attitude to Nature.[24] Both the *Phenomenology* and *The Philosophy of Mind* trace this development, through various inadequate or limited forms of consciousness, which all strive (either knowingly or unknowingly) to find the Idea present in the object. This development culminates in the standpoint of Absolute Spirit, a standpoint occupied by Philosophy itself, to which the world is fully and completely intelligible:

> The love of truth, faith in the power of the mind, is the first condition in Philosophy. Man, because he is Mind, should and must deem himself worthy of the highest; he cannot think too highly of the greatness and the power of his mind, and, with this belief, nothing will be so difficult and hard that it will not reveal itself to him (*das sich ihm eröffnete*). The Essence (*Wesen*) of the universe, at first hidden and concealed, has no power which can offer resistance to the search for knowledge; it has to lay itself open before the seeker – to set before his eyes and give for his enjoyment, its riches and its depths.
>
> (LHP, I p. xiii; translation modified: HW XVIII pp. 13–14)

Mind therefore serves as the mediating element between Idea and Nature because it can discern the intelligible structure of the Idea behind the extrinsicality of Nature, and reveal the latter as implicitly ideal.

In order to do this, however, Mind does not *itself* determine Nature as ideal, but merely brings to light the prior existence of the Idea in Nature.

The second syllogism therefore gives way to the third syllogism, in which the Idea constitutes the mediating element between the two extremes of Spirit and Nature:

> The third syllogism is the Idea of philosophy, which has self-knowing reason, the absolutely universal, for its middle term: a middle, which divides itself into Mind and Nature, making the former its presupposition, as process of the Idea's subjective activity, and the latter its universal extreme, as process of the objectively and implicitly existing Idea. The self-judging of the Idea into its two appearances (§§ 575, 576) characterizes both as its (the self-knowing reason's) manifestations: and in it there is a unification of the two aspects: – it is the nature of the fact, the notion, which causes the movement and development, yet this same movement is equally the action of cognition. The eternal Idea, in full fruition of its essence, eternally sets itself to work, engenders and enjoys itself as absolute Mind.
>
> (EM §577, pp. 314–15)

This third syllogism makes clear all that is different between absolute and subjective idealism: for Hegel it is not Mind that brings together Idea and Nature, but ultimately Idea that makes possible the unity of Nature and Mind.[25]

For, by recognizing the Idea in Nature, Mind is able to overcome the opposition between itself and the object, in so far as it too is informed by the Idea. Given that both Nature and Mind share in the movement of the Idea, there can be no ultimate antithesis between them:

> That is why here [Mind] still lacks the *determinate* knowledge of the rationality of the object. To attain this, Mind must liberate the intrinsically rational object from the form of contingency, singleness, and externality [*Zufälligkeit, Einzelheit und Äußerlichkeit*] which at first clings to it, and thereby free *itself* from the connection which for it is an Other. It is on the path of this liberation that mind continues to be finite. For so long as it has not yet reached its goal, it does not yet know itself as absolutely identical with its object, but finds itself limited by it.
>
> (EM §441Z p. 182)

In recognizing itself as explicitly Idea, and Nature as implicitly Idea, Mind overcomes its opposition to the other, in so far as the Idea is shared between them. In this way, Logic, not Mind, constitutes the ultimate mediator for absolute idealism.

In one of the introductory chapters of the *Encyclopaedia Logic*, Hegel comments that 'the universal' as brought to consciousness by reflective thought, 'contains the value of the thing – is the essential, inward and true.'[26] This belief that the substance-universal constitutes the essence of the individual object is, I have argued, characteristic of Hegel's objective idealism, which rests on his acceptance of a realist theory of universals as substance-forms.[27] It has been shown that for Hegel the role of the subject is to become conscious of the unified substance-universal which the object exemplifies, and thus to see beyond the plurality of apparently unrelated atomistic qualities that the object displays in our sensory experience. As I have stressed throughout, however, Hegel is only able to make this move towards absolute idealism because he denies that the object is reducible to the kinds of atomistic representations that Kant made the basis of his doctrine of synthesis: only in this way could Hegel liberate the object from the synthesizing activity of Kant's transcendental subject, and so make possible the shift from subjective to absolute idealism.

Conclusion

In his article, 'On the Very Idea of a Conceptual Scheme', Donald Davidson identifies the 'dualism of scheme and content, of organizing system and something waiting to be organized' as the third dogma of empiricism.[1] I hope it has become clear that acceptance of this dogma, which forms a central part of Kant's transcendental idealism, is in fact inseparable from a fourth: that an individual object is just a bundle of sensible properties, which needs to be organized by the subject if the object is to come into being. I have argued that only by accepting this reduction of the object to a plurality of properties can the Kantian doctrine of synthesis get a grip on us, and that the bundle theory of the object leads immediately to the idealist position, that objects as they appear to us are in fact products of some unifying conceptual scheme imposed by the subject on an intrinsically unstructured manifold.

Hegel escaped this third dogma, I have suggested, because his quasi-Aristotelian account of the object led him to reject the fourth. For Hegel, the object is not reducible to a plurality of properties needing to be organized, but rather is the exemplification of a universal from the category of substance: such universals constitute the essential nature or form of the object *as a whole*, and cannot be reduced to a plurality. In basing his ontology and his account of things on substance-universals in this way, Hegel could avoid treating the unity of the object as if it were the outcome of some act of synthesis; because the individual is the exemplification of a substance-kind, and because the substance-kind is irreducible, the pluralistic framework of an object as a synthesis of intuitions is no longer intelligible as an account of the structure and realization of things. The individual as a whole is the primary sort of being, because the individual is the exemplification of an indivisible substance-kind: the object is thereby given to us as a unity at the beginning of the ontological enterprise, and is not, as Kant's reductionist atomism implied, something that we must construct for ourselves.

What makes Hegel's critique of Kant on this issue important is that much metaphysics, epistemology, science, social theory, and philosophy of mind and language is dominated by the same sort of pluralistic ontology that we find in Kant, which treats all apparent unities as if they could be explained as the combination of pre-existing and mutually independent elements. The implication of Hegel's more holistic outlook, however, is that certain fundamental totalities (for example, the mind, language, the self, or living organisms) cannot be reduced to a plurality of ontologically self-subsistent building blocks, and it is wrong to treat these totalities as if they were constructed out of atomistic entities in this way; rather, it is claimed, the totality as a whole is the ontologically primary substance, and the parts into which it is properly analysable could not exist outside or prior to their instantiation in the whole. Thus, there is no suggestion on this account that nothing regarding the *structure* of these totalities can possibly be known, or that they form homogeneous unities; the claim is merely that the elements which form genuine and functional *parts* of these totalities are not ultimately divisible from one another, and that in dealing with these totalities it is wrong to assume that it is always with a plurality of such atomistic elements that any account of their genesis and structure should begin.

In his *Lectures on the Philosophy of Religion*, Hegel declares that 'the whole of philosophy is nothing other than the study of the determinations of unity'.[2] In this book, the aim has been to study how Kant and Hegel differed over what they conceived these determinations to be, and how this difference, both for them and for us, constitutes a pivotal issue in any metaphysical account of the nature and realization of things.

Notes

Introduction

1 In some discussions of these issues, particularly as they arise in the social sciences, holism is constrasted to *individualism*. I have not used this term, and have preferred the more general term 'pluralism' because in this book it is precisely the nature of the *individual* which is at issue.

2 In the third of his *Logical Investigations*, 'On the Theory of Wholes and Parts', Edmund Husserl draws a formal distinction between collections and real wholes on the grounds that the parts of the former are 'independent' (*selbständig*) and the parts of the latter are 'dependent' (*unselbständig*). He calls the former 'pieces' (*Stücke*) and the latter 'parts' (*Teile*). Husserl outlines the nature of this distinction as follows: 'We have independent contents wherever the elements of a presentational complex (complex of contents) by their very nature *permit their separated presentation*; we have dependent contents wherever this is not the case' (Edmund Husserl, *Logical Investigations*, translated by J. N. Findlay [2 vols, Routledge & Kegan Paul, London; Humanities Press, New York, 1970], Vol. 2, Pt III Chap. 1 §2, p. 439). In Husserl's terminology, then, we may say that whereas the pluralist treats the given unity as a compound formed out of independent pieces, the holist argues it is an irreducible unity of dependent parts, which 'cannot be, if the other contents are not together with [them].' (ibid., §5, p. 443.)

3 A third position, with which holism should not be confused, is that of *monism*, which treats the totality as an absolutely unanalysable and unstructured one. The contrast between holism and monism may be defined as follows: whereas holism treats the totality as internally analysable into parts but as irreducible into atomistic and independent pieces, monism denies that the totality is analysable *at all*, and argues that it even lacks *parts* (using the terms 'pieces' and 'parts' in the Husserlian sense outlined above).

4 Michael J. Loux, *Substance and Attribute: A Study in Ontology* (D. Reidel, Dordrecht, 1978), pp. 158–66. In fairness to Loux, I should emphasize that while my main aim is to stress the anti-reductionist implications of this model, he himself does not see this as any great consideration in its favour: see ibid., pp. 165–6.

5 The phrase is Hume's: see *A Treatise of Human Nature*, edited by L. A. Selby-Bigge and revised by P. H. Nidditch, 2nd edn (Oxford University Press,

Oxford, 1978), Bk I Pt 1 §6, p. 16.

6 There is of course much debate among Aristotelian scholars as to whether substantial forms are particular, universal, or neither. I would follow G. J. Hughes in arguing that although universal *predicates* are not substantial forms, universals which constitute the *essence* of an individual are: see Gerald J. Hughes, 'Universals as Potential Substances: The Interpretation of Metaphysics Z 13', in M. F. Burnyeat (ed.), *Notes on Book Zeta of Aristotle's Metaphysics* (Oxford Study Series, Oxford Sub Faculty of Philosophy, 1981), pp. 107–26. For a clear and comprehensive discussion of this issue, see Jonathan Lear, *Aristotle: The Desire to Understand* (Cambridge University Press, Cambridge, 1988), pp. 273–93.

7 This is not to say that for Hegel *any* sort of analysis is impossible, and that the whole should be treated as a totally homogeneous one. Hegel accepted that wholes do have parts, and that the identification of these parts and the tracing of interconnections between them is an important aspect of cognition. What he did object to, however, was then treating these parts as if they could exist *outside* and *prior to* their instantiation in the whole, for it is *this* step (he argued) that causes us to treat them as atomistic entities in their own right, which then leads to the misleading question: how do these entities come to form a unity? This question is misleading (Hegel believed) because once it is put, it is difficult to avoid some form of Kantian constructivism.

8 For example, on the structure of consciousness and the self see Thomas Nagel, *The View from Nowhere* (Oxford University Press, Oxford, 1986), pp. 49–51 and Robert Nozick, *Philosophical Explanations* (Oxford University Press, Oxford, 1981), pp. 94–104; on the structure of communities see D. H. Ruben, 'Social Wholes and Parts', *Mind*, Vol. 92 (1983), pp. 219–38, and Philip Pettit, 'The Varieties of Collectivism', in O. Neumaier (ed.), *Mind, Language and Society* (Verband der wissenschaftlichen Gesellschaften Österreichs, Vienna, 1984), pp. 158–66; and on the nature of the physical world see Paul Teller, 'Relational Holism and Quantum Mechanics', *British Journal for the Philosophy of Science*, Vol. 37 (1986), pp. 71–81.

9 I borrow this phrase from W. D. Hart, 'The Anatomy of Thought', *Mind*, Vol. 92 (1983), pp. 264–9 (p. 266).

1 Kant and the doctrine of synthesis

1 As a result of his assumption that the unity and structure of empirical reality is imposed by the cognizing subject, Kant describes himself as a *formal* idealist, in that he takes the organizing frameworks of space, time, and the categories to be brought to experience us. (See Prol. p. 146: KW IV p. 375; cf. also CPR B519.) This idealistic account of the origins of order and unity in our experience is of course to be distinguished from those varieties of idealism which treat all objects as only existing in the individual consciousness; such forms of idealism are distinct from Kant's in that they treat all objects as ideas and sensations that are contained in the 'inner' space of the mind, which means (*contra* Kant) that they thereby locate them *outside* the frameworks of space, time, and the categories. As we shall see in Chapter 5, where Hegel accuses Kant of 'subjective idealism', it is the former doctrine

and not the latter he is referring to, and which his holistic conception of the object led him to reject.

2 cf. Edwin Hartman, *Substance, Body and Soul: Aristotelian Investigations* (Princeton University Press, Princeton, 1977), pp. 10–56. For a modern philosophical defence of the primacy of individual objects (including persons) in our ontology, see P. F. Strawson, *Individuals: An Essay in Descriptive Metaphysics* (Methuen, London, 1959).

3 Bertrand Russell, *A Critical Exposition of the Philosophy of Leibniz* (Cambridge University Press, Cambridge, 1900) p. 14.

4 John Locke, *An Essay Concerning Human Understanding*, edited with a foreword by P. H. Nidditch (Oxford University Press, Oxford, 1975), II xxiii §1, p. 295.

5 ibid., II xxiii §15, p. 305. See also ibid., II xiii §19, p. 175.

6 ibid., II xii §§4–6, p. 165–6.

7 'We are now in the next place to consider those we call *Mixed Modes*, such are the Complex *Ideas*, we mark by the names *Obligation, Drunkenness*, a *Lye*, etc. which consisting of several Combinations of simple *Ideas* of different kinds, I have called *Mixed Modes*, to distinguish them from the more simple Modes, which consist only of simple *Ideas* of the same kind. These mixed Modes being also such Combinations of simple *Ideas*, as are not looked upon to be the characteristical Marks of any real Beings that have a steady existence, but scattered and independent *Ideas*, put together by the Mind, are thereby distinguished from the complex *Ideas* of Substances.' (ibid., II xxii §1, p. 288.)

8 ibid., III vi §2, p. 439.

9 ibid., IV iii §10, p. 544.

10 ibid., IV vi §9, p. 583.

11 ibid., III vi §6, p. 442.

12 M. R. Ayers, 'The Ideas of Power and Substance in Locke's Philosophy' in I. C. Tipton (ed.), *Locke on Human Understanding* (Oxford University Press, Oxford, 1977), pp. 77–104 (p. 96).

13 D. Hume, *A Treatise of Human Nature*, edited by L.A. Selby-Bigge and revised by P.H. Nidditch, 2nd edn (Oxford University Press, Oxford, 1978) Bk I Pt 1 §6, pp. 15–16.

14 ibid., Bk I Pt 4 §3, p. 221.

15 ibid., Bk I Pt 1 §4, pp. 10–13. See also David Hume, *Enquiries Concerning Human Understanding and Concerning the Principles of Morals*, edited by L. A. Selby-Bigge, revised and notes by P. H. Nidditch, 3rd edn (Oxford University Press, Oxford, 1975), Pt 1 §3, p. 24.

16 Hume, *Treatise*, Bk I Pt 1 §6, p. 16.

17 Reinhardt Grossmann, *The Categorial Structure of the World* (Indiana University Press, Bloomington, 1983), pp. 155–6. See also D. S. Mackay, 'An Historical Sketch of the Problem of Relations', in *Studies in the Problem of Relations*, University of California Publications in Philosophy, Vol. 13 (1930), pp. 1–34 (pp. 16–19). This view of Aristotle (which ultimately derives from Russell and A. N. Whitehead) has not gone unchallenged, however: see (for example) R. Demos, 'Types of Unity According to Plato and Aristotle', *Philosophy and Phenomenological Research*, Vol. 6 (1945–6), pp. 534–45 (pp. 536–7).

18 The nature of relations was also discussed by Kant's more immediate predecessors and contemporaries, such as Wolff, Crusius, and Lambert: see Peter Schulthess, *Relation und Funktion: Eine systematische und entwicklungsgeschichtliche Untersuchung zur theoretischen Philosophie Kants* (de Gruyter, Berlin and New York, 1981), pp. 144–55.

19 Russell, *The Philosophy of Leibniz*, pp. 14–15. See also Gottfried Martin, *Kant's Metaphysics and Theory of Science*, translated by P. G. Lucas (Manchester University Press, Manchester, 1955), pp. 2–4 and pp. 118–22.

20 Gottfried Wilhelm Leibniz, *Philosophical Papers and Letters: A Selection*, translated and edited with an introduction by L. E. Loemker, 2nd edn (D. Reidel, Dordrecht, 1969), p. 704.

21 Martin, *Kant's Metaphysics*, p. 4 and pp. 119–20. Martin quotes the following passage from the draft of a letter to Des Bosses as the clearest statement of Leibniz's position: 'Thus God not only perceives the individual monads and all their modifications, but also their relations, and in this consists the reality of relations and truths' (*Die philosophischen Schriften von Gottfried Willhelm Leibniz*, edited by C. J. Gerhardt (7 vols, *Berlin Ausgabe*, 1879; reprint edn, Georg Olms, Hildesheim, 1960), Vol. 2, p. 438; cited Martin, *Kant's Metaphysics*, p. 120).

22 Kant, CPR Bxvi-xvii.

23 Kant, CPR A9/B13.

24 Kant, CPR A9/B13.

25 Gerd Buchdahl's phrase.

26 Again, I borrow this term from Gerd Buchdahl: see his paper 'Reduction-Realization: A Key to the Structure of Kant's Thought', in J. N. Mohanty and Robert W. Shahan (eds), *Essays on Kant's Critique of Pure Reason* (University of Oklahoma Press, Norman, 1982), pp. 39–98.

27 Many commentators, therefore, have gone wrong in treating Kant's account of *a priori* knowledge as the *direct* or *only* route to his idealism. Thus, for example, while Paul Guyer notes that 'like his empiricist predecessors as well as the rationalists themselves, Kant harbored a prejudice against the ultimate reality of relations', he still insists that 'Kant's most fundamental argument for transcendental idealism is to be found in his understanding of the conditions of possibility of *a priori* knowledge, thus in his epistemology' (Paul Guyer, *Kant and the Claims of Knowledge* (Cambridge University Press, Cambridge, 1987), p. 351 and p. 354). In my view the framework model that explains this knowledge is only made conceivable for Kant by his *ontological* conviction, noted by Guyer but not sufficiently appreciated by him, that the object as we experience it has its relational unity imposed on it by us.

28 'Metaphysical Deduction' is the more convenient name given by commentators to the section of the 'Transcendental Analytic' entitled 'The Clue to the Discovery of All Pure Concepts of the Understanding' (CPR, A76–83/B102–16). Kant himself referred to this section as the metaphysical deduction later in the *Critique* (CPR B159).

29 H. E. Allison, *Kant's Transcendental Idealism: An Interpretation and Defense* (Yale University Press, New Haven and London, 1983), p. 145.

30 Kant, CPR A77/B102.

31 Kant, CPR A69/B94.

32　Kant, CPR A68/B93.

33　For an elaboration of this view see Jonathan Bennett, *Kant's Analytic* (Cambridge University Press, Cambridge, 1966), pp. 71–6.

34　Kant, CPR A70/B95.

35　Kant, CPR A80/B106.

36　Kant, CPR A79/B104–5.

37　P. F. Strawson, *The Bounds of Sense* (Methuen, London, 1966), p. 32.

38　Kant, CPR A111.

39　See Kant, CPR A90/B123.

40　This doctrine that the combination of intuitions cannot be given, but is the result of our synthesizing activity, is already present in Kant's pre-critical writings, and survived unchallenged in his *Opus postumum*. See H-G. Hoppe, 'Ist alle Verbindung eine Verstandeshandlung?', in G. Funke (ed.), *Akten des 5. Internationalen Kant-Kongresses* (3 vols, Bouvier, Bonn, 1981–2), Vol. 1, pp. 221–31 (p. 223, notes 8 and 9). See also F. Kaulbach, 'Die Entwicklung der Synthesis-Gedankens bei Kant', in H. Heimsoeth, D. Henrich, and G. Tonelli (eds), *Studien zu Kants Philosophischer Entwicklung* (Georg Olms, Hildesheim, 1967), pp. 56–92.

41　Kant, CPR B133.

42　cf. also CPR A122: 'According to this principle all appearances, without exception, must so enter the mind or be apprehended, that they conform to the unity of apperception. Without synthetic unity in their connection, this would be impossible; and such synthetic unity is itself, therefore, objectively necessary.'

43　Hume, *Treatise*, BkI Pt4 §6, p. 252. For a full treatment of Kant's response to Hume's attack on the identity of the self, see Patricia Kitcher, 'Kant on Self-Identity', *The Philosophical Review*, Vol. 91 (1982), pp. 41–72.

44　Kant's conception of the transcendental object is of course notoriously many-sided, but I would argue that this is at least *one* of the major uses of the term in the *Critique*.

45　Kant, CPR A341–405/B399–432.

46　This attack by Kant on the soul, and his insistence on the empty formalism of the self, earned him rare praise from that other great enemy of the 'soul-concept', Friedrich Nietzsche. See *Beyond Good and Evil: Prelude to a Philosophy of the Future*, translated by W. Kaufmann (Random House, New York, 1966), §54, pp. 66–7.

47　'We are now in a position to have a clear view of the outcome of the whole Transcendental Dialectic, and accordingly to define the final purpose of the ideas of pure reason, which become dialectical only through heedlessness and misapprehension. . . . The unity of reason is the unity of system; and this systematic unity does not serve objectively as a principle that extends the application of reason to objects, but subjectively as a maxim that extends its application to all possible empirical knowledge of objects. . . . / We misapprehend the meaning of this idea if we regard it as the assertion or even as the assumption of a real thing, to which we may proceed to ascribe the ground of the systematic order of the world. On the contrary, what this ground which eludes our concepts may be in its own inherent constitution is left entirely undetermined; the idea is posited only as being the point of view from which alone that unity, which is so essential to reason and so beneficial to the understanding, can be further extended. In short, this transcendental thing is only the schema of the regulative principle by which reason, so far as lies in its power, extends systematic unity over the whole field of experience' (Kant, CPR A679–80/B707–8 and A681–2/B709–10).

48 cf. also: 'Further, since the one condition which accompanies all thought is the "I" in the universal proposition "I think", reason has to deal with this condition in so far as it is itself unconditioned. It is only the formal condition, namely, the logical unity of every thought, in which I abstract from all objects; but nevertheless it is represented as an object which I think, namely, I myself and its unconditioned unity' (Kant, CPR A398).

49 In this book, my main aim is to show how Hegel attacked Kant's pluralistic model of the object. I have argued elsewhere that he sought to undermine Kant's pluralistic model of the *subject* as well. See my paper, 'Kant, Hegel and the Place of the Subject', in Proceedings of the International Hegel Congress of the Hegel-Gesellschaft, 1988; publication forthcoming in the *Hegel-Jahrbuch*.

2 Hegel contra Kant

1 Hegel, DFS p. 90: HW II p. 21. For a recent account of how one of these antitheses – that between faith and intellect – dominated German philosophy in the period prior to the emergence of post-Kantian idealism, see Frederick C. Beiser, *The Fate of Reason: German Philosophy from Kant to Fichte* (Harvard University Press, Cambridge, Mass., and London, 1987).

2 M. H. Abrams has observed: 'In the several decades beginning with the 1780s. . . a number of the keenest and most sensitive minds found radically inadequate, both to immediate human experience and to basic human needs, the intellectual ambiance of the Enlightenment, with (as they saw it) its mechanistic world-view, its analytic divisiveness (which undertook to explain all physical and mental phenomena by breaking them down into irreducible parts, and regarded all wholes as a collocation of such elementary parts), and its conception of the human mind as totally diverse and alien from its nonmental environment' (M. H. Abrams, *Natural Supernaturalism: Tradition and Revolution in Romantic Literature* (W. W. Norton, New York and London, 1973), pp. 170–1). For a general account of the preoccupations and aims of thinkers in Hegel's period, see Edward Craig, *The Mind of God and the Works of Man* (Oxford University Press, Oxford, 1987), pp. 131–72.

3 cf. also: 'When the might of union vanishes from the life of men and the antitheses lose their living connection and reciprocity and gain independence, the need of philosophy arises' (DFS p. 91: HW II p. 22).

4 Friedrich Schiller, *On the Aesthetic Education of Man, in a Series of Letters*, edited and translated by E. M. Wilkinson and L. A. Willoughby (Oxford University Press, Oxford, 1967), 6th Letter, § 3, pp. 31 and 33. For a (rather lurid) account of the influence of Hellenism on German writers during this period, see E. M. Butler, *The Tyranny of Greece over Germany* (Cambridge University Press, Cambridge, 1935). It should be noted that this nostalgia for the ancient world was not shared by all, and as the new century began,

'modernists' became increasingly impatient with the elegiac outlook of those who continually harked back to the glories of classical Greece. For a fascinating account of how Goethe's classicism became increasingly embattled, see Nicholas Boyle, '*Die Natürliche Tochter* and the Origins of "Entsagung"', forthcoming in *London German Studies*.

5 Hegel makes a similar point in the following criticism of empirical psychology: 'For though this psychology also demands that the various spiritual forces shall be harmoniously integrated. . . this gives expression to a unity of mind which only *ought* to be, not to the original unity. . . . This harmonious integration remains, therefore, a vacuous idea which expresses itself in high-sounding but empty phrases but remains ineffective in face of the spiritual forces presupposed as independent' (EM §378 p. 4).

6 This point is echoed by Friedrich Hölderlin at the end of his poetic novel *Hyperion*: 'It is a hard saying, and yet I must speak it because it is the truth: I can think of no people more at odds with themselves than the Germans. You see artisans, but no men, thinkers, but no men, priests, but no men, masters and servants, but no men, minors and adults, but no men – is this not like a battlefield on which hacked-off hands and arms and every other member lie pell-mell, while the life-blood flows from them to vanish in the sand?' (F. Hölderlin, *Hyperion*, translated by W. R. Trask (The New American Library, New York, 1965), p. 164.)

7   He who would study organic existence,
           First drives out the soul with rigid persistence;
           Then the parts in his hand he may hold and class,
           But the spiritual link is lost, alas!
           Encheiresin naturae, this Chemistry names,
           Nor knows how herself she banters and blames!

(J. W. von Goethe, *Faust*, lines 1936–41; translated by Bayard Taylor (The Modern Library, New York, 1950), p. 66.) Hegel cites these lines (while putting them in a different order) at EL §38Z p. 63 and EN §246Z, I p. 202. The phrase *Encheiresis naturae* (meaning 'manipulating nature') has been traced back to the chemist Jacob Reinhold Spielmann, with whom Goethe studied in Strassburg: see E. O. von Lippmann, 'Encheiresis Naturae', in *Abhandlungen und Vorträge zur Geschichte der Naturwissenschaften* (2 vols, von Veit, Leipzig, 1906–13), Vol. 2, pp. 439–69.

8 There is an fairly extensive literature on *Naturphilosophie* and its development during this period. The following general studies should be mentioned: C. Siegel, *Geschichte der deutschen Naturphilosophie* (Akademische Verlagsgesellschaft, Leipzig, 1913), pp. 131–247; R. Ayrault, *La Genèse du romantisme allemand* (4 vols, Editions Montaigne, Paris, 1961–76), Vol. 4, pp. 11–167; A. Faivre, 'La Philosophie de la nature dans la romantisme allemand', in Y. Belaval (ed.), *Histoire de la philosophie III: du XIX siècle à nos jours* (Editions Gallimard, Paris, 1974), pp. 14–45; B. Gower, 'Speculation in Physics: The History and Practice of "Naturphilosophie" ', *Studies in History and Philosophy of Science*, Vol. 3, (1972–3), pp. 301–56; D. M. Knight, 'German Science in the Romantic Period', in M. Crosland (ed.), *The Emergence of Science in Western Europe* (Macmillan, London, 1975), pp. 161–78; H. A. M. Snelders, 'Romanticism

and "Naturphilosophie" and the Inorganic Natural Sciences 1797–1840: An
Introductory Survey', *Studies in Romanticism*, Vol. 9 (1970), pp. 193–215;
A. Gode von Aesch, *Natural Science in German Romanticism* (Columbia
University Press, New York, 1941); W. D. Wetzels, 'Aspects of Natural
Science in German Romanticism', *Studies in Romanticism*, Vol. 10 (1971),
pp. 44–59.

9 J. W. von Goethe, *Elective Affinities*, translated with an introduction by R. J.
Hollingdale (Penguin Books, Harmondsworth, 1971), pp. 53–4. The pun in
Eduard's comment vanishes in translation: in German *Scheidung* means
'division' and *Scheidekünstler* means 'analytical chemist'. Jeremy Adler has
pointed out that Goethe breaks from the normal scientific accounts of
elective affinity in so far as the discussion in the novel begins with a reference
to the unity of the phenomena of nature [*Naturwesen*] with themselves (ibid.,
p. 51); Goethe thereby underlines his view that the category of unity is prior
to that of difference and diversity. See Jeremy Adler, *'Eine fast magische
Anziehungskraft': Goethes 'Wahlverwandtschaften' und die Chemie seiner
Zeit* (C. H. Beck, Munich, 1987), p. 88.

10 Schiller, *On the Aesthetic Education of Man*, 1st Letter, §4, p. 5.

11 If anyone could be expected to feel keenly the dangers and disadvantages of
extreme social and political pluralism, it must be someone living in the
fragmented German Empire at the turn of the eighteenth century. As a result
of the Treaty of Westphalia, which concluded the Thirty Years War in 1648,
Germany was broken up into some three hundred principalities with only a
nominal unity. Hegel never ceased to be critical of the treaty and its
consequences. In his *Lectures on the Philosophy of History* he described the
Germany that resulted from the treaty as 'organised anarchy' (*konstituierte
Anarchie*) (LPH p. 454: HW XII p. 518).

12 Schiller, *On the Aesthetic Education of Man*, 6th Letter, §7, p. 35.

13 See F. W. Coker, *Organismic Theories of the State: Nineteenth Century
Interpretations of the State as an Organism or Person* (AMS Press, New
York, 1967).

14 Michael Rosen has commented on the impatience Hegel and his
contemporaries felt towards Kant's reductionist and atomistic conception of
experience: 'Kant had rejected the ruling empiricist–associationist doctrine
of the passivity of the human mind. It appeared only natural to challenge at
the same time empiricism–associationism's other key doctrine – the doctrine
of the atomic character of experience, and the external character of the
relations introduced by the mind. But Kant, as we saw, does not take this
further step; although he was aware of the current thought which was trying
to rehabilitate conceptions of intrinsic unity, such conceptions feature in his
own thought only as subjective propensities of our power of judgement, not
as objective features of cognition' (M. Rosen, *Hegel's Dialectic and Its
Criticism* (Cambridge University Press, Cambridge, 1982) p. 118).

15 Hegel, EM §420 p. 161; translation modified.

16 Hegel, PS p. 68: HW III p. 95.

17 'The object is defined as having within it an essential property which
constitutes its simple being-for-self; but along with this simple nature the
object is also to contain diversity which, though *necessary*, is not to

constitute its *essential* determinateness. This, however, is a distinction that is still only nominal; the unessential, which is none the less supposed to be necessary, cancels itself out. It is what has just been called the negation of itself' (Hegel, PS p. 76: HW III pp. 103–4).

18 Hegel, SL p. 589: HW VI p. 261. Hegel may be alluding here to the use of the term synthesis as it occurs in Aristotle, where Aristotle uses it to mean the putting together of ingredients in a compound in which the ingredients remain separate and distinct, like grains of barley and wheat in a heap constituted of both. As a result, in this kind of compound there is a mere aggregate juxtaposition of the constitutents. In this connection, Ivor Leclerc cites Aristotle, *Of Generation and Corruption*, 328a 2–4. (See Ivor Leclerc, *The Nature of Physical Existence* (George Allen & Unwin, London, 1972), p. 141.)

3 Ontology and structure in Hegel's *Logic*

1 This ambiguity stems from the fact that although the *Phenomenology* is described by Hegel as a 'ladder' to the absolute systematic standpoint (PS p. 14: HW III p. 29), much of the *content* of the *Phenomenology* is reduplicated within the third part of the *Encyclopaedia*, in Hegel's *Philosophy of Mind*; thus, the *Phenomenology* appears to be not just an introduction to the system, but also *part of* the system itself.

2 This claim to be talking about 'humanity in general', when at the same time his outlook is more narrowly European, has led to claims that Hegel's philosophy is imperialistic and flawed by Eurocentrism. I have some sympathy with this claim, though it does not in itself undermine Hegel's more substantive insight, that it is permissible to talk about the development of 'cultures' as well as of individuals.

3 For an account of the *Phenomenology* that emphasizes its character as a spiritual journey and *Bildungsroman*, see M. H. Abrams, *Natural Supernaturalism: Tradition and Revolution in Romantic Literature* (W.W. Norton, New York and London, 1973), pp. 225–37.

4 I would reject any reading of the *Phenomenology* which attempts to associate *Geist* with anything *extra*-human or divine. Hegel says quite clearly that it is nothing more than the collective human consciousness: 'What still lies ahead for consciousness is the experience of what Spirit is – this absolute substance which is the unity of the different independent self-consciousnesses which, in their opposition, enjoy perfect freedom and independence: "I" that is "We" and "We" that is "I" ' (PS p. 110: HW III p. 145).

5 Hegel, PS pp. 64–5: HW III p. 90.

6 In the corresponding passage from his *Philosophical Propaedeutic* Hegel comments: 'Therefore what in truth is before us is not the abstract, sensuous determinateness but the universal' (PP p. 57: HW IV p. 114).

7 'The question has been asked, why slavery has vanished from modern Europe. One special circumstance after another has been adduced in explanation of this phenomenon. But the real ground why there are no more slaves in Christian Europe is only to be found in the very principle of Christianity itself, the religion of absolute freedom. Only in Christendom is man respected as man, in his infinitude and universality. What the slave is

without, is the recognition that he is a person: and the principle of
personality is universality. The master looks upon his slave not as a person,
but as a selfless thing. The slave is not himself reckoned an "I" – his "I" is his
master ' (Hegel, EL §163Z pp. 227–8).

8 For example, Hegel comments on those laws which relate the nature of the
organism to its environment: 'But laws of this kind: animals belonging to the
air have the nature of birds, those belonging to water have the nature of fish,
animals in northern latitudes have thick, hairy pelts, and so on – such laws
are seen at a glance to display a poverty which does not do justice to the
manifold variety of organic Nature. Besides the fact that organic Nature in
its freedom can divest its forms of these characteristics, and of necessity
everywhere presents exceptions to such laws, or rules as we might call them,
the characterization of the creatures to which they do apply is so superficial
that even the necessity of the laws cannot be other than superficial, and
amounts to no more than the *great influence* of the environment; and this
does not tell us what does and what does not strictly belong to this influence.
Such relations of organisms to the elements [they live in] cannot therefore in
fact be called *laws*' (PS p. 155: HW III p. 197).

9 'In thus establishing himself – and each moment, because it is a moment of
the essence, must succeed in exhibiting itself as the essence – the individual
has thereby placed himself in opposition to the laws and customs. These are
regarded as mere ideas having no absolute essentiality, an abstract theory
without any reality, while he as this particular "I" is his own living truth'
(Hegel, PS pp. 214–15: HW III p. 267).

10 For an account of Hegel's association of death with universality, see M. J.
Inwood, 'Hegel on Death', *International Journal of Moral and Social Studies*,
Vol. 1, No. 2 (1986), pp. 109–22 (pp. 111–12).

11 Hegel, PS pp. 236–62: HW III pp. 292–323.

12 'The simple substance of Spirit, as consciousness, is divided. In other words,
just as consciousness of abstract sensuous being passes over into perception,
so also does the immediate certainty of a real ethical situation; and just as for
sense-perception simple being becomes a Thing of many properties, so for
ethical perception a given action is an actual situation with many ethical
connections. For the former, however, the superfluous plurality of
properties concentrates itself into the essential antithesis of individuality and
universality; and still more for ethical perception, which is the purified
substantial consciousness, does the plurality of ethical moments become the
duality of a law of individuality and a law of universality. But each of these
divisions of substance remains Spirit in its entirety; if in sense-perception
things have no other substance than the two determinations of individuality
and universality, here these determinations express only the superficial
antithesis of the two sides' (Hegel, PS p. 267: HW III pp. 328–9).

13 Hegel, PS p. 293: HW III p. 358.

14 'The two extremes, the state power and the noble consciousness, are split up
by the latter: the state power into the abstract universal which is obeyed, and
into the self-centered will which, however, does not yet conform to the
universal; and the noble consciousness into the obedience rendered by the
existence which is not self-centered, or the *intrinsic being* of self-respect and

honour, and into the still unsurrendered being-for-self, the will that still reserves its independence. The two moments into which both sides are purified and which, therefore, are moments of language, are the *abstract universal*, called "the general good", and *pure self* which, in serving the state, renounced its own many and various interests' (Hegel, PS pp. 309–10: HW III pp. 377–8).

15 Hegel, PS p. 357: HW III p. 433.

16 'In the actual "doing", however, consciousness behaves as this particular self, as completely individual; it is directed towards reality as such, and has this for its purpose, for it wills to achieve something. Duty in general thus falls outside of it into another being, which is consciousness and the sacred law-giver of pure duty' (Hegel, PS p. 371: HW III p. 449).

17 The tension that exists between the individuality of the moral agent with a determinate 'character' and the abstract claims of the universal moral standpoint has recently been recognized by modern moral philosophers – such as Bernard Williams and Robert Nozick – who have argued that it is too much to expect the moral individual to rise above what Nagel has called his 'individualistic baggage' (Thomas Nagel, *The View from Nowhere* (Oxford University Press, Oxford, 1986), p. 199). For Nozick, see *Philosophical Explanations* (Oxford University Press, Oxford, 1981), pp. 452–3; for Williams, see his 'Persons, Character and Morality' in *Moral Luck* (Cambridge University Press, Cambridge, 1981), pp. 1–19, and *Ethics and the Limits of Philosophy* (Fontana Press, London, 1985). For an account of how Hegel tries to resolve this tension between individuality and universality in the political domain, see my 'Unity and Difference in Hegel's Political Philosophy', *Ratio*, new series, Vol. 2 (1989), pp. 75–88.

18 Julian Roberts has recently summarized the importance of this dialectic in the *Phenomenology* as follows: 'The recurring motif in Hegel, which guides notions like negation and continuity, or consciousness and its other, is the opposition *and the union* of individuality and generality. The individual is material singularity, the *hic et nunc*; the general is concept, rule, law, prescription. For "reality", whether it be the reality of experience, of morality, or of politics, *both* sides must play their part. A thing is not only the example of a genus, it is a singular piece of matter. A person is not merely a function, he or she is a living flesh-and-blood individual. A political leader is not merely the representative of a group, he or she is an entirely unique character with unique fears and hopes. But, beyond either of the two sides, the reality of change is a unity, the unity of freedom, practice and reason. Reason is an eternally beckoning vision, equally detached from the individual and the general, and yet in the end more "real" than either of them' (Julian Roberts, *German Philosophy: An Introduction* (Polity Press, Cambridge, 1988), p. 78).

19 cf. the following passage from the introduction to Hegel's *Lectures on the History of Philosophy*: 'everyone possesses and uses the wholly abstract category of *being*. The sun *is* in the sky; these grapes *are* ripe, and so on *ad infinitum*. Or, in a higher sphere of education [*oder in höhrer Bildung*], we proceed to the relation of cause and effect, force and its manifestation, etc. All our knowledge and ideas are entwined with metaphysics like this and

governed by it; it is the net which holds together all the concrete material which occupies us in our action and endeavour. But this net and its knots are sunk in our ordinary consciousness beneath numerous layers of stuff. This stuff comprises our known interests and the objects that are before our minds, while the universal threads of the net remain out of sight and are not explicitly made the subject of our reflection' (ILHP pp. 27–8: HW XVIII, p. 77).

20 See for example Hegel, EL §45Z p. 73. For an illuminating discussion of how Hegel's conception of reason as a power of reconciliation came under attack from later critics, see Jürgen Habermas, *The Philosophical Discourse of Modernity*, translated by Frederick Lawrence (Polity Press, Cambridge, 1987).

21 'Thus the antinomy of pure reason in its cosmological ideas vanishes when it is shown that it is merely dialectical, and that it is a conflict due to an illusion which arises from our applying to appearances that exist only in our representations, and therefore, so far as they form a series, not otherwise than in a successive regress, that idea of absolute totality which holds only as a condition of things in themselves' (Kant, CPR A506/B534).

22 Hegel, EL §79 p. 113.

23 Hegel, EL §80 p. 113; translation modified.

24 Hegel, EL §81 p. 115; translation modified.

25 Hegel, EL §82 p. 119; translation modified.

26 One of the first commentators to notice this transformation was J. M. E. McTaggart, who remarked on the fact that 'The further the dialectic goes from its starting-point, the less prominent becomes the apparent stability of the individual finite categories, and the less do they seem to be self-centred and independent' (J. M. E. McTaggart, *Studies in the Hegelian Dialectic*, 2nd edn (Cambridge University Press, Cambridge, 1922), p. 21; cf. also *A Commentary on Hegel's Logic* (Cambridge University Press, Cambridge, 1910), p. 12). More recently, Dieter Henrich has warned against trying to reduce the dialectic to some standardized formula, commenting that 'Whoever wants to find a key [for the whole *Logic*] must disregard Hegel's repeated statement, that the *Logic* changes its method in its three branches [*Disziplinen*]' (D. Henrich, *Hegel im Kontext* (Suhrkamp, Frankfurt am Main, 1967), p. 148; my translation).

27 Hegel, SL p. 603: HW VI p. 276.

28 Hegel, SL p. 602: HW VI p. 276.

29 Hegel, SL p. 619: HW VI p. 297. cf. also: ' we must recognize the infinite force of the understanding in splitting the concrete into abstract determinatenesses and plumbing the depth of the difference, the force that at the same time is alone the power that effects their transition. The concrete of *intuition* is a *totality*, but a sensuous one – a real material which has an indifferent, *sundered* existence in space and time; but surely this absence of unity in the manifold, where it is the content of intuition, ought not to be counted to it for merit and superiority over intellectual existence' (Hegel, SL p. 610: HW VI p. 286).

30 See Hegel, SL p. 625: HW VI p. 304. In this, Hegel was following Hölderlin. See F. Hölderlin, *Urteil und Sein* in *Sämtliche Werke* (*Kleine Stuttgarter Ausgabe*), edited by Friedrich Beissner (W. Kohlkammer, Stuttgart, 1962), Vol. 4, pp. 226–7. For recent commentaries on Hölderlin's conception of

judgment see Dieter Henrich, 'Hölderlin über Urteil und Sein', *Hölderlin Jahrbuch*, Vol. 14 (1965–6), pp. 73–96, and Klaus Düsing, *Das Problem der Subjektivität in Hegels Logik, Hegel-Studien*, supplementary Vol. 15 (Bouvier, Bonn, 1976), pp. 66–8.

31 Hegel, EL §174Z p. 239.

32 'The predicate in this judgement [of reflection] no longer *inheres* in the subject; it is rather the *implicit being* under which this individual is *subsumed* as an accidental. If the judgements of existence may also be defined as *judgements* of *inherence*, judgements of reflection are, on the contrary, *judgements of subsumption*' (Hegel, SL p. 645: HW VI p. 328).

33 Hegel, PP p. 111: HW IV p. 147.

34 cf. G. E. M. Anscombe and P. T. Geach, *Three Philosophers* (Basil Blackwell, Oxford, 1961), pp. 33–4. Aristotle also held that sentences in which a substance-term is apparently predicated of a subject are in fact identity-statements rather than cases of predication. Hegel is clearly echoing this point when he states: 'No doubt there is also a distinction between terms like individual and universal, subject and predicate: but it is none the less the universal fact, that every judgement states them to be identical'. (EL §166 p. 231). For Aristotle see *Metaphysics* Γ 4 (1007a 20ff.); and see Kirwan's note on this passage in his translation of Aristotle's *Metaphysics* Γ, Δ, E (Oxford University Press, Oxford, 1971), pp. 100–1; and Gerald J. Hughes, 'Universals as Potential Substances':The Interpretation of Metaphysics Z 13', in M.F. Burnyeat and others, *Notes on Book Zeta of Aristotle's Metaphysics* (Oxford Study Series, Oxford Sub Faculty of Philosophy, 1981), p. 115.

35 'It betrays a defective logical training to place upon the same level judgements like "gold is dear" and judgements like "gold is a metal". That "gold is dear" is a matter of external connection between it and our wants or inclinations, the cost of obtaining it, and other circumstances. Gold remains the same as it was, though that external reference is altered or removed. Metalleity, on the contrary, constitutes the substantial nature of gold, apart from which it, and all else that is in it, or can be predicated of it, would be unable to subsist' (EL §177Z p. 242).

36 Hegel, EL §181 p. 244 (translation modified) and SL p. 664: HW VI p. 352. Hegel was enamoured with the syllogism from the very start of his philosophical career, stating in the second of his *Habilitationsthesen*: 'Syllogismus est principium Idealismi [Syllogism is the principle of Idealism]'. (See N. Waszek, 'Hegel's *Habilitationsthesen*: A Translation with Introduction and Annotated Bibliography', in D. Lamb (ed.), *Hegel and Modern Philosophy* (Croom Helm, London, 1987), pp. 249–60 (p. 253).)

37 See above pp. 55–8.

38 cf. also Hegel, SL p. 664: HW VI p. 351.

39 Hegel, EL §183Z p. 237.

40 Hegel, SL pp. 697–8: HW VI pp. 394–5.

41 It may occur to some readers that in arguing that Hegel's holism derives from his account of the substance-universal, I am mistaken in overlooking the place of the *dialectic* in his holistic approach. I am not wholly antipathetic to this view, and in my PhD dissertation I argued strongly for an account of

Hegel's holism along these lines. However, I now think that to argue for holism simply on the basis of the interrelation of the categories is too formalistic, and relies on imputing to Hegel a type of 'onto-logic' more extravagant than any he actually possessed. In short, I would argue that Hegel's holism rests less on a 'dialectical overcoming of difference', and more on his account of the categories of universal, particular, and individual, and the kind of anti-reductionist ontology that this account implies.

42 A. J. Ayer has observed that in the work of Russell and W. V. Quine 'we at last have a proof of Berkeley's contention that things are bundles of qualities, and with it the solution of an old philosophical problem' (A. J. Ayer, *Russell and Moore: The Analytical Heritage* (Macmillan, London, 1971), p. 47; cf. also A. J. Ayer, 'Names and Descriptions', in *The Concept of a Person and Other Essays* (Macmillan, London, 1963), pp. 129–61 (p. 61)). Russell's classic exposition of his theory of descriptions is in 'On Denoting', *Mind*, Vol. 14 (1905), pp. 479–93.

43 For an interesting discussion of the feasibility of doing without singular terms in a natural language, see Ian Hacking, 'A Language Without Particulars', *Mind*, Vol. 77 (1968), pp. 168–85.

44 cf. Anthony Quinton, *The Nature of Things* (Routledge & Kegan Paul, London, 1973), p. 43: 'The idea of a thing in general can be acquired from the use and understanding of existential statements provided that the predicative element of these statements is of the thing, rather than the stuff or quality, kind. The language proposed by Quine would not enable the idea of a thing in general to be acquired if all its predicates, its Fs, were quality-predicates. But there is no reason why they should all be of this kind and, as a matter of fact, thing-predicates are the first we learn.' cf. also Stanley Rosen, *The Limits of Analysis*, paperback edn (Yale University Press, New Haven and London, 1985), p. 107: 'As analysts, we attempt to establish "scientifically" or "rigorously" the unity of an entity by establishing its identity via the entity's predicates. However, we require a pre-analytical intuition of the unity of an entity in order to recognize that such-and-such predicates belong to it. It follows that a whole is not the same as the sum of its parts. We cannot arrive at the unity of a whole by listing its predicates, even upon the very rash assumption that the list is complete.'

45 See Ian Hacking, 'Individual Substance', in Harry G. Frankfurt (ed.), *Leibniz: A Collection of Critical Essays* (University of Notre Dame Press, Notre Dame and London, 1976), pp. 137–54.

46 'The subject of a judgement, in the representation of which is combined the ground of the synthetic unity of a manifold of predicates, is an object' (Kant, Reflexion 6350, KW XVIII p. 676; cited and translated in H. Allison, *Kant's Transcendental Idealism: An Interpretation and Defense*, (Yale University Press, New Haven and London, 1983), p. 147).

4 Unity and structure in Hegel's *Philosophy of Nature*

1 cf. M. J. Loux, *Substance and Attribute: A Study in Ontology* (D. Reidel, Dordrecht, 1978), pp. 170–3.

2 'External Nature, too, like mind, is rational, divine, a representation of the

Idea. But in Nature, the Idea appears in the element of asunderness [*im Elemente des Außereinander*]' (Hegel, EM §381Z p. 9).

3 cf. also: 'It is easy to *understand* something, to get an idea of it. Red, for example, is an abstract idea of our sense-perception, and when in ordinary parlance we talk of "red" we do not mean we are dealing with an abstraction; but a rose which is red is a concrete red, it is a unity of leaves, shape, colour, smell, something living, growing; in it in many ways something abstract can be distinguished and isolated, which can be destroyed and rent apart and yet in the multiplicity of its parts it is still *one* subject, one Idea. Thus the pure abstract Idea is not itself an abstraction, an empty simplicity like red, but a flower, something inherently concrete' (Hegel, ILHP, p. 19 (*Vorlesungen über die Geschichte der Philosophie*, edited by J. Hoffmeister (Felix Meiner, Leipzig, 1938), pp. 30–1)).

4 'If in pursuance of the foregoing remarks we consider Logic to be the system of the pure types of thought, we find that the other philosophical sciences, the Philosophy of Nature and the Philosophy of Mind, take the place, as it were, of an Applied Logic, and that Logic is the soul which animates them both' (Hegel, EL §24 p. 39). Although this passage would seem to more than justify my move from the abstract metaphysics of the *Logic* to the *Philosophy of Nature*, not everyone working on the latter would agree: see M. J. Petry, 'Scientific Method: Francoeur, Hegel and Pohl' in R-P. Horstmann and M. J. Petry (eds), *Hegels Philosophie der Natur: Beziehungen zwischen empirischer und speculativer Naturerkenntnis* (Klett-Cotta, Stuttgart, 1986), pp. 11–29 (pp. 13–14).

5 cf. also: 'The object (1) in its immediacy is the notion only potentially; the notion as subjective is primarily outside it; and all its specific character is imposed from without. As a unity of differents, therefore, it is a composite, an aggregate; and its capacity of acting on anything else continues to be an external relation' (Hegel, EL §195 pp. 261–2).

6 Hegel, EL §195Z p. 262. Cf. also: 'A favourite reflectional form is that of powers and faculties of soul, intelligence or mind. . . . In this lies the want of organic unity which by this reflectional form, treating mind as a "lot" of forces, is brought into mind, as it is by the same method brought into nature. Any aspect which can be distinguished in mental action is stereotyped as an independent entity, and the mind thus made a skeleton-like mechanical collection' (Hegel, EM §445 p. 189).

7 A. N. Whitehead, *Adventures of Ideas* (Penguin Books, Harmondsworth, 1942), p. 185.

8 Hegel, EL §198 p. 264.

9 See my introduction to F. W. J. Schelling, *Ideas for a Philosophy of Nature*, translated by E. E. Harris and P. Heath (Cambridge University Press, Cambridge, 1988). Cf. also F. Moiso, 'Die Hegelische Theorie der Physik und der Chemie in ihrer Beziehung zu Schellings Naturphilosophie', in R-P. Horstmann and M. J. Petry (eds), *Hegels Philosophie der Natur: Beziehungen zwischen empirische and speculativer Naturerkenntnis* (Klett-Cotta, Stuttgart, 1986), pp. 54–87.

10 Gideon Freudenthal, *Atom and Individual in the Age of Newton: On the Genesis of the Mechanistic World View* (D. Reidel, Dordrecht, 1986), p. 98;

cf. also ibid. p. 27. See also P. Teller, 'Relational Holism and Quantum Mechanics', *British Journal for the Philosophy of Science*, Vol. 37 (1986) pp. 71–6.

11 Hegel, EN §254, I p. 223.

12 'It is an ancient proposition that the one is many and especially that the many is one. We may repeat here the observation that the truth of the one and the many expressed in propositions appears in an inappropriate form, and that this truth is to be grasped and expressed only as a becoming, as a process, a repulsion and attraction – not as being, which in a proposition has the character of a stable unity' (Hegel, SL p. 172: HW V p. 193).

13 'The relation of attraction to repulsion is such that the former has the latter for *presupposition*. Repulsion provides the material for attraction. If there were no ones there would be nothing to attract; the conception of a perpetual attraction, of an absorption of the ones, presupposes an equally perpetual production of them' (Hegel, SL p. 173: HW V p. 194).

14 'If repulsion is thus taken merely by itself, then it is the dispersion of the many ones into somewhere undetermined, outside the sphere of repulsion itself; for repulsion is this, to negate the inter-relatedness of the many: the absence of any relation between them is the determination of the many taken abstractly. But repulsion is not merely the void; the ones, as unrelated, do not repel or exclude one another, this constitutes their determination. Repulsion is, although negative, still essentially *relation*. . . . But this moment of relation is attraction and thus is in repulsion itself; it is the negating of that abstract repulsion according to which the ones would be only self-related affirmative beings not excluding one another' (Hegel, SL p. 175: HW V pp. 195–6).

15 Hegel says of the centre of gravitational attraction: 'Its determinateness is essentially different from a mere *order* or *arrangement* and *external connexion* of parts; as determinateness in and for itself it is an *immanent* form, a self-determining principle in which the objects inhere and by which they are bound together into a genuine One' (SL p. 723: HW VI p. 424).

16 '[The unity of gravity] is a mere should, a yearning; this is the most afflicted of efforts, and matter is damned to it eternally, for the unity does not fulfil itself, and is never reached. If matter reached what it aspires to in gravity, it would fuse together into a single point. It is because repulsion is as essential a moment as attraction, that unity is not attained here' (Hegel, EN §262Z, I p. 243).

17 See Hegel, EN §270Z, I p. 276.

18 M. J. Inwood, *Hegel* (Routledge & Kegan Paul, London, 1983), p. 457.

19 Plato, *Timaeus*, 55d ff.

20 Compare the following passage from Hegel's *Lectures on Aesthetics*: 'If, for example, three natural realms are identified, the mineral, the vegetable, the animal, then in this series we see foreshadowed a universally necessary articulation in accordance with the Concept [*Begriff*], without abiding by the mere idea of an external purposefulness. Even in the multiplicity of products within these three realms, sensuous observation divines a rationally ordered advance, in the different geological formations, and in the series of vegetable and animal species. Similarly, the individual animal organism – this insect with its subdivisions into head, breast, belly and extremities – is envisaged as

an inherently rational articulation, and in the five senses, although at first sight they may seem to be just an accidental plurality, there is likewise found a correspondence with the Concept' (Hegel, LA p. 129: HW XIII, pp. 173–4).

21 'Primarily, the solar system is a number of independent bodies, which maintain themselves in this relation, and posit an external unity within another' (Hegel, EN §269Z, I p. 261).

22 See Hegel, EN §271, I p. 282.

23 Hegel, EN §276Z, II p. 19.

24 'Weighted matter is *divisible* into *masses*, since it is concrete, quantitative being-for-self; but in the quite *abstract* ideality of light there is no such difference; a limit to the infinite expansion of light does not destroy its absolute continuity in itself. The conception of *aggregations* of discrete and simple *light-rays* and *particles*, out of which a light which is limited in its diffusion is supposed to arise, belong to the barbarous categories which have continued to dominate physics, since *Newton* made them current' (Hegel, EN §276, II pp. 17–18).

25 The classic formulation of this view can be found in Newton's *Opticks*: 'it seems probable to me, that God in the Beginning form'd Matter in solid, massy, hard, impenetrable, moveable Particles, of such Sizes and Figures, and with such other Properties, and in such Proportion to Space, as most conduced to the End for which he form'd them. . . . While the Particles continue entire, they may compose Bodies of one and the same Nature and Texture in all Ages: But should they wear away, or break in pieces, the Nature of Things depending on them, would be changed. . . . And therefore, that Nature may be lasting, the Changes of corporeal Things are to be placed only in the various Separations and new Associations and Motions of these permanent Particles' (Isaac Newton, *Opticks or a Treatise of the Reflections, Refractions, Inflections and Colours of Light*, based on the 4th edn, London, 1730 (Dover Publications, New York, 1952) Query 31, p. 400).

26 Hegel, EN §286Z, II p. 45.

27 Hegel, EN §286Z, II p. 46.

28 'Curved lines do not yet occur in inorganic being however, which displays geometrical regular figures with equal and correspondent angles, everything being necessitated by the progression of identity' (Hegel, EN §310Z, II p. 98). P. C. Ritterbush has pointed out that it was not until Häuy had demonstrated in 1801 that the crystalline form is governed by strict geometrical principles, that any real distinction was drawn between the form of crystals and organic form. See P. C. Ritterbush, 'Organic Form: Aesthetics and Objectivity in the Study of Form in the Life Sciences', in G. S. Rousseau (ed.), *Organic Form: The Life of an Idea* (Routledge & Kegan Paul, London, 1972), pp. 25–60 (pp. 32–3).

29 For a full account of the concept of form in crystallography, see Norma E. Emerton, *The Scientific Reinterpretation of Form* (Cornell University Press, Ithaca and London, 1984).

30 Newton, *Opticks*, Bk I Pt 2 Prop. 5 theorem 4, p. 134. Cf. also: 'But the most surprising and wonderful composition was that of *Whiteness*. . . . 'Tis ever compounded, and to its composition are requisite all the aforesaid primary

Colours, mixed in a due proportion. . . . Hence therefore it comes to pass, that *Whiteness* is the usual colour of *Light*; for Light is a confused aggregation of Rays, indued with all sorts of Colours, as they are promiscuously darted from the various parts of luminous bodies. And of such a confused aggregate, as I said, is generated Whiteness' (*Philosophical Transactions of the Royal Society*, No. 80, 9 Feb., 1671/2, p. 3083; reprinted in *Isaac Newton's Papers and Letters on Natural Philosophy*, edited with a general introduction by I. Bernard Cohen, assisted by R. E. Schofield, 2nd edn (Harvard University Press, Cambridge, Mass., and London, 1978), p. 55).

31 EN, II p. 353. As Goethe himself commented: '[Newton's] whole mistake rests on the fact that the complicated phenomenon [colour] was supposed to be laid as the foundation and the simpler [light] to be explained from out of the composite' (*Goethes Werke* (*Hamburger Ausgabe*), edited by E. Trunz (14 vols, Beck, Munich, 1981), Vol. 14, p. 363; cited in Dennis L. Sepper, *Goethe Contra Newton: Polemics and the Project for a New Science of Color* (Cambridge University Press, Cambridge, 1988), p. 37). For a full account of the dispute between Newton and Goethe, see Sepper.

32 Hegel, EN §320Z, II p. 142.

33 A. I. Sabra, *Theories of Light from Descartes to Newton*, new edn, (Cambridge University Press, Cambridge, 1981), pp. 281–2 and pp. 296–7.

34 This remark is quoted by Hegel at EN §324Z, II p. 173. For a brief account of Pohl's career, see Petry's note on this subject, EN, II p. 408.

35 'The chemical process is therefore the unity of magnetism and electricity' (Hegel, EN §326Z, II p. 179). For a full account of Hegel's treatment of chemistry, and its background in the history of science, see Dietrich von Engelhardt, *Hegel und die Chemie: Studie zur Philosophie und Wissenschaft der Natur um 1800* (Guido Pressler, Wiesbaden, 1976).

36 'We have the whole shape therefore, as in magnetism, but it is not single, for there are now distinct wholes. The two sides into which form divides itself are the whole bodies therefore, such as metals, acids, and alkalies, the truth of which consists in their entering into relation. The electrical moment here consists of these sides falling apart into a distinct independence which is not yet present in magnetism. The indivisible unity of magnetism is however the governing principle here; this identity of both bodies, whereby they return once more into the magnetic relationship, is lacking in the electrical process' (Hegel, EN §326Z, II p. 179).

37 cf. also: 'It is in this way that we reach the Notion of the totality of the chemical process in general, and have the concept of it as containing the Notion within the entirety of its differences; that is to say, as positing its negation and yet remaining completely by itself. Consequently, each side constitutes the whole. Acidity is certainly not alkaline, and vice versa, and both are therefore exclusive. Implicitly however, each side is also the other, and is the totality of itself and of the other' (Hegel, EN §326Z, II p. 182).

38 Hegel, EN §327, II p. 183.

39 Hegel, EN §328Z, II p. 185. Cf. also: 'The dissolution of the neutral body initiates the reversion to the particular chemical form, i.e. through a series of partly particular processes, to the form of undifferentiated bodies. On the other hand, each and every separation of this kind is itself inseparably linked

with a combination, while the processes classified as involved in the course of combination also contain the other moment of separation' (Hegel, EN §334, II pp. 213–14).

40 Alessandro Volta, *Opere* (Florence, 1816), II, Pt 2, p. 158; cited in A. R. Hall, *The Scientific Revolution 1500–1800: The Formation of the Modern Scientific Attitude*, 2nd edn (Longmans, London, 1962), p. 360.

41 See Edmund Whittaker, *A History of the Theories of Aether and Electricity*, revised and enlarged edn (2 vols, Thomas Nelson, London, 1951), Vol. 1, p. 75.

42 'An outstanding example of the ignoring of facts in this field is the conception of water as *consisting* of oxygen and hydrogen. When water is submitted to the active current of a pile, oxygen appears at one of its poles and hydrogen at the other. This is taken as evidence of *decomposition*.' Hegel calls this theory 'intrinsically indefensible' (EN §330, II pp. 193–4).

43 'In general, it is therefore by means of fire that that which is still in a state of neutrality, of torpid and indifferent differentiation, is activated into the chemical opposition of acid and caustic alkali' (Hegel, EN §331, II p. 205).

44 On the chemical background to Goethe's *Elective Affinities*, see Jeremy Adler, *'Eine fast magische Anziehungskraft': Goethes 'Wahlverwandtschaften' und die Chemie seiner Zeit* (C.H. Beck, Munich, 1987).

45 Hegel explains this process at EN §333Z, II pp. 211–12.

46 In the final chapter of the third part of the *Encyclopaedia*, the *Philosophy of Mind*, Hegel declares: 'the ordinary physicist (chemist included) takes up only one [determination], the most external and the worst, viz. *composition*, applies only it to the whole range of natural structures, which he thus renders for ever inexplicable' (EM §573 p. 312).

47 Friedrich Schlegel, *Werke* (*Kritische Ausgabe*), edited by E. Behler, J-J. Anstatt, and H. Eichner (35 vols, Thomas, Munich and Vienna, 1967), Vol. 2, pp. 248–9; my translation.

48 'This insistence on the primacy of organism was, I think, common to all of the *Naturphilosophen*, and can be taken as one of their distinctive characteristics as a group' (H. S. Harris, *Hegel's Development II: Night Thoughts (Jena 1801–1806)* (Oxford University Press, Oxford, 1983), p. 286 note 1.

49 'We rightly say, therefore, that not freedom but necessity reigns in Nature; for this latter in its strictest meaning is precisely the merely internal, and for that reason also merely external, connection of mutually independent existences. Thus, for example, light and the [four] elements appear as mutually independent; similarly the planets, although attracted by the sun and despite this relation to their centre, appear to be independent of it and of one another, this contradiction being represented by the motion of the planet around the sun' (Hegel, EM §381Z p. 9).

50 Kant, CJ Pt 2 §75 p. 51: KW V p. 398.

51 Charles Taylor, *Hegel* (Cambridge University Press, Cambridge, 1975), pp. 321–2.

52 Hegel, EL §213 p. 274.

53 Hegel, EN §337Z, III p. 12.

54 Hegel, EN §343Z, III p. 46.

55 cf. Arthur Koestler, *Janus: A Summing Up* (Hutchinson, London, 1978), p. 57.

56 See for example F. W. J. Schelling, *Schellings Werke*, edited by M. Schröter (13 vols, Beck, Munich, 1946–59), Vol. 2, p. 171ff.; and Carl Friedrich von Kielmeyer, *Gesammelte Schriften*, edited by F. H. Holler (Keiper, Berlin, 1938), p. 67ff.

57 Albrecht von Haller, 'A Dissertation on the Sensible and Irritable Parts of Animals', reprinted with an introduction by O. Temkin, *Bulletin of the Institute of the History of Medicine*, Vol. 4 (1936), pp. 651–99 (pp. 658–9).

58 'I proceed now to irritability, which is so different from sensibility, that the most irritable parts are not at all sensible, and vice versa, the most sensible parts are not irritable. I shall demonstrate, that irritability does not depend upon the nerves, but on the original fabric of the parts which are susceptible of it' (ibid., p. 675).

59 On the debate between Haller and Whytt, see R. K. French, *Robert Whytt, the Soul and Medicine* (The Wellcome Institute of the History of Medicine, London, 1969), Chap. VI.

60 Hegel, EN §354, III pp. 111–12. Hegel also mounts an attack on Haller's account for being too rigid in its division of the organic systems in PS p. 166ff: HW III p. 210ff.

61 The quotation from Treviranus is taken from his *Biologie, oder Philosophie der lebenden Natur für Naturforscher und Aerzte* (6 vols, Göttingen, 1802–22), Vol. 1, p. 166; cited by Hegel EN §354Z, III p. 112.

62 cf. also: 'the chemist e. g. places a piece of flesh in his retort, tortures it in many ways, and then informs us that it consists of nitrogen, carbon, hydrogen, etc. True: but these abstract matters have ceased to be flesh' (Hegel, EL §227Z p. 285).

63 'Fever facilitates recovery on account of its motivating the totality of the organism into activity. Once motivated in this way, the organism as a whole is animated, and lifts itself out of its submergence in a particularity' (Hegel, EN §372Z, III p. 202).

64 See also Hegel, EL §216Z p. 280. Cf. also Aristotle, *Metaphysics* Z 10, 1035b 19–25: 'the body and its parts are posterior to this its substance, and it is not the substance [the soul] but the concrete thing that is divided into these parts as its matter. To the concrete thing these are in a sense prior, but in a sense they are not. For they cannot even exist if severed from the whole; for it is not a finger in *any* state that is the finger of a living thing, but the dead finger is a finger only homonymously' (translated by W. D. Ross in J. Barnes (eds.) *The Complete Works of Aristotle*, the revised Oxford translation (2 vols, Princeton University Press, Princeton, 1985), Vol. 2, p. 1635).

65 David Lamb, *Hegel: From Foundation to System* (Martinus Nijhoff, The Hague, 1980), pp. 111–25.

66 A study of the place of organicism in the work of the biologists Ross G. Harrison, Joseph Needham, and Paul Weiss can be found in Donna Jeanne Haraway, *Crystals, Fabrics and Fields: Metaphors of Organicism in Twentieth-Century Developmental Biology* (Yale University Press, New Haven and London, 1976). For a brief outline of the theory of organicism in modern biology, and an account of the major figures in its development see

ibid., pp. 33–63.
67 Paul A. Weiss, *Within the Gates of Science and Beyond* (Hafner, New York, 1971), p. 267.
68 Some *have* been prepared to make this extravagant claim: Sean Kelly, for example, has recently asserted that 'Hegel is the founder of what is commonly referred to as the new science' (Sean Kelly, 'Hegel and Morin: The Science of Wisdom and the Wisdom of the New Science' *The Owl of Minerva*, Vol. 20 (1988), 51–67). While exciting and intriguing parallels between Hegelian thought and the new physics do exist, it seems injudicious to treat Hegel as the father of the movement, when there is little evidence that he exercised any significant influence upon it.

5 The unity of the object and the unity of the subject

1 'It is the union of the Notion with reality which constitutes the true determination of life. This reality no longer has an immediate and independent mode of being as a plurality of properties existing apart from each other, for the Notion is simply the identity of indifferent subsistence [*des gleichgültigen Bestehens*]' (Hegel, EN §337Z, III p. 11).
2 Paul Weiss also saw how the acceptance of holism makes any form of 'constructivism' redundant: 'This, then, concludes my argument. If nature were atomized and inherently chaotic, only creative mind could see and carve into it and from it those patterns of higher order to which we concede consistency and beauty. But nature is not atomized. Its patterning is inherent and primary, and the order underlying beauty is demonstrably there; what is more, human mind can perceive it only because it is itself part and parcel of that order.' (Paul A. Weiss, *Within the Gates of Science and Beyond* (Hafner, New York, 1971), pp. 199–200).
3 Kantian commentators have recently begun to see how phenomenalistic readings of Kant offered by Strawson *et al.* in the 1960s were mistaken, and have sought to defend Kant from Hegel by finding the latter guilty of the same misreading. To see this strategy at its clearest, cf. Graham Bird's two articles, 'Kant's Transcendental Idealism', in G. Vesey (ed.), *Idealism Past and Present*, Royal Institute of Philosophy Lecture Series, 13 (Cambridge University Press, Cambridge, 1982), pp. 71–92 and 'Hegel's Account of Kant's Epistemology in the *Lectures on the History of Philosophy*', in Stephen Priest (ed.), *Hegel's Critique of Kant* (Oxford University Press, Oxford, 1987), pp. 65–76. As I have argued, however, Hegel's main objection to Kant was not that the latter failed to show how we can have objective knowledge; it follows that new readings of Kant's epistemology do not save Kant from the main thrust of Hegel's critique, which turns on his entirely different explanation of the genesis and structure of things.
4 William James saw very clearly how this Kantian subject had replaced substance as the ground of unity for the object: 'The notion of one instantaneous or eternal Knower – either adjective here means the same thing – is, as I said, the great intellectualist achievement of our time. It has practically driven out that conception of 'Substance' which earlier philosophers set such store by, and by which so much unifying work used to

be done. . . . Substance has succumbed to the pragmatic criticisms of the English school. It appears now only as another name for the fact that phenomena as they come are actually grouped and given in coherent form, the very form in which we finite knowers experience or think them together' (William James, *'Pragmatism' and 'The Meaning of Truth'*, with an introduction by A. J. Ayer (Harvard University Press, Cambridge, Mass., and London, 1978), p. 72).

5 Hegel, EL §42Z p. 69.

6 'The unity of apperception might be said at a pinch to subdue or appropriate the manifold of sense by forcing the latter to enter into relations with itself' (W. H. Walsh, 'Kant as Seen by Hegel', in G. Vesey (ed.), *Idealism Past and Present*, Royal Institute of Philosophy Lecture Series, 13 (Cambridge University Press, Cambridge, 1982), pp. 93–109 p. 98).

7 R. C. Solomon, 'Hegel's Concept of "Geist"', *Review of Metaphysics*, Vol. 23 (1969–70), pp. 642–61 (p. 660). Solomon puts forward the same account in his more recent study of the *Phenomenology*: see R. C. Solomon, *In the Spirit of Hegel: A Study of G. W. F. Hegel's Phenomenology of Spirit* (Oxford University Press, New York and Oxford, 1983), pp. 201–3 and pp. 304–6. Walsh has also expressed the view that Hegel's *Geist* is analogous to Kant's transcendental ego: 'The Kantian unity of apperception is the germ of Hegel's doctrine of Spirit' (Walsh, 'Kant as Seen by Hegel', p. 98). For an account of *Geist* that is closer to my own, and which also explicitly rejects Solomon's 'Kantian' reading, see Robert R. Williams, 'Hegel's Concept of *Geist*', in Peter G. Stillman (ed.), *Hegel's Philosophy of Spirit* (State University of New York, Albany, 1987), pp. 1–20.

8 Solomon, *In the Spirit of Hegel*, p. 284.

9 'The Concept of *'Geist'* is a successor to both Kant's *Transcendental Ego* or *'I Think'* and Descartes' celebrated *'Cogito*" (Solomon, 'Hegel's Concept of "Geist" ', p. 650).

10 Hegel, EL §24Z p. 37.

11 Aside from the fact that the apparent unrelatedness of our intuitions leads us into pluralism, Hegel was also extremely critical of the *arithmetical* approach of mathematics, which he argues can also lead us astray in the same way: 'Arithmetic is an analytical science because all the combinations and differences which occur in its subject matter are not intrinsic to it but are effected on it in a wholly external manner. It does not have a concrete subject matter possessing inner, intrinsic, relationships, which, as at first concealed, as not given in our immediate acquaintance with them, have first to be elicited by the efforts of cognition' (Hegel SL pp. 212–13: HW V p. 244).

12 cf. also: 'A thought is the universal as such; even in nature we find thoughts present as its *species* and laws, and thus they are not merely present in the form of consciousness, but absolutely and therefore objectively. The reason of the world is not subjective reason' (Hegel, ILHP, p. 90 (*Vorlesungen über die Geschichte der Philosophie*, edited by J. Hoffmeister, p. 121); my emphasis).

13 Hegel, EL §42Z p. 70.

14 '*Thought* is an expression which attributes the determinations contained therein primarily to consciousness. But inasmuch as it is said that

understanding, reason, is in the objective world, that mind and nature have universal laws to which their life and changes conform, then it is conceded that the determinations of thought equally have objective value and existence' (Hegel, SL p. 51: HW V p. 45).

15 David Wiggins has remarked of Heraclitus: 'Heraclitus lived before the moment when concepts became ideas and took up residence in the head' (D. Wiggins, 'Heraclitus' Conception of Fire, Flux and Material Persistence', in M. Schofield and M. C. Nussbaum (eds.), *Language and Logos* (Cambridge University Press, Cambridge, 1982), pp. 1–31 (p. 29)). This realism with respect to concepts was of course a major feature of classical philosophy, and although there are clear and important differences between Hegel's doctrine and that of the ancients, I would suggest that his *realist* account of universals and concepts means that he is closer to the latter variety of idealism than to Kant's distinctively modern, post-Cartesian approach. For a clear account of the difference Descartes' 'invention' of mind made to the development of idealism, see M. F. Burnyeat, 'Idealism and Greek Philosophy: What Descartes Saw and Berkeley Missed', in G. N. A Vesey (ed.), *Idealism Past and Present* (Cambridge University Press, Cambridge, 1982), pp. 19–50.

16 '*Geist*' is of course notoriously difficult to translate into English, and it is usually rendered as either Spirit or Mind. In what follows I will use both translations interchangeably.

17 Hegel, EM §§575–7, pp. 314–15.

18 I believe that Emil Fackenheim was the first to draw attention to the importance of these three syllogisms in interpreting Hegel's philosophical system, and my account of them is largely in agreement with his analysis: see Emil L. Fackenheim, *The Religious Dimension in Hegel's Thought*, reprint edition (University of Chicago Press, Chicago, 1982), pp. 83–106. However, rather than basing his exposition of these three syllogisms on the last three sections of the *Encyclopaedia*, Fackenheim bases his analysis on an earlier account of the syllogisms given at EL §187Z pp. 250–1, stating that the former are too 'obscure' (ibid., p. 85). By contrast, I will concentrate my attentions on the account given in the *Philosophy of Mind*, first because it is part of the main text and not taken from the student notes, and second because Fackenheim's analysis of the account of these three syllogisms in the *Logic* itself helps to make the later account in the *Philosophy of Mind* less 'obscure'.

19 'But after all, objectivity of thought, in Kant's sense, is again to a certain extent subjective. Thoughts, according to Kant, although universal and necessary categories, are *only our* thoughts – separated by an impassable gulf from the thing, as it exists apart from our knowledge. But the true objectivity of thinking means that the thoughts, far from being merely ours, must at the same time be the real essence of the things, and of whatever is an object to us' (Hegel, EL §41Z pp. 67–8).

20 Solomon, *In the Spirit of Hegel*, p. 192.

21 'First, Nature mediates. That is Nature *itself*. It is by no means either a transcendent Idea of Nature or a subjective experience we may have of it. Nature as such may be 'immediate', i.e., subject to both logical and spiritual mediation. It is, however, an 'immediate *Totality*', i.e., a self-existent Whole

in its own right, and it persists in such self-existence throughout all mediation' (Fackenheim, *The Religious Dimension in Hegel's Thought*, p. 85).

22 'The movement of the solar system is governed by unalterable laws; these laws are its inherent reason. But neither the sun nor the planets which revolve around it in accordance with these laws are conscious of them. It is man who abstracts the laws from empirical reality and acquires knowledge of them' (Hegel, LPWH p. 34 (*Vorlesungen über die Philosophie der Weltgeschichte I: Einleitung: Die Vernunft in der Geschichte*, edited by G. Lasson, 3rd edn (Felix Meiner, Leipzig, 1930), p. 13)). Cf. also: 'To consider a thing rationally means not to bring reason to bear on the object from the outside and so to tamper with it, but to find that the object is rational on its own account . . . . The sole task of philosophic science is to bring into consciousness this proper work of the reason of the thing itself' (Hegel, PR §31 p. 35).

23 'In §5 the old belief was quoted that the reality in object, circumstance, or event, the thing on which everything depends, is not a self-evident datum of consciousness, or coincident with the first appearance and impression of the object; that, on the contrary, Reflection [*Nachdenken*] is required in order to discover the real constitution of the object – and that by such reflection it will be ascertained' (Hegel, EL §21 p. 33).

24 'As a matter of fact, the need to occupy oneself with pure thought presupposes that the human spirit must already have travelled a long road' (Hegel, SL p. 34: HW V p. 23).

25 Failure to recognize the Idea as a third mediating element in Hegel's system has led some commentators to see only Mind and Nature as the only significant elements in Hegel's philosophy. For example, M. H. Abrams observes: 'The tendency in innovative Romantic thought . . . is greatly to diminish, and at the extreme to eliminate, the role of God, leaving as the prime agencies man and the world, mind and nature, the ego and the non-ego, the self and the not-self, spirit and the other, or (in the favourite antithesis of post-Kantian philosophers) subject and object' (M. H. Abrams, *Natural Supernaturalism: Tradition and Revolution in Romantic Literature* (W. W. Norton, New York and London, 1973), p. 91). Whatever the justice of this observation with respect to Fichte and to Schelling, to reduce Hegel's essentially tripartite scheme to a subject–object polarity is to miss all that is new in Hegel's doctrine of the Logic.

26 Hegel, EL §21 p. 33.

27 Given this reading of Hegel's absolute idealism, it follows that the most telling criticism of Hegel's system is not that of the epistemological realists, but rather of the materialists, like Feuerbach, Engels, and Marx, who questioned the pre-eminence given to the Idea in Hegel's ontology. If Hegel's realist account of universals had placed concepts 'outside the head', Marx wanted to put them back in again: 'For Hegel, the process of thinking, which he even transforms into an independent subject, under the name of "the Idea", is the creator of the real world, and the real world is only the external appearance of the Idea. With me, the reverse is true: the ideal is nothing but the material world reflected in the mind of man, and translated into forms of thought' (Karl Marx, *Capital*, Vol. 1, Preface to the Second Edition, translated by Ben Fowkes (Penguin Books, Harmondsworth, 1976), p. 102).

Conclusion

1 Donald Davidson, 'On the Very Idea of a Conceptual Scheme', in *Inquiries into Truth and Interpretation* (Oxford University Press, Oxford, 1985), pp. 183–98 (p. 189). Davidson also points out how the concept of an 'organizing scheme' makes sense only in so far as it is used to structure a *plurality*: 'We cannot attach a clear meaning to the notion of organizing a single object (the world, nature etc.) unless that object is understood to contain or consist in other objects. Someone who sets out to organize a closet arranges the things in it. If you are told not to organize the shoes and shirts, but the closet itself, you would be bewildered. How would you organize the Pacific Ocean? Straighten out its shores, perhaps, or relocate its islands, or destroy its fish' (Davidson, ibid., p. 192).

2 Hegel, LPR I p. 100: HW XVI p. 100.

Bibliography

This bibliography includes all the works cited in the notes (whether they have been consulted in full or only in part) and a selection of other works which I have found useful in the preparation of this book.

Abrams, M. H., *Natural Supernaturalism: Tradition and Revolution in Romantic Literature* (W. W. Norton, New York and London, 1973).

Adler, J., *'Eine fast magische Anziehungskraft': Goethes 'Wahlverwandtschaften' und die Chemie seiner Zeit* (C. H. Beck, Munich, 1987).

Al-Azm, S. J., *The Origins of Kant's Arguments in the Antinomies* (Oxford University Press, Oxford, 1972).

Alexander, P., *Ideas, Qualities and Corpuscles: Locke and Boyle on the External World* (Cambridge University Press, Cambridge, 1985).

Allaire, E. B., 'Existence, Independence and Universals', *Philosophical Review*, Vol. 69 (1960), pp. 485–96.

Allison, H. E., *Kant's Transcendental Idealism: An Interpretation and Defense* (Yale University Press, New Haven and London, 1983).

Anscombe, G. E. M., and Geach, P. T., *Three Philosophers* (Basil Blackwell, Oxford, 1961).

Aquila, R. E., 'Kant's Theory of Concepts', *Kant-Studien*, Vol. 65 (1974), pp. 1–19.

Aquila, R. E., 'Predication and Hegel's Metaphysics', *Kant-Studien*, Vol. 64 (1973), pp. 231–45.

Aquila, R. E., *Representational Mind: A Study of Kant's Theory of Knowledge* (Indiana University Press, Bloomington, 1983).

Arber, A., *The Natural Philosophy of Plant Form* (Cambridge University Press, Cambridge, 1950).

Aristotle, *The Complete Works of Aristotle*, the revised Oxford translation, ed. by J. Barnes (2 vols, Princeton University Press, Princeton, 1985).

Aristotle, *Metaphysics* Γ, Δ, E, trans. by C. Kirwan (Oxford University Press, Oxford, 1971).

Ayer, A. J., 'Names and Descriptions', in *The Concept of a Person and Other Essays* (Macmillan, London, 1963).

Ayer, A. J., *Russell and Moore: The Analytical Heritage* (Macmillan, London, 1971).

Ayers, M. R., 'Berkeley's Immaterialism and Kant's Transcendental Idealism', in G. Vesey (ed.), *Idealism Past and Present*, Royal Institute of Philosophy Lecture Series, 13 (Cambridge University Press, Cambridge, 1982), pp. 51–69.

Ayers, M. R., 'The Ideas of Power and Substance in Locke's Philosophy', in I. C. Tipton (ed.), *Locke on Human Understanding* (Oxford University Press, Oxford, 1977), pp. 77–104.

Ayrault, R., *La Genèse du romantisme allemand* (4 vols, Editions Montaigne, Paris, 1961–76).

Bahm, A. J., 'Organicism: The Philosophy of Interdependence', *International Philosophical Quarterly*, Vol. 7 (1967), pp. 251–84.

Ballauff, T., *Die Wissenschaft von Leben I: Eine Geschichte der Biologie von Altertum bis zur Romantik* (Karl Alber, Freiburg and Munich, 1954).

Baum, M., 'Zur Methode der Logik und Metaphysik beim Jenaer Hegel', in D. Henrich and K. Düsing (eds), *Hegel in Jena, Hegel-Studien*, supp. Vol. 20 (Bouvier, Bonn, 1980), pp. 119–38.

Beck, L. W., *Early German Philosophy: Kant and his Predecessors* (Harvard University Press, Cambridge, Mass., and London, 1969).

Beck, L. W., 'Kant's Strategy', in T. Penelhum and J. J. MacIntosh (eds), *The First Critique* (Wadsworth, California, 1969), pp. 4–17.

Bedell, G., 'Bradley and Hegel', *Idealistic Studies*, Vol. 7 (1977), pp. 262–90.

Beiser, F. C., *The Fate of Reason: German Philosophy from Kant to Fichte* (Harvard University Press, Cambridge, Mass., and London, 1987).

Bennett, J., *Kant's Analytic* (Cambridge University Press, Cambridge, 1966).

Berkeley, G., *Philosophical Works, Including the Works on Vision*, with an introduction and notes by M. R. Ayers, new edn, revised and enlarged (J. M. Dent, London, 1975).

Berry, A. J., *From Classical to Modern Chemistry: Some Historical Sketches* (Cambridge University Press, Cambridge, 1954).

Bird, G., 'Hegel's Account of Kant's Epistemology in the *Lectures on the History of Philosophy*', in S. Priest (ed.), *Hegel's Critique of Kant* (Oxford University Press, Oxford, 1987), pp. 65–76.

Bird, G., 'Kant's Transcendental Idealism', in G. Vesey (ed.), *Idealism Past and Present*, Royal Institute of Philosophy Lecture Series, 13 (Cambridge University Press, Cambridge, 1982), pp. 71–92.

Boas, M., 'Structure of Matter and Chemical Theory in the Seventeenth and Eighteenth Centuries', in M. Clagett (ed.), *Critical Problems in the History of Science* (University of Wisconsin Press, Madison, 1959), pp. 499–514.

Bohm, D., *Wholeness and the Implicate Order* (Ark Paperbacks, London, 1983).

Boyle, N., '*Die Natürliche Tochter* and the Origins of "Entsagung"', in *London German Studies* (forthcoming).

Bradley, F. H., *Appearance and Reality: A Metaphysical Essay*, 2nd edn, corrected with an appendix (Oxford University Press, Oxford, 1930).

Bradley, F. H., *Collected Essays* (2 vols, Oxford University Press, Oxford, 1935).

Bradley, F. H., *Essays on Truth and Reality* (Oxford University Press, Oxford, 1914).

Bradley, F. H., *The Principles of Logic*, 2nd edn, revised, with commentary and terminal essays (2 vols, Oxford University Press, Oxford, 1922).

Breidbach, O., *Das Organische in Hegels Denken: Studie zur Naturphilosophie und Biologie um 1800* (Königshausen and Neumann, Würzburg, 1982).

Bubner, R., *Modern German Philosophy*, trans. by E. Matthews (Cambridge University Press, Cambridge, 1981).

Buchdahl, G., 'Conceptual Analysis and Scientific Theory in Hegel's Philosophy of Nature (with special reference to Hegel's optics)', in R. S. Cohen and M. W. Wartofsky (eds), *Hegel and the Sciences*, Boston Studies in the Philosophy of Science, 64 (D. Reidel, Dordrecht, 1984), pp. 13–36.

Buchdahl, G., 'Hegel's Philosophy of Nature', review, *British Journal for the Philosophy of Science*, Vol. 23 (1972), pp. 257–66.

Buchdahl, G., 'Hegel's Philosophy of Nature and the Structure of Science', *Ratio*, Vol. 15 (1973), pp. 1–27.

Buchdahl, G., *Metaphysics and the Philosophy of Science* (Basil Blackwell, Oxford, 1969).

Buchdahl, G., 'Reduction–Realization: A Key to the Structure of Kant's Thought', in J. N. Mohanty and R. W. Shahan (eds), *Essays on Kant's Critique of Pure Reason* (University of Oklahoma Press, Norman, 1982), pp. 39–98.

Buchdahl, G., 'The Relation between "Understanding" and "Reason" in the Architectonic of Kant's Philosophy', *Proceedings of the Aristotelian Society*, Vol. 67 (1966–7), pp. 209–26.

Burbidge, J., *On Hegel's Logic: Fragments of a Commentary* (Humanities Press, Atlantic Highlands NJ, 1981).

Burbidge, J., 'Transition or Reflection', *Revue Internationale de Philosophie*, Vol. 36 (1982), pp. 111–24.

Burnyeat, M., 'Idealism and Greek Philosophy: What Descartes Saw and Berkeley Missed', in G. N. A. Vesey (ed.), *Idealism Past and Present*, Royal Institute of Philosophy Lecture Series, 13 (Cambridge University Press, Cambridge, 1982), pp. 19–50.

Butchvarov, P., *Being qua Being: A Theory of Identity, Existence and Predication* (Indiana University Press, Bloomington, 1979).

Butchvarov, P., 'The Ontology of Philosophical Analysis', *Nous*, Vol. 15 (1981), pp. 3–14.

Butler, E. M., *The Tyranny of Greece over Germany* (Cambridge University Press, Cambridge, 1935).

Cantor, G. N., *Optics after Newton: Theories of Light in Britain and Ireland, 1704–1840* (Manchester University Press, Manchester, 1983).

Čapek, M., 'Hegel and the Organic View of Nature', in R. S. Cohen and M. W. Wartofsky, *Hegel and the Sciences*, Boston Studies in the Philosophy of Science, Vol. 64 (D. Reidel, Dordrecht, 1984), pp. 109–21.

Cassirer, E., *Rousseau, Kant, Goethe: Two Essays*, trans. by J. Gutmann, P. O. Kristeller, and J. H. Randall Jr, with an introduction by P. Gay, 3rd printing (Princeton University Press, Princeton, 1970).

Cassirer, E., *Substance and Function, and Einstein's Theory of Relativity*, trans. by W. C. Swabey and M. C. Swabey (Open Court, Chicago, 1923).

Chipman, L., 'Kant's Categories and Their Schematism', *Kant-Studien*, Vol. 63 (1972), pp. 36–50.

Clark, M., *Logic and System: A Study of the Transition from 'Vorstellung' to Thought in the Philosophy of Hegel* (Martinus Nijhoff, The Hague, 1971).

Code, A., 'Aristotle: Essence and Accident', in R. E. Grandy and R. Warner (eds), *Philosophical Grounds of Rationality: Intentions, Categories, Ends* (Oxford University Press, Oxford, 1986), pp. 411–40.

Code, A., 'On the Origin of Some Aristotelian Theses about Predication', in J. Bogen and J. E. McGuire (eds), *How Things Are: Studies in Predication and the History of Philosophy and Science* (D. Reidel, Dordrecht, 1985), pp. 101–31.

Coker, F. W., *Organismic Theories of the State: Nineteenth Century Interpretations of the State as an Organism or Person*, (AMS Press, New York, 1967).

Colletti, L., 'Hegel und die "Dialektik der Materie"', in R-P. Horstmann (ed.), *Seminar: Dialektik in der Philosophie Hegels*, (Suhrkamp, Frankfurt am Main, 1978), pp. 394–414.

Collingwood, R. G., *The Idea of Nature*, ed. by T. M. Knox (Oxford University Press, Oxford, 1945).

Collins, J., *Descartes' Philosophy of Nature*, The American Philosophical *Quarterly*, monograph 5 (Basil Blackwell, Oxford, 1971).

Craig, E. J., *The Mind of God and the Works of Man* (Oxford University Press, Oxford, 1987).

Croce, B., *What is Living and What is Dead of the Philosophy of Hegel*, trans. by D. Ainslie (Macmillan, London, 1915).

Cullen, B., *Hegel's Social and Political Thought: An Introduction* (Gill & Macmillan, Dublin, 1979).

Culotta, C. A., 'German Biophysics, Objective Knowledge, and Romanticism', *Historical Studies in the Physical Sciences*, Vol. 4 (1974), pp. 3–38.

Daudet, L., *Goethe et la synthèse* (Editions Bernard Grasset, Paris, 1932).

Davidson, D., 'On the Very Idea of a Conceptual Scheme', in *Inquiries into Truth and Interpretation* (Oxford University Press, Oxford, 1985), pp. 183–98.

Dawes Hicks, G., 'Symposium: Is the "Concrete Universal" the True Type of Universality?', *Proceedings of the Aristotelian Society*, Vol. 20 (1919–20), pp. 147–56.

Demos, R., 'Types of Unity According to Plato and Aristotle', *Philosophy and Phenomenological Research*, Vol. 6 (1945–6), pp. 534–45.

de Vleeschauwer, H-J., *The Development of Kantian Thought: The History of a Doctrine*, trans. by A. R. C. Duncan (Thomas Nelson, London, 1962).

di Giovanni, G., 'The Category of Contingency in the Hegelian Logic', in W. E. Steinkraus and K. I. Schmitz (eds), *Art and Logic in Hegel's Philosophy* (Humanities Press, New Jersey and Sussex, 1980), pp. 179–200.

di Giovanni, G., 'More Comments on the Place of the Organism in Hegel's Philosophy of Nature', in R. S. Cohen and M. W. Wartofsky (eds), *Hegel and the Sciences*, Boston Studies in the Philosophy of Science, 64 (D. Reidel, Dordrecht, 1984), pp. 101–7.

di Giovanni, G., 'Reflection and Contradiction: A Commentary on Some Passages of Hegel's Science of Logic', *Hegel-Studien*, Vol. 8 (1973), pp. 131–62.

Donnelley, S., 'Whitehead and Jonas: On Biological Organisms and Real Individuals', in S. F. Spicker (ed.), *Organism, Medicine and Metaphysics* (D. Reidel, Dordrecht, 1978), pp. 155–75.

Driesch, H., 'Kant und das Ganze', *Kant-Studien*, Vol. 29 (1924), pp. 365–76.

Düsing, K., 'Constitution and Structure of Self-Identity: Kant's Theory of Apperception and Hegel's Criticism', *Midwest Studies in Philosophy*, Vol. 8 (1983), pp. 409–31.

Düsing, K., *Das Problem der Subjektivität in Hegels Logik*, Hegel-Studien, supp. Vol. 15 (Bouvier, Bonn, 1976).

Echelard-Dumas, M., 'Der Begriff des Organismus bei Leibniz: "Biologische Tatsache" und "Fundierung"', *Studia Leibnitiana*, Vol. 8 (1976), pp. 160–86.

Emerton, N. E., *The Scientific Reinterpretation of Form* (Cornell University Press, Ithaca and London, 1984).

Emmett, D., *Whitehead's Philosophy of Organism*, 2nd edn (Macmillan, London, 1966).

Engelhardt, D. von, 'The Chemical System of Substances, Forces and Processes in Hegel's Philosophy of Nature and the Science of his Time', in R. S. Cohen and M. W. Wartofsky (eds), *Hegel and the Sciences*, Boston Studies in the Philosophy of Science, 64 (D. Reidel, Dordrecht, 1984), pp. 41–54.

Engelhardt, D. von, *Hegel und die Chemie: Studie zur Philosophie und Wissenschaft der Natur um 1800* (Guido Pressler, Wiesbaden, 1976).

Engelhardt, D. von, 'Romanticism in Germany', in R. Porter and M. Teich (eds), *Romanticism in National Context* (Cambridge University Press, Cambridge, 1988), pp. 109–33.

Engels, F., *Anti-Dühring: Herr Eugen Dühring's Revolution in Science*, 2nd edn (Foreign Languages Publishing House, Moscow, 1959).

Engels, F., *Dialectics of Nature*, ed. and trans. by C. Dutt, with a preface and notes by J. B. S. Haldene (Lawrence & Wishardt, London, 1940).

Engels, F., *Ludwig Feuerbach and the Outcome of Classical German Philosophy*, ed. and trans. by C. Dutt, with a preface by L. Rudas (Martin Rudas, London, 1934).

Eposito, J. L., *Schelling's Idealism and Philosophy of Nature* (Associated University Press, New Jersey and London, 1977).

Ewing, A. C., *Idealism: A Critical Survey*, 3rd edn (Methuen, London, 1961).

Fackenheim, E. L., *The Religious Dimension in Hegel's Thought*, reprint edn (University of Chicago Press, Chicago, 1982).

Faivre, A., 'La Philosophie de la nature dans la romantisme allemand', in Y. Beleval (ed.), *Histoire de la philosophie III: du XIX siècle à nos jours* (Editions Gallimard, Paris, 1974), pp. 14–45.

Falkenburg, B., *Die Form der Materie: zur Metaphysik der Natur bei Kant und Hegel* (Athenäum, Frankfurt am Main, 1987).

Farber, M., 'Types of Unity and the Problem of Monism', *Philosophy and Phenomenological Research*, Vol. 4 (1943), pp. 37–59.

Fichte, J. G., *The Science of Knowledge*, ed. and trans. by P. Heath and J. Lachs (Cambridge University Press, Cambridge, 1970).

Findlay, J. N., *Hegel: A Re-examination* (George Allen & Unwin, London, 1958).

Findlay, J. N., 'Hegel and the Philosophy of Physics', in J. O'Malley, J.W. Alogozin, H.P. Kainz, and L.L. Rice (eds), *The Legacy of Hegel*, Proceedings of the Marquette Hegel Symposium, 1970 (Martinus Nijhoff, The Hague, 1973), pp. 72–89.

Findlay, J. N., 'The Hegelian Treatment of Biology and Life', in R. S. Cohen and

M. W. Wartofsky (eds), *Hegel and the Sciences*, Boston Studies in the Philosophy of Science, 64 (D. Reidel, Dordrecht, 1984), pp. 87–100.

Fleischmann, E., 'Le Concept de science "speculative": son origine et son développement de Kant à Hegel', in *Science et dialectique chez Hegel et Marx*, by the 'Groupe de recherche sur science et dialectique', under the direction of M. Vadee (Editions du Centre National de la Recherche Scientifique, Paris, 1980), pp. 5–14.

Frede, M., 'Individuals in Aristotle', in *Essays in Ancient Philosophy* (Oxford University Press, Oxford, 1987), pp. 49–71.

Frede, M., 'Substance in Aristotle's *Metaphysics*', in *Essays in Ancient Philosophy* (Oxford University Press, Oxford, 1987), pp. 72–80.

French, R. K., *Robert Whytt, the Soul and Medicine* (The Wellcome Institute of the History of Medicine, London, 1969).

Freudenthal, G., *Atom and Individual in the Age of Newton: On the Genesis of the Mechanistic World View* (D. Reidel, Dordrecht, 1986).

Fulda, H. F., 'Hegels Dialektik als Begriffsbewegung und Darstellungsweise', in R-P. Horstmann (ed.), *Seminar: Dialektik in der Philosophie Hegels* (Suhrkamp, Frankfurt am Main, 1978), pp. 124–74.

Gadamer, H-G., *Hegels Dialektik: Fünf hermeneutische Studien* (J. C. B. Mohr (Paul Siebeck), Tübingen, 1971).

Gillespie, C. M., 'The Aristotelian Categories', in J. Barnes, M. Schofield, and R. Sorabji (eds), *Articles on Aristotle* (4 vols, Duckworth, London, 1979), Vol. III: *Metaphysics*, pp. 1–12.

Gloy, K., *Einheit und Mannigfaltigkeit: Eine Strukturanalyse des 'Und'* (W. de Gruyter, Berlin and New York, 1981).

Gode von Aesch, A., *Natural Science in German Romanticism* (Columbia University Press, New York, 1941).

Goethe, J. W. von, *Goethes Werke (Hamburger Ausgabe)*, ed. by E. Trunz (14 vols, Beck, Munich, 1981).

Goethe, J. W. von, *Goethe's Botany: The Metamorphosis of Plants, 1790*, trans. with an introduction by A. Arber, *Chronica Botanica*, Vol. 10 (1946), pp. 63–115.

Goethe, J. W. von, *Elective Affinities*, trans. with an introduction by R. J. Hollingdale (Penguin Books, Harmondsworth, 1971).

Goethe, J. W. von, *Faust*, trans. by B. Taylor (The Modern Library, New York, 1950).

Gower, B., 'Speculation in Physics: The History and Practice of "Naturphilosophie" ', *Studies in History and Philosophy of Science*, Vol. 3 (1972–3), pp. 301–56.

Gram, M. S., *Kant, Ontology and the A Priori* (Northwestern University Press, Evanston, 1968).

Gray, J. G., *Hegel and Greek Thought* (Harper & Row, New York, 1968).

Greene, M., 'Hegel's Concept of Logical Life', in W. E. Steinkraus and K. I. Schmitz (eds), *Art and Logic in Hegel's Philosophy* (Humanities Press, New Jersey and Sussex, 1980), pp. 121–49.

Grossmann, R., *The Categorial Structure of the World* (Indiana University Press, Bloomington, 1983).

Guthrie, W. K. C., *A History of Greek Philosophy* (6 vols, Cambridge University Press, Cambridge, 1962–81).

Guyer, P., *Kant and the Claims of Knowledge* (Cambridge University Press, Cambridge, 1987).

Habermas, J., *The Philosophical Discourse of Modernity*, trans. by F. Lawrence (Polity Press, Cambridge, 1987).

Hacking, I., 'Individual Substance', in H. G. Frankfurt (ed.), *Leibniz: A Collection of Critical Essays* (University of Notre Dame Press, Notre Dame, 1976), pp. 137–54.

Hacking, I., 'A Language without Particulars', *Mind*, Vol. 77 (1968), pp. 168–85.

Hall, A. R., *The Scientific Revolution 1500–1800: The Formation of the Modern Scientific Attitude*, 2nd edn (Longmans, London, 1962).

Haller, A. von, 'A Dissertation on the Sensible and Irritable Parts of Animals', reprinted with an introduction by O. Temkin, *Bulletin of the Institution of the History of Medicine*, Vol. 4 (1936), pp. 651–99.

Haraway, D. J., *Crystals, Fabrics and Fields: Metaphors of Organicism in Twentieth-Century Developmental Biology* (Yale University Press, New Haven and London, 1976).

Haring, E. S., 'Substantial Form in Aristotle, *Metaphysics Z*', *Review of Metaphysics*, Vol. 10 (1956–7), pp. 308–32, pp. 482–501, pp. 698–713.

Harman, P. M., *Metaphysics and Natural Philosophy: The Problem of Substance in Classical Physics* (Harvester Press, Sussex, 1982).

Harris, E. E., 'The Dialectical Structure of Scientific Thinking', in R. S. Cohen and M. W. Wartofsky (eds), *Hegel and the Sciences*, Boston Studies in the Philosophy of Science, 64 (D. Reidel, Dordrecht, 1984), pp. 195–213.

Harris, E. E., 'Hegel and the Natural Sciences', in F. G. Weiss (ed.), *Beyond Epistemology* (Martinus Nijhoff, The Hague, 1974), pp. 129–53.

Harris, E. E., *An Interpretation of the Logic of Hegel* (University Press of America, Lanham and London, 1983).

Harris, E. E., *Nature, Mind and Modern Science*, (George Allen & Unwin, London, 1954).

Harris, E. E., 'The Philosophy of Nature in Hegel's System', *Review of Metaphysics*, Vol. 3 (1949), pp. 213–28.

Harris, H. S., *Hegel's Development I: Toward the Sunlight (1770–1801)* (Oxford University Press, Oxford, 1972).

Harris, H. S., *Hegel's Development II: Night Thoughts (Jena 1801–1806)* (Oxford University Press, Oxford, 1983).

Hart, W. D., 'The Anatomy of Thought', *Mind*, Vol. 92 (1983), pp. 264–9.

Hartman, E., *Substance, Body and Soul: Aristotelian Investigations* (Princeton University Press, Princeton, 1977).

Hartmann, K., 'Hegel: A Non-metaphysical View', in A. MacIntyre (ed.), *Hegel: A Collection of Critical Essays* (Anchor Books, New York, 1972), pp. 101–24.

Hartmann, K., 'Die ontologische Option', in K. Hartmann (ed.), *Die Ontologische Option* (W. de Gruyter, Berlin, 1976), pp. 1–30.

Hegel, G. W. F., *Aesthetics: Lectures on Fine Art*, trans. by T. M. Knox (2 vols, Oxford University Press, Oxford, 1975).

Hegel, G. W. F., *The Difference between Fichte's and Schelling's System of Philosophy*, trans. by W. Cerf and H. S. Harris (State University of New York, Albany, 1977).

Hegel, G. W. F., *Dissertatio philosophica de Orbitis Planetarum*, in *Erste Druckschriften*, ed. by G. Lasson (Felix Meiner, Leipzig, 1928), pp. 347–401.

Hegel, G. W. F., *Faith and Knowledge*, trans. by W. Cerf and H. S. Harris (State University of New York, Albany, 1977).

Hegel, G. W. F., *Hegel: The Letters*, trans. by C. Butler and C. Seiler, with a commentary by C. Butler (Indiana University Press, Bloomington, 1984).

Hegel, G. W. F., 'Hegel's *Habilitationsthesen*: A Translation with Introduction and Annotated Bibliography' by N. Waszek, in D. Lamb (ed.), *Hegel and Modern Philosophy* (Croom Helm, London, 1987), pp. 249–60.

Hegel, G. W. F., *Hegel's Logic*, trans. by W. Wallace, 3rd edn (Oxford University Press, Oxford, 1975).

Hegel, G. W. F., *Hegel's Phenomenology of Spirit*, trans. by A. V. Miller, with analysis of the text and foreword by J. N. Findlay, (Oxford University Press, Oxford, 1977).

Hegel, G. W. F., *Hegel's Philosophy of Mind*, trans. by W. Wallace and A. V. Miller (Oxford University Press, Oxford, 1971).

Hegel, G. W. F., *Hegel's Philosophy of Nature*, trans. with an introduction and explanatory notes by M. J. Petry (3 vols, George Allen & Unwin, London, 1970).

Hegel, G. W. F., *Hegel's Philosophy of Right*, trans. by T. M. Knox (Oxford University Press, Oxford, 1952).

Hegel, G. W. F., *Hegel's Philosophy of Subjective Spirit*, ed. and trans. with an introduction and explanatory notes by M. J. Petry (3 vols, D. Reidel, Dordrecht, 1978).

Hegel, G. W. F., *Hegel's Political Writings*, trans. by T. M. Knox, with an introductory essay by Z. A. Pelczynski (Oxford University Press, Oxford, 1964).

Hegel, G. W. F., *Hegel's Science of Logic*, trans. by A. V. Miller (George Allen & Unwin, London, 1969).

Hegel, G. W. F., *Introduction to the Lectures on the History of Philosophy*, trans. by T. M. Knox and A. V. Miller (Oxford University Press, Oxford, 1985).

Hegel, G. W. F., *Jenaer Systementwürfe II*, ed. by R-P. Horstmann and J. H. Trede, *Gesammelte Werke*, VII (Felix Meiner, Hamburg, 1971).

Hegel, G. W. F., *Lectures on the History of Philosophy*, trans. by E. S. Haldane and F. H. Simson (3 vols, Humanities Press, London, 1892–6).

Hegel, G. W. F., *Lectures on the Philosophy of History*, trans. by J. Sibree (George Bell, London, 1881).

Hegel, G. W. F., *Lectures on the Philosophy of Religion*, trans. by E. B. Speirs and J. B. Sanderson, new edn (3 vols, Humanities Press, London, 1962).

Hegel, G. W. F., *Lectures on the Philosophy of World History; Introduction: Reason in History*, trans. by H. B. Nisbet with an introduction by D. Forbes (Cambridge University Press, Cambridge, 1975).

Hegel, G. W. F., *Natural Law*, trans. by T. M. Knox with an intoduction by H. B. Acton (University of Pennsylvania Press, Pennsylvania, 1975).

Hegel, G. W. F., *The Philosophical Propaedeutic*, trans. by A. V. Miller, ed. by M. George and A. Vincent (Basil Blackwell, Oxford, 1986).

Hegel, G. W. F., *Theorie Werkausgabe*, ed. by E. Moldenhauer and K. M. Michel (20 vols and Index, Suhrkamp, Frankfurt am Main, 1969–71).

Hegel, G. W. F., *Vorlesungen über die Geschichte der Philosophie*, ed. by
J. Hoffmeister (Felix Meiner, Leipzig, 1938).

Hegel, G. W. F., *Vorlesungen über die Philosophie der Weltgeschichte I;
Einleitung: Die Vernunft in der Geschichte*, ed. by G. Lasson, 3rd edn (Felix
Meiner, Leipzig, 1930).

Heidegger, M., *Hegel's Concept of Experience* (Harper & Row, New York,
1970).

Heidegger, M., *Identity and Difference*, trans. with an introduction by
J. Stambaugh (Harper & Row, New York, 1974).

Heidegger, M., *Kant and the Problem of Metaphysics*, trans. by J. S. Churchill
(Indiana University Press, Bloomington, 1962).

Heidegger, M., *What is a Thing?*, trans. by W. B. Barton Jr and V. Deutsch with
an analysis by E. T. Gendlin (Regnery/Gateway, South Bend, Indiana, 1967).

Henrich, D., 'Die Formationsbedingungen der Dialektik', *Revue Internationale
de Philosophie*, Vol. 36 (1982), pp. 139–62.

Henrich, D., *Hegel im Kontext* (Suhrkamp, Frankfurt am Main, 1967).

Henrich, D., 'Hölderlin über Urteil und Sein', *Hölderlin Jahrbuch*, Vol. 14
(1965–6), pp. 73–96.

Henrich, D., *Identität und Objectivität: eine Untersuchung über Kants
transzendentaler Deduktion* (Carl Winter, Heidelberg, 1976).

Henrich, D., 'The Proof Structure of Kant's Transcendental Deduction', *Review
of Metaphysics*, Vol. 22 (1968–9), pp. 640–59.

Hochberg, H., 'Universals, Particulars and Predication', *Review of Metaphysics*,
Vol. 19 (1965–6), pp. 87–102.

Hoffman, P., *The Anatomy of Idealism: Passivity and Activity in Kant, Hegel and
Marx* (Martinus Nijhoff, The Hague, 1982).

Hölderlin, F., *Hyperion*, trans. by W. R. Trask (The New American Library,
New York, 1965).

Hölderlin, F., *Urteil und Sein*, in *Sämtliche Werke* (*Kleine Stuttgarter Ausgabe*),
ed. by F. Beissner (5 vols, W. Kohlkammer, Stuttgart, 1944–62), Vol. 4, pp.
226–7.

Hoppe, H-G., 'Ist alle Verbindung eine Verstandeshandlung?', in G. Funke (ed.)
Akten des 5. Internationalen Kant-Kongresses (3 vols, Bouvier, Bonn, 1981–
2), Vol. 1, pp. 221–31.

Hoppe, H-G., *Synthesis bei Kant* (W. de Gruyter, Berlin, 1983).

Horstmann, R-P., *Ontologie und Relationen: Hegel, Bradley, Russell und die
Kontroverse über interne und externe Beziehungen* (Athenäum, Hain, 1984).

Houlgate, S., *Hegel, Nietzsche and the Criticism of Metaphysics* (Cambridge
University Press, Cambridge, 1986).

Hughes, G. J., 'Universals as Potential Substances: The Interpretation of
Metaphysics Z 13', in M. F. Burnyeat (ed.), *Notes on Book Zeta of Aristotle's
Metaphysics* (Oxford Study Series, Oxford Sub Faculty of Philosophy, 1981),
pp. 107–26.

Hume, D., *Enquiries Concerning Human Understanding and Concerning the
Principles of Morals*, ed. by L. A. Selby-Bigge, revised and notes by P. H.
Nidditch, 3rd edn (Oxford University Press, Oxford, 1975).

Hume, D., *A Treatise of Human Nature*, ed. by L. A. Selby-Bigge and revised by
P. H. Nidditch, 2nd edn (Oxford University Press, Oxford, 1978).

Husserl, E., *Logical Investigations*, trans. J. N. Findlay (2 vols, Routledge & Kegan Paul, London/Humanities Press, New York, 1970).

Hylton, P., 'The Nature of the Proposition and the Revolt against Idealism', in R. Rorty, J. B. Schneewind, and Q. Skinner (eds), *Philosophy in History: Essays on the Historiography of Philosophy* (Cambridge University Press, Cambridge, 1984), pp. 375–97.

Hyppolite, J., *Genesis and Structure of Hegel's Phenomenology of Spirit*, trans. by S. Cherniak and J. Heckman (Northwestern University Press, Evanston, 1974).

Hyppolite, J., *Studies on Marx and Hegel*, trans. with an introduction, notes, and bibliography by J. O'Neill (Heinemann, London, 1969).

Inwood, M., *Hegel* (Routledge & Kegan Paul, London, 1983).

Inwood, M., 'Hegel on Death', *International Journal of Moral and Social Studies*, Vol. 1 (1986), pp. 109–22.

James, W., *A Pluralistic Universe* (Longmans, London, 1909).

James, W., *'Pragmatism' and 'The Meaning of Truth'*, with an introduction by A. J. Ayer (Harvard University Press, Cambridge, Mass., and London, 1978).

Jonas, H., *The Phenomenon of Life: Toward a Philosophical Biology* (Harper & Row, New York, 1966).

Kant, I., *Critique of Judgement*, trans. by J. C. Meredith (Oxford University Press, Oxford, 1952).

Kant, I., *Critique of Pure Reason*, trans. by N. Kemp Smith, 2nd edn with corrections (Macmillan, London, 1933).

Kant, I., *Kants gesammelte Schriften*, *Akademische Textausgabe* (Georg Reimer (subsequently W. de Guyter), Berlin, 1902–).

Kant, I., *Prolegomena to any Future Metaphysics that Will be Able to Present Itself as a Science*, trans. by P. Gray Lucas (Manchester University Press, Manchester, 1953).

Kaulbach, F., 'Die Entwicklung des Synthesis-Gedankes bei Kant', in H. Heimsoeth, D. Henrich, and G. Tonelli (eds), *Studien zu Kants Philosophischer Entwicklung* (Georg Olms, Hildesheim, 1967), pp. 56–92.

Kelly, S., 'Hegel and Morin: The Science of Wisdom and the Wisdom of the New Science', *The Owl of Minerva*, Vol. 20 (1988), pp. 51–67.

Kemp Smith, N., 'The Nature of Universals', *Mind*, Vol. 36 (1927), pp. 137–57, pp. 265–80, pp. 393–422.

Kielmeyer, C. F. von, *Gesammelte Scriften*, ed. by F. H. Holler (Keiper, Berlin, 1938).

Kitcher, P., 'Kant on Self-Identity', *The Philosophical Review*, Vol. 91 (1982), pp. 41–72.

Kitcher, P., 'Kant's Paralogisms', *The Philosophical Review*, Vol. 91 (1982), pp. 515–47.

Kitcher, P., 'Kant's Real Self', in A. W. Wood (ed.), *Self and Nature in Kant's Philosophy* (Cornell University Press, Ithaca and London, 1984), pp. 113–47.

Kneale, W., 'The Notion of a Substance', *Proceedings of the Aristotelian Society*, Vol. 40 (1940), pp. 103–34.

Knight, D. M., 'Chemistry, Physiology and Materialism in the Romantic Period', *Durham University Journal*, Vol. 64 (1971–2), pp. 139–45.

Knight, D. M., 'German Science in the Romantic Period', in M. Crosland (ed.) *The Emergence of Science in Western Europe* (Macmillan, London, 1975), pp. 161–78.

Koestler, A., *Janus: A Summing Up* (Hutchinson, London, 1978).
Kojève, A., *Introduction to the Reading of Hegel: Lectures on the Phenomenology of Spirit*, ed. by A. Bloom, trans. by J. H. Nichols (Basic Books, New York and London, 1969).
Körner, S., *Categorial Frameworks* (Basil Blackwell, Oxford, 1970).
Körner, S., *Kant* (Penguin Books, Harmondsworth, 1955).
Kosman, L. A., 'Animals and Other Beings in Aristotle', in A. Gotthelf and J. G. Lennox (eds), *Philosophical Issues in Aristotle's Biology* (Cambridge University Press, Cambridge, 1987), pp. 360–91.
Kroner, R., *Von Kant bis Hegel* (2 vols, J. C. B. Mohr, Tübingen, 1921–4).
Kuhn, T. S., *The Structure of Scientific Revolutions*, 2nd edn enlarged (The University of Chicago Press, Chicago, 1970).
Lacey, A. R., 'Οὐσία and Form in Aristotle', *Phronesis*, Vol. 10 (1965), pp. 54–69.
Lamb, D., *Hegel: From Foundation to System* (Martinus Nijhoff, The Hague, 1980).
Laszlo, E., *The Systems View of the World* (Basil Blackwell, Oxford, 1972).
Lear, J., *Aristotle: The Desire to Understand* (Cambridge University Press, Cambridge, 1988).
Leclerc, I., *The Nature of Physical Existence* (George Allen & Unwin, London, 1972).
Leibniz, G. W., *New Essays on Human Understanding*, trans. and ed. by P. Remnant and J. Bennett (Cambridge University Press, Cambridge, 1981).
Leibniz, G. W., *Philosophical Papers and Letters: A Selection*, trans. and ed. with an introduction by L. E. Loemker, 2nd edn (D. Reidel, Dordrecht, 1969).
Leibniz, G. W., *Die philosophische Schriften von Gottfried Willhelm Leibniz* (*Berlin Ausgabe*) (7 vols, Berlin, 1879; reprint edn, Georg Olms, Hildesheim, 1960).
Lenoir, T., 'Generational Factors in the Origin of "Romantische Naturphilosophie" ', *Journal of the History of Biology*, Vol. 11 (1978), pp. 57–100.
Lenoir, T., 'The Gottingen School and the Development of Transcendental Naturphilosophie in the Romantic Era', *Studies in History of Biology*, vol. 5 (1981), pp. 111–205.
Lescher, J. H., 'Aristotle on Form, Substance and Universals: A Dilemma', *Phronesis*, Vol. 16 (1971), pp. 169–78.
Levere, T. H., *Affinity and Matter: Elements of Chemical Philosophy 1800–1865* (Oxford University Press, Oxford, 1971).
Lippmann, E.O. von, 'Encheiresis Naturae', in *Abhandlungen and Vorträge zur Geschichte der Naturwissenschaften* (2 vols, von Veit, Leipzig, 1906–13).
Lloyd, A. C., *Form and Universal in Aristotle* (F. Cairns, Liverpool, 1981).
Lloyd, G. E. R., *Polarity and Analogy: Two Types of Argumentation in Early Greek Thought* (Cambridge University Press, Cambridge, 1966).
Locke, J., *An Essay Concerning Human Understanding*, ed. with a foreword by P. H. Nidditch (Oxford University Press, Oxford, 1975).
Loux, M. J., 'Form, Species and Predication in Metaphysics Z, H and Θ', *Mind*, Vol. 88 (1979), pp. 1–23.

Loux, M. J., *Substance and Attribute: A Study in Ontology* (D. Reidel, Dordrecht, 1978).

Löw, R., *Philosophie des Lebendigen: Der Begriff des Organischen bei Kant, sein Grund und seine Aktualität* (Suhrkamp, Frankfurt am Main, 1980).

Lucas, G. R., 'A Re-interpretation of Hegel's Philosophy of Nature', *Journal of the History of Philosophy*, Vol. 22 (1984), pp. 103–113.

Lugarini, L., 'Die Bedeutung des Problems des Ganzen in der Hegelschen Logik', in D. Henrich (ed.), *Die Wissenschaft der Logik und die Logik der Reflexion, Hegel-Studien*, supp. Vol. 18 (Bouvier, Bonn, 1978), pp. 19–36.

Lukács, G., *The Ontology of Social Being I: Hegel's False and his Genuine Ontology*, trans. by D. Fernbach (Merlin Press, London, 1978).

Lukács, G., *The Young Hegel*, trans. by R. Livingstone, (Merlin Press, London, 1975).

McFarland, J. D., *Kant's Concept of Teleology* (University of Edinburgh Press, Edinburgh, 1970).

Mackay, D. S., 'An Historical Sketch of the Problem of Relations', in *Studies in the Problem of Relations*, University of California Publications in Philosophy, Vol. 13 (1930), pp. 1–34.

Mackie, J. L., *Problems from Locke* (Oxford University Press, Oxford, 1976).

McMullin, E., 'Philosophies of Nature', *The New Scholasticism*, Vol. 43 (1969), pp. 29–74.

McRae, R., *Leibniz: Perception, Apperception and Thought*, (University of Toronto Press, Toronto, 1976).

McTaggart, J. M. E., *A Commentary of Hegel's Logic* (Cambridge University Press, Cambridge, 1910).

McTaggart, J. M. E., *The Nature of Existence*, ed. by C. D. Broad, reprint (2 vols, Cambridge University Press, Cambridge, 1968).

McTaggart, J. M. E., *Studies in the Hegelian Dialectic*, 2nd edn (Cambridge University Press, Cambridge, 1922).

Manser, A. R., 'Bradley and Internal Relations', in G. Vesey (ed.), *Idealism Past and Present*, Royal Institute of Philosophy Lecture Series, 13 (Cambridge University Press, Cambridge, 1982), pp. 181–96.

Marcuse, H., *Reason and Revolution: Hegel and the Rise of Social Theory* (Routledge & Kegan Paul, London, 1941).

Martin, G., *Kant's Metaphysics and Theory of Science*, trans. by P. G. Lucas (Manchester University Press, Manchester, 1955).

Martin, G., *Leibniz: Logic and Metaphysics*, trans. by K. J. Northcott and P. G. Lucas (Manchester University Press, Manchester, 1964).

Marx, K., *Capital*, Vol. 1, trans. by B. Fowkes (Penguin Books, Harmondsworth, 1976).

Marx, K., *Critique of Hegel's Philosophy of Right*, trans. by A. Jolin and J. O'Malley, ed. with an introduction and notes by J. O'Malley (Cambridge University Press, Cambridge, 1970).

Marx, K., *Early Writings*, trans. by R. Livingstone and G. Benton, with an introduction by L. Colletti (Penguin Books, Harmondsworth, 1975).

Matthews, H. E., 'Strawson on Transcendental Idealism', *Philosophical Quarterly*, Vol. 19 (1969), pp. 204–20.

Mellor, D. H., 'The Reduction of Society', *Philosophy*, Vol. 57 (1982), pp. 51–76.

Mendelsohn, E., 'The Biological Sciences in the Nineteenth Century: Some Problems and Sources', *History of Science*, Vol. 3 (1964), pp. 39–59.

Mendelsohn, E., 'Physical Models and Physiological Concepts: Explanation in Nineteenth Century Biology', in R. S. Cohen and M. W. Wartofsky (eds), Boston Studies in the Philosophy of Science, 2 (Humanities Press, New York, 1965), pp. 127–50.

Moiso, F., 'Die Hegelsche Theorie der Physik und der Chemie in ihrer Beziehung zu Schellings Naturphilosophie', in R-P. Horstmann and M. J. Petry (eds), *Hegels Philosophie der Natur: Beziehungen zwischen empirischer und speculativer Naturerkenntnis* (Klett-Cotta, Stuttgart, 1986), pp. 54–87.

Müller, G. E., 'The Hegel Legend of Thesis – Antithesis – Synthesis', *Journal of the History of Ideas*, Vol. 19 (1958), pp. 411–14.

Mure, G. R. G., *Aristotle* (Ernest Benn, London, 1932).

Mure, G. R. G., *An Introduction to Hegel* (Oxford University Press, Oxford, 1940).

Mure, G. R. G., *The Philosophy of Hegel* (Oxford University Press, Oxford, 1965).

Mure, G. R. G., *A Study of Hegel's Logic* (Oxford University Press, Oxford, 1950).

Nagel, E., 'Wholes, Sums and Organic Unities', in D. Lerner (ed.), *Parts and Wholes: The Hayden Colloqium on Scientific Method and Concept* (The Free Press of Glencoe, New York/Macmillan, London, 1963), pp. 135–56.

Nagel, T., *The View From Nowhere* (Oxford University Press, Oxford, 1986).

Newton, I., *Isaac Newton's Papers and Letters on Natural Philosophy*, ed. with a general introduction by I. Bernard Cohen assisted by R. E. Schofield, 2nd edn (Harvard University Press, Cambridge, Mass., and London, 1978).

Newton, I., *Opticks or A Treatise of the Reflections, Refractions, Inflections and Colours of Light*, based on the 4th edn, London, 1730 (Dover Publications, New York, 1952).

Nietzsche, F., *Beyond Good and Evil: Prelude to a Philosophy of the Future*, trans. by W. Kaufmann (Random House, New York, 1966).

Nisbet, H. B., *Goethe and the Scientific Tradition* (Institute of Germanic Studies, London, 1972).

Nisbet, H. B., *Herder and the Philosophy and History of Science* (The Modern Humanities Research Association, Cambridge, 1970).

Norman, R., *Hegel's Phenomenology: A Philosophical Introduction* (Harvester Press, New Jersey and Sussex, 1981).

Nozick, R., *Philosophical Explanations* (Oxford University Press, Oxford, 1981).

Oersted, H. C., *The Soul in Nature*, trans. by L. Horner and J. B. Horner, reprint edn (Dawsons, London, 1966).

Oliver, H. H., *A Relational Metaphysic* (Martinus Nijhoff, The Hague, 1981).

Olivier, H., 'Philosophie de la nature et sciences positive selon Hegel', in *Science et dialectique chez Hegel et Marx*, by the 'Groupe de recherche sur science et dialectique', under the direction of M. Vadee (Editions du Centre National de la Recherche Scientifique, Paris, 1980), pp. 15–26.

Orsini, G. N., 'The Ancient Roots of a Modern Idea', in G. S. Rousseau (ed.), *Organic Form: The Life of an Idea* (Routledge & Kegan Paul, London, 1972), pp. 7–24.

Owen, G. E. L., 'Logic and Metaphysics in Some Earlier Works of Aristotle', in J. Barnes, M. Schofield, and R. Sorabji (eds), *Articles on Aristotle* (4 vols, Duckworth, London, 1975–9), Vol. III: *Metaphysics*, pp. 13–32.

Owens, J., *The Doctrine of Being in the Aristotelian Metaphysics* (Pontifical Institute of Mediaeval Studies, Toronto, 1957).

Partington, J. R., *A History of Chemistry* (4 vols, Macmillan, London, 1961–4).

Pearce Williams, L., 'Kant, "Naturphilosophie" and Scientific Method', in R. N. Giere and R. S. Westfall (eds), *Foundations of Scientific Method: The Nineteenth Century* (Indiana University Press, Bloomington and London, 1973), pp. 3–22.

Pelletier, F. J., 'Locke's Doctrine of Substance', in C. E. Jarrett, J. King-Furlow, and F. J. Pelletier (eds), *New Essays on Rationalism and Empiricism, Canadian Journal of Philosophy*, supp. Vol. 4 (1978), pp. 121–40.

Petry, M. J., 'Scientific Method: Francoeur, Hegel and Pohl', in R-P. Horstmann and M. J. Petry (eds), *Hegels Philosophie der Natur: Beziehungen zwischen empirischer und speculativer Naturerkenntnis* (Klett-Cotta, Stuttgart, 1986), pp. 11–29.

Pettit, P., 'The Varieties of Collectivism', in O. Neumaier (ed.), *Mind, Language and Society* (Verband der wissentschaftliche Gesellschaften Österreichs, Vienna, 1984), pp. 158–66.

Phillips, D. G., 'Organicism in the Late Nineteenth and Early Twentieth Centuries', *Journal of the History of Ideas*, Vol. 31 (1970), pp. 413–32.

Pichler, H., 'Über die Einheit und die Immanenz des Ganzen', *Kant-Studien*, Vol. 48 (1956–7), pp. 55–72.

Pinkard, T., 'The Logic of Hegel's *Logic*', *Journal of the History of Philosophy*, Vol. 17 (1979), pp. 417–35.

Pippin, R. B., *Kant's Theory of Form* (Yale University Press, New Haven and London, 1982).

Plant, R., *Hegel: An Introduction*, 2nd edn, (Oxford University Press, Oxford, 1983).

Plato, *The Collected Dialogues*, ed. by E. Hamilton and H. Cairns (Princeton University Press, New Jersey, 1963).

Popper, K., 'What is Dialectic?', in *Conjectures and Refutations: The Growth of Scientific Knowledge*, 3rd edn (Routledge & Kegan Paul, London, 1969), pp. 312–35.

Priest, S., 'Subjectivity and Objectivity in Kant and Hegel', in S. Priest (ed.), *Hegel's Critique of Kant* (Oxford University Press, Oxford, 1987), pp. 103–18.

Quine, W. V., 'Things and Their Place in Theories', in *Theories and Things* (Harvard University Press, Cambridge, Mass., and London, 1981), pp. 1–23.

Quine, W. V., 'Variables Explained Away', in *Selected Logical Papers* (Random House, New York, 1966), pp. 227–35.

Quine, W. V., *Word and Object* (MIT Press, Cambridge, Mass., 1960).

Quinton, A., 'Absolute Idealism', *Proceedings of the British Academy*, Vol. 57 (1971), pp. 303–29.

Quinton, A., *The Nature of Things* (Routledge & Kegan Paul, London, 1973).

Reinach, A., 'Kant's Interpretation of Hume's Problem', trans. by J. N. Mohanty, *Southwestern Journal of Philosophy*, Vol. 7 (1976), pp. 161–88.

Rescher, N., *The Philosophy of Leibniz* (Prentice Hall, Englewood Cliffs, 1967).

Richter, L. G., *Hegels begreifende Naturbetrachtung als Versöhnung der Spekulation mit der Erfahrung* (Köningshausen and Newmann, Würzburg/Rodlophin, Amsterdam, 1985).

Ritterbush, P. C., 'Organic Form: Aesthetics and Objectivity in the Study of Form in the Life Sciences', in G. S. Rousseau (ed.), *Organic Form: The Life of an Idea* (Routledge & Kegan Paul, London, 1972), pp. 25–60.

Roberts, J., *German Philosophy: An Introduction* (Polity Press, Cambridge, 1988).

Robinson, H. M., 'Prime Matter in Aristotle', *Phronesis*, Vol. 19 (1974), pp. 168–88.

Roqué, A. J., 'Self-Organisation: Kant's Concept of Teleology and Modern Chemistry', *Review of Metaphysics*, Vol. 39 (1985), pp. 107–35.

Rorty, R., *Philosophy and the Mirror of Nature* (Basil Blackwell, Oxford, 1980).

Rorty, R., 'Relations, Internal and External', *The Encyclopedia of Philosophy* (8 vols, Macmillan, New York and London, 1967), Vol. 7, pp. 125–33.

Rorty, R., 'Strawson's Objectivity Argument', *Review of Metaphysics*, Vol. 24 (1970), pp. 207–44.

Rosen, M., *Hegel's Dialectic and Its Criticism* (Cambridge University Press, Cambridge, 1982).

Rosen, S., *G. W. F. Hegel: An Introduction to the Science of Wisdom* (Yale University Press, New Haven and London, 1974).

Rosen, S., *The Limits of Analysis*, paperback edn (Yale University Press, New Haven and London, 1985).

Rotenstreich, N., *From Substance to Subject: Studies in Hegel* (Martinus Nijhoff, The Hague, 1974).

Ruben, D. H., 'Social Wholes and Parts', *Mind*, Vol. 92 (1983), pp. 219–38.

Russell, B., *A Critical Exposition of the Philosophy of Leibniz* (Cambridge University Press, Cambridge, 1900).

Russell, B., 'On Denoting', *Mind*, Vol. 14 (1905), pp. 479–93.

Russell, B., *The Philosophy of Logical Atomism*, ed. with an introduction by D. Pears (Open Court, La Salle, 1985).

Sabine, G. H., 'Professor Bosanquet's *Logic* and the Concrete Universal', *Philosophical Review*, Vol. 21 (1912), pp. 546–65.

Sabra, A. I., *Theories of Light from Descartes to Newton*, new edn (Cambridge University Press, Cambridge, 1981).

Sambursky, S., 'Hegel's Philosophy of Nature', in Y. Elkana (ed.), *The Interaction Between Science and Philosophy* (Humanities Press, Atlantic Highlands, 1974), pp. 143–54.

Sarlemijn, A., *Hegel's Dialectic*, trans. by P. Kirschenmann (D. Reidel, Dordrecht, 1975).

Schelling, F. W. J., *Ideas for a Philosophy of Nature*, trans. by E. E. Harris and P. Heath, with an introduction by R. Stern (Cambridge University Press, Cambridge, 1988).

Schelling, F. W. J., *Schellings Werke*, ed. by M. Schröter (13 vols, C. H. Beck, Munich, 1946–59).

Schiller, F., *On the Aesthetic Education of Man, in a Series of Letters*, ed. and trans. by E. M. Wilkinson and L. A. Willoughby, with an introduction and commentary, German and English parallel texts (Oxford University Press, Oxford, 1967).

Schlegel, F., *Werke* (*Kritische Ausgabe*), ed. by E. Behler, J-J. Anstatt, and H. Eichner (35 vols, Thomas, Munich and Vienna, 1967).

Schulthess, P., *Relation und Funktion: Eine systematische und entwicklungs-geschichtliche Untersuchung zur theoretischen Philosophie Kants* (W. de Gruyter, Berlin and New York, 1981).

Schulz-Seitz, R-E., ' "Sein" in Hegels Logik: "Einfache Beziehung auf sich" ', in H. Fahrenbach (ed.), *Wirklichkeit und Reflexion: Walter Schulz zum 60. Geburtstag* (Günther Neske, Pfulligen, 1973), pp. 365–84.

Seidel, G. J., *Activity and Ground: Fichte, Schelling and Hegel* (Georg Olms, Hildesheim, 1976).

Sepper, D. L., *Goethe Contra Newton: Polemics and the Project for a New Science of Color* (Cambridge University Press, Cambridge, 1988).

Shklar, J. N., *Freedom and Independence: A Study of the Political Ideas of Hegel's Phenomenology of Mind* (Cambridge University Press, Cambridge, 1976).

Siegel, C., *Geschichte der deutschen Naturphilosophie* (Akademische Verlagsgesellschaft, Leipzig, 1913).

Simons, P. M., *Parts: A Study in Ontology* (Oxford University Press, Oxford, 1987).

Simons, P. M., 'Three Essays in Formal Ontology', in B. Smith (ed.), *Parts and Moments: Studies in Logic and Formal Ontology* (Philosophia Verlag, Munich and Vienna, 1982), pp. 111–260.

Smith, B., and Mulligen, K., 'Pieces of a Theory', in B. Smith (ed.), *Parts and Moments: Studies in Logic and Formal Ontology*, (Philosophia Verlag, Munich and Vienna, 1982), pp. 15–110.

Snelders, H. A. M., 'Romanticism and "Naturphilosophie" and the Inorganic Natural Sciences 1797–80: An Introductory Survey', *Studies in Romanticism*, Vol. 9 (1970), pp. 193–215.

Sokolowski, R., 'The Logic of Parts and Wholes in Husserl's Investigations', *Philosophy and Phenomenological Research*, Vol. 28 (1968), pp. 537–53.

Soll, I., *An Introduction to Hegel's Metaphysics* (Chicago University Press, Chicago, 1969).

Solomon, R. C., 'Hegel's Concept of "Geist" ', *Review of Metaphysics*, Vol. 23 (1969–70), pp. 642–61.

Solomon, R. C., 'Hegel's Epistemology', *American Philosophical Quarterly*, vol. 11 (1974), pp. 277–89.

Solomon, R. C., *In the Spirit of Hegel: A Study of G. W. F. Hegel's Phenomenology of Spirit* (Oxford University Press, New York and Oxford, 1983).

Spinoza, B., *The Collected Works of Spinoza*, ed. and trans. by E. Curley, (2 vols, Princeton University Press, Princeton, 1985–).

Spinoza, B., *Spinoza Opera*, ed. by C. Gebhardt (4 vols, Carl Winters, Heidelberg, 1925).

Sprigge, T. L. S., 'Intrinsic Connectedness', *Proceedings of the Aristotelian Society*, Vol. 88 (1987–8), pp. 129–45.

Sprigge, T. L. S., 'Russell and Bradley on Relations', in G. W. Roberts (ed.), *Bertrand Russell Memorial Volume* (George Allen & Unwin, London/ Humanities Press, New York, 1979), pp. 150–70.

Stauffer, R. C., 'Speculation and Experiment in the Background of Oersted's Discovery of Electromagentism', *Isis*, Vol. 48 (1957), pp. 33–50.

Stern, R., 'Hegel and the Structure of the Whole: Relation and Unity in the Philosophy of G. W. F. Hegel', Cambridge PhD dissertation, 1986.

Stern, R., 'Kant, Hegel and the Place of the Subject', Proceedings of the International Congress of the Hegel-Gesellschaft, 1988, forthcoming in the *Hegel-Jahrbuch*.

Stern, R., 'Unity and Difference in Hegel's Political Philosophy', *Ratio*, new series, Vol 2. (1989), pp. 75–88.

Stokes, M. C., *One and Many in Presocratic Philosophy* (Centre for Hellenic Studies, Washington, 1971).

Strawson, P. F., *The Bounds of Sense* (Methuen, London, 1966).

Strawson, P. F., *Individuals: An Essay in Descriptive Metaphysics* (Methuen, London, 1959).

Strawson, P. F., *Subject and Predicate in Logic and Grammar* (Methuen, London, 1974).

Taminaux, J., *La Nostalgie de la Grèce à l'Aube de l'idéalisme allemand: Kant et les Grecs dans l'itinéraire de Schiller, de Hölderlin et de Hegel* (Martinus Nijhoff, The Hague, 1967).

Tanabe, H., 'Zu Hegels Lehre vom Urteil', *Hegel-Studien*, Vol. 6 (1971), pp. 211–30.

Taylor, C., *Hegel* (Cambridge University Press, Cambridge, 1975).

Teller, P., 'Relational Holism and Quantum Mechanics', *British Journal for the Philosophy of Science*, Vol. 37 (1986), pp. 71–81.

Theunissen, M., *Sein und Schein: Die kritische Funktion der Hegelschen Logik* (Suhrkamp, Frankfurt am Main, 1980).

Toulmin, S., and Goodfield, J., *The Architecture of Matter* (Hutchinson, London, 1962).

Toulmin, S., and Goodfield, J., *The Fabric of the Heavens* (Hutchinson, London, 1961).

Vaught, C. G., 'Subject, Object and Representation: A Critique of Hegel's Dialectic of Perception', *International Philosophical Quarterly*, Vol. 26 (1986), pp. 117–29.

Vesey, G., 'A History of "Ideas" ', in G. Vesey (ed.), *Idealism Past and Present*, Royal Institute of Philosophy Lecture Series, 13 (Cambridge University Press, Cambridge, 1982), pp. 1–18.

Vieillard-Baron, J-L., 'La Notion de matière et la materialisme vrai selon Hegel et Schelling à l'époque d'Iéna', in D. Henrich and K. Düsing (eds), *Hegel in Jena*, supp. Vol. 20 (Bouvier, Bonn, 1980), pp. 197–206.

Vlastos, G., 'Organic Categories in Whitehead', in G. C. Kline (ed.), *Alfred North Whitehead: Essays in His Philosophy* (Englewood Cliffs, New York, 1963), pp. 158–67.

Walker, R. C. S., *Kant* (Routledge & Kegan Paul, London, 1978).

Wall, K., *Relation in Hegel*, reprint edn (University Press of America, Washington, 1983).

Walsh, W. H., 'Kant as Seen by Hegel', in G. Vesey (ed.), *Idealism Past and Present*, Royal Institute of Philosophy Lecture Series, 13 (Cambridge University Press, Cambridge, 1982), pp. 93–109.

Walsh, W. H., *Reason and Experience* (Oxford University Press, Oxford, 1947).

Walsh, W. H., 'Subjective and Objective Idealism', in D. Henrich (ed.), *Kant oder Hegel: über Formen der Begründung in der Philosophie*, Veröffentlichen der Internationalen Hegel-Vereinigung, Vol. 12 (Klett-Cotta, Stuttgart, 1983), pp. 83–98.

Weiss, P., 'On Being Together', *Review of Metaphysics*, Vol. 9 (1955–6), pp. 391–403.

Weiss, P. A., *Within the Gates of Science and Beyond* (Hafner, New York, 1971).

Westphal, M., 'Hegel's Theory of the Concept', in W. E. Steinkraus and K. I. Schmitz (eds), *Art and Logic in Hegel's Philosophy* (Humanities Press, New Jersey and Sussex, 1980), pp. 103–120.

Wetzels, W. D., 'Art and Science: Organicism and Goethe's Classical Aesthetics', in F. Burwick (ed.), *Approaches to Organic Form: Permutations in Science and Culture* (D. Reidel, Dordrecht, 1987), pp. 71–85.

Wetzels, W. D., 'Aspects of Natural Science in German Romanticism', *Studies in Romanticism*, Vol. 10 (1971), pp. 44–59.

Whitehead, A. N., *Adventures of Ideas* (Penguin Books, Harmondsworth, 1942).

Whittaker, E., *A History of the Theories of Aether and Electricity*, revised and enlarged edn (2 vols, Thomas Nelson, London, 1951).

Wiggins, D., 'Heraclitus' Conception of Fire, Flux, and Material Persistence', in M. Schofield and M. C. Nussbaum (eds), *Language and Logos* (Cambridge University Press, Cambridge, 1982), pp. 1–32.

Williams, B., *Ethics and the Limits of Philosophy* (Fontana Press, London, 1985).

Williams, B., 'Persons, Character and Morality', in *Moral Luck* (Cambridge University Press, Cambridge, 1981), pp. 1–19.

Williams, R. R., 'Hegel's Concept of *Geist*', in P. G. Stillman (ed.), *Hegel's Philosophy of Spirit* (State University of New York, Albany, 1987), pp. 1–20.

Wimsatt, W. K., 'Organic Form: Some Questions About a Metaphor', in G. S. Rousseau (ed.), *Organic Form: The Life of an Idea* (Routledge & Kegan Paul, London, 1972), pp. 61–82.

Wolff, R. P., *Kant's Theory of Mental Activity* (Harvard University Press, Cambridge, Mass., 1963).

Yolton, J. W. , 'Ideas and Knowledge in Seventeenth-Century Philosophy', *Journal of the History of Philosophy*, Vol. 13 (1975), pp. 145–65.

Zaidi, S. A. R., 'Towards a Relational Metaphysics', *The Review of Metaphysics*, Vol. 26 (1973), pp. 412–37.

Zumbach, C., *The Transcendent Science: Kant's Conception of Biological Methodology* (Martinus Nijhoff, The Hague, 1984).

Index